ART MEETS
ECOLOGY

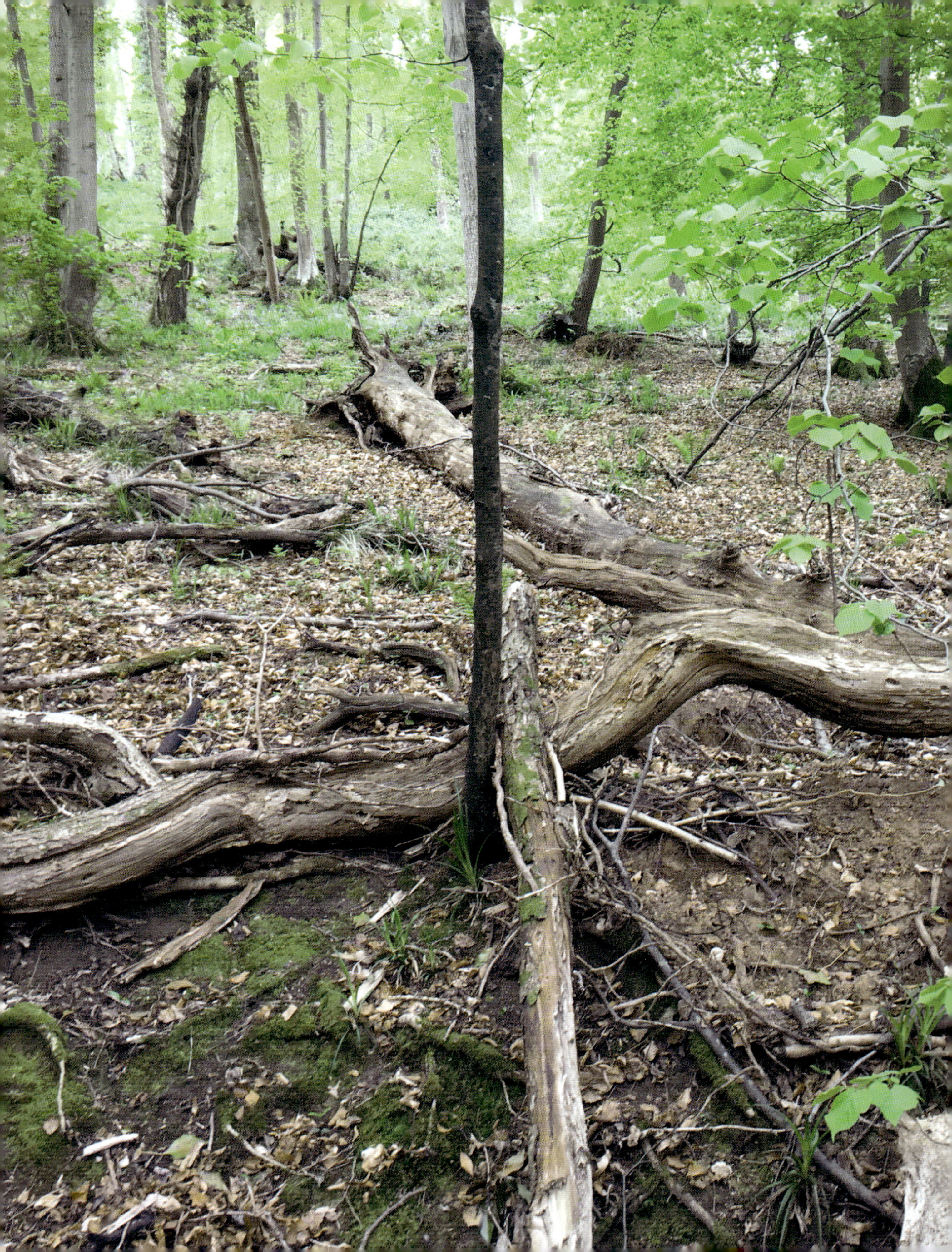

ART MEETS

ECOLOGY

THE ARBOREALISTS
In Lady Park Wood

George Peterken
Tim Craven
Christiana Payne

Foreword by Anne Rainsbury
Edited by Ann Kay

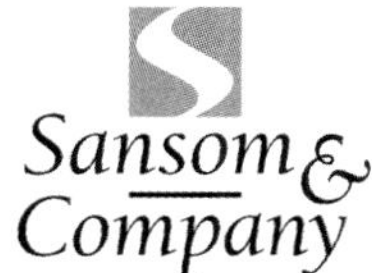

Sansom &
Company

Reprinted November 2021. First published in 2020 by Sansom and Company,
a publishing imprint of Redcliffe Press Ltd.,
81g Pembroke Road, Bristol BS8 3EA
www.sansomandcompany.co.uk | info@sansomandcompany.co.uk

ISBN 978-1-911408-68-0
© Text: George Peterken, Tim Craven, Christiana Payne
© Images: The Arborealists

Photographs on pp 2, 6, 8, 10, 12, 16, 30, 35, 38, 44, 59, 60, 65, 66, 73, 92,
102, 103, 104, 105, 106, 107, 108 ©Martin Urmson.
Paul Nash, *We are Making a New World* ©Imperial War Museum (Art.IWM ART 1146)
Samuel Palmer, *Oak Trees, Lullingstone Park* ©Bridgeman Images 6322894
Front cover detail, above: Richard Bavin, *Regeneration*, 2019 (fig 24).
Front cover detail, below: Fiona McIntyre, *Wild Wood*, 2018 (fig 71).

British Library Cataloguing-in-Publication Data
A catalogue record for this book is available from the British Library.
All rights reserved.

Design and typesetting Fiona McIntyre (fiona.me.mcintyre@gmail.com)
Printed in Wales by Zenith Media (01495 750033)

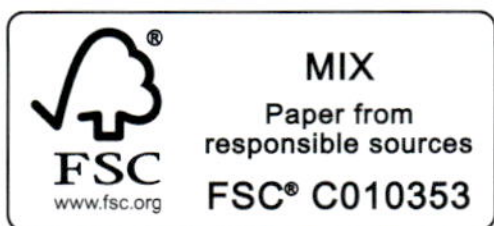

Sansom & Co is committed to being an environmentally friendly publisher.
This book is made from Forest Stewardship Council® certified paper.

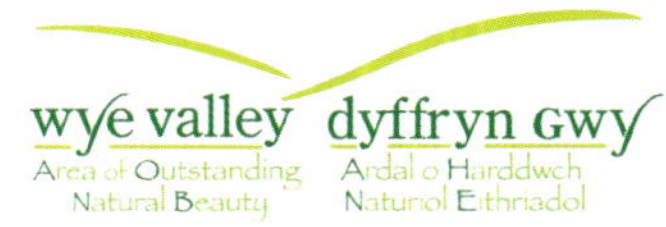

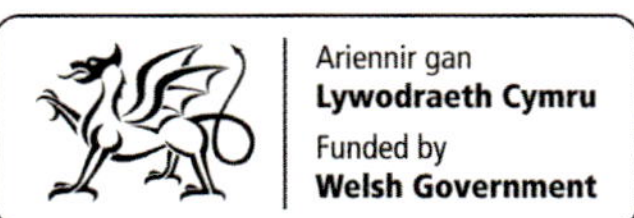

This project has been supported by the Sustainable Development Fund, a Welsh
Government Initiative in the Wye Valley Area of Outstanding Natural Beauty.

CONTENTS

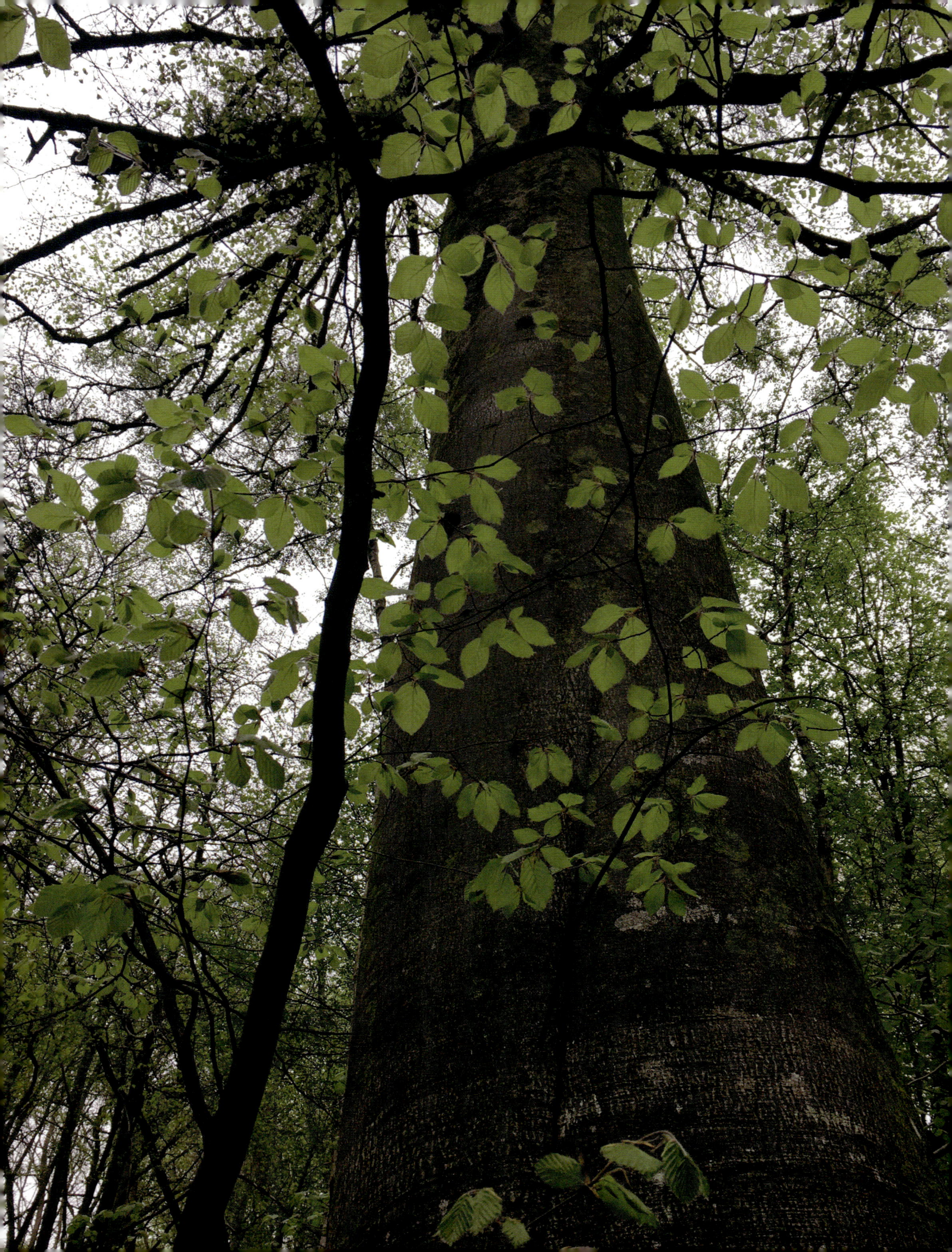

FOREWORD

ANNE RAINSBURY

When I first heard of the project that The Arborealists were undertaking in Lady Park Wood, the idea was both intriguing and enticing. This area of woodland, untouched by man since World War II, except for the ecologists monitoring and measuring, unvisited and to a large extent unknown to most locals, was being made accessible to artists – and not just any artists, but a group of professionals whose practice centred around the depiction of trees. These were people who habitually focused intently and intensively on trees, so their perception of this unique piece of unmanaged woodland would be acute. The work that they would produce would undoubtedly be sensitive to its special qualities and portray its particular characteristics. An exhibition of their work would provide the public with a window into this hidden place in the heart of the Wye Valley; a vision of wood and run wild without any human intervention for several generations; and with the artists' individual interpretations of their experience in this untouched landscape.

The lower Wye Valley has famously attracted artists for some 250 years: the river winding through its steeply wooded banks and cliffs, its water-powered and charcoal-fuelled industry, and its romantic ruins of castles and abbey provided many ideal landscapes for professional and amateur artists and writers originally in pursuit of picturesque beauty. Once discovered it has never lapsed in popularity and its scenery still inspires artists to this day. So art and nature have enjoyed a long and happy life together here in the Wye Valley.

In May 2018, coinciding with the theme of trees and woodland chosen for that year's Wye Valley River Festival (a biennial festival of the Wye Valley Area of Outstanding Natural Beauty), we were able to display at Monmouth Museum the first glimpse of the work that the Arborealists had been able to produce since their site visits in 2017. Together with their sketches and the film that contextualised their work and ideas, it whetted appetites for the large-scale exhibition in 2019–20 ('A Wye Valley Woodland through Artists' Eyes', Nelson Museum, Monmouth), which showed the full realisation and resolution of their Lady Park Wood experience.

It was also an important opportunity to highlight the Lady Park Wood project itself, this piece of uniquely unmanaged woodland in one sense devoid of human intervention, but in another the subject of intensive human interest for over 70 years. It has also brought into focus how much the future of that scientific study now relies on the work of one man to maintain it – woodland ecologist and author George Peterken CBE.

Not only did George Peterken open the virtual door to Lady Park Wood for The Arborealists and guide them through it, but his continued relationship with their work has been extraordinary. His responses to their work in the initial show, and their subsequent responses to him, have maintained a very special dialogue between artist and scientist that we have been able to share with visitors and now with readers of this book.

It has been a privilege to work with Tim Craven and the members of The Arborealists to display this project to the public, to show an exhibition of art focused solely on trees – not just anywhere, but in one very special woodland in our very own Wye Valley, which they have had the privilege of entering and we have been able to see through their eyes. It has also been an immense privilege to work with George Peterken, whose intimate knowledge not just of Lady Park Wood but of the ecology of the whole Wye Valley has enriched this experience. Never was it so true to say that, without him, none of this would have happened.

Anne Rainsbury, 2020
Monmouthshire Community Museums Curator

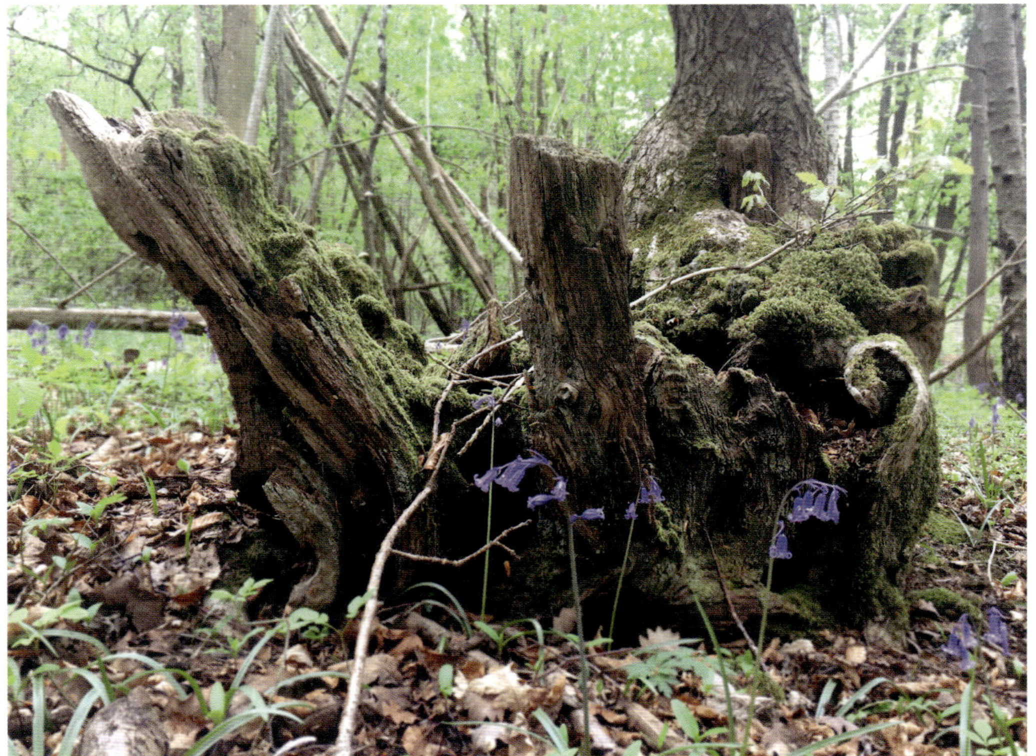

Lady Park Wood in spring. Photographed by Fiona McIntyre, April 2017.

INTRODUCTION

GEORGE PETERKEN

Woodland has long been studied and appreciated by artists and ecologists, but these two communities of interest have rarely met on equal terms. This book is a record of a project that took place on the flanks of the Wye gorge in which a group of artists sketched and painted in a wood that has been studied in detail by ecologists as it has become ever more natural.

Lady Park is a wood overlooking the Wye gorge that has been left to grow naturally for 75 years and in places for 150 years. Its significance for ecologists is that we can gain some understanding of how individual tree species and woodland as a whole behave when left to themselves; we can learn how wild species survive and compete naturally; and we can use it as a baseline against which to measure the impacts of people elsewhere. It also shows what truly wild countryside looks like and how attractive or otherwise it is to those who want to 'get away from it all' for a while. We can demonstrate the likely destiny of those rewilding projects now springing up throughout Britain that hope to provide a touch of wild nature on a larger scale than we currently enjoy.

Lady Park is also significant for artists. It formed part of the 'side screens' for the Wye Tourists of the eighteenth and nineteenth centuries, boating down the river in search of picturesque scenes with a sketchbook in one hand and William Gilpin's *Observations on the River Wye* (1770s/80s) in the other. It also provides contemporary artists with an opportunity to follow in the footsteps of the Hudson Bay school of artists in North America, the Barbizon school in France, Ivan Shishkin in Russia and even some sixteenth- and seventeenth-century Flemish and German artists, who painted 'virgin forests', or forests that at least looked untouched. Their works contrast with most tree and woodland art, which shows scenes that have clearly been shaped by people.

In 2017, The Arborealists, a loose association of artists who share the subject of trees and woodland, were invited to work in Lady Park Wood, and this book is a record of the resulting project. It includes all the artworks exhibited during 2019 and 2020 at the Nelson Museum, Monmouth – in 'A Wye Valley Woodland through Artists' Eyes' – and a matching ecological commentary on the scenes depicted.

The hope underlying this project was that we would be able to place artistic interpretations of the wood beside ecological interpretations, and that this would give artists, ecologists and people in general an enhanced appreciation of both the wood and how other people see it. It worked for the participants and we now hope that this book will enable others to see woods in new ways. This book collects together the prints, drawings and paintings derived from the artists' study of the wood. The commentaries link each artwork to the wood's ecology. Lady Park lies within the Wye Valley Area of Outstanding Natural Beauty, where the woods are one of the principal features, just as they were for William Gilpin. The first works from this project formed part of the AONB woodland-themed River Festival of 2018.

References:
George Peterken and Edward Mountford, *Woodland Development: A Long-term Study of Lady Park Wood* (CABI Publishing, 2017).

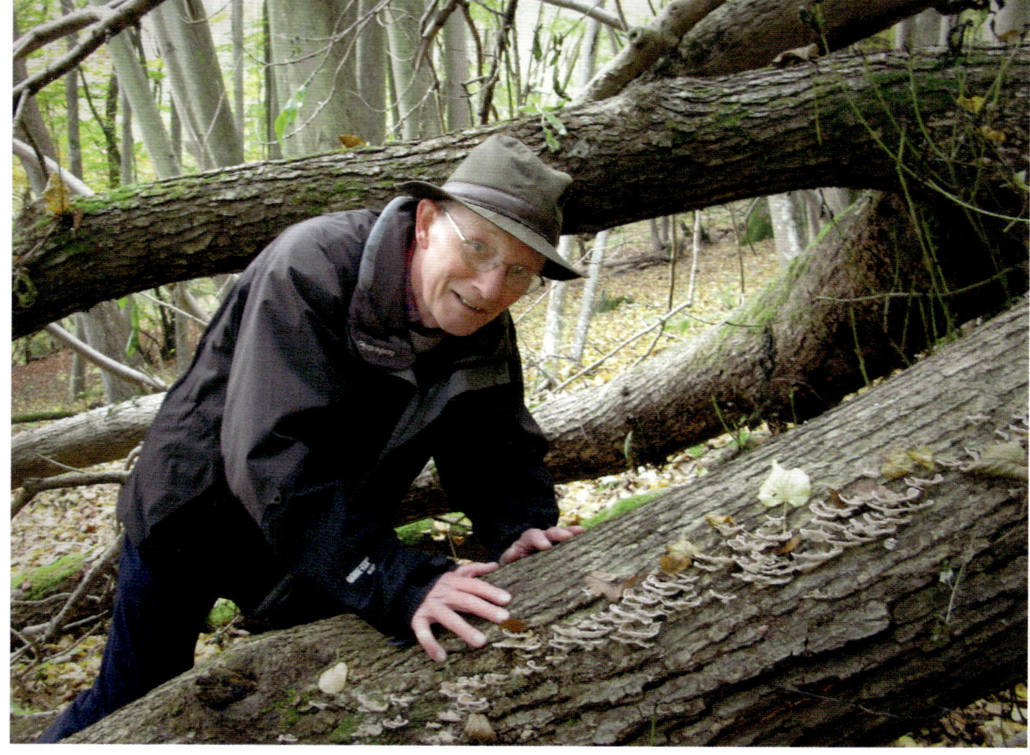

George Peterken in Lady Park Wood. Photographed by Richard Bavin, September 2018.

THE ARBOREALISTS

TIM CRAVEN

The Arborealists were founded in 2013 by artist and curator Tim Craven following the seminal exhibition 'Under the Greenwood: Picturing the British Tree', staged at St Barbe Museum and Art Gallery, Lymington, in the heart of the New Forest. The group's inaugural exhibition was staged at the Royal West of England Academy, Bristol, in 2014/15 and attracted national media coverage; it was described by *The Daily Telegraph* as 'spellbinding'.

The Arborealists are a loose association of some 60 professional artists of diverse art practice who share the subject of the tree. There are no rules, and there is no subscription fee. Members of the group are far flung, from the Welsh borders and the Cotswolds to East Anglia and London and every southern county from Kent to Cornwall. Outposts include Yorkshire, France and Ireland. The group enjoys an international profile and has already staged 23 exhibitions to acclaim in the UK and France with many more planned for the future, including site-specific projects. It has also produced four illustrated publications to complement its exhibitions to date, and has worked in partnership with various environmental organisations, including Exmoor and Dartmoor National Park authorities, the National Trust and the Woodland Trust.

Although united by their subject, these artists employ a wide range of working practices: scale, medium, philosophy, style and technique. The results are by turn dramatic, contemplative, expressive, abstracted, hyperreal and surreal. They demonstrate that trees still have a great relevance in contemporary art and retain their power to move us as a vital element in our landscape. Trees are a potent symbol of our threatened, fragile environment and are now at the top of the world's political agenda – indeed, they have never been more important to the human race.

Trees provide a wonderfully versatile subject for artists, not only in terms of the rich variety of form, texture and colour they provide, whether individually or collectively, but also through the wealth of association – myth, folklore, religious and symbolic significance – that they have come to embody over many centuries. In Britain, trees as a subject have inspired artists from Gainsborough and Constable through to the Pre-Raphaelites, the Neo-Romantics and the Ruralists. Piet Mondrian and Victor Pasmore used the tree as a device to turn abstract and Paul Nash famously stated that he loved and worshipped trees and believed they were people.

Previous publications by The Arborealists:
The Arborealists: The Art of the Tree (Bristol: Sansom & Co, 2016).
The Arborealists: The Art of Trees (London: Plato-Beale Productions, 2017).
The Arborealists and Other Painters (Moreton-in-Marsh: John Davies Gallery, 2018).
Being With Trees 1 (London: Plato-Beale Productions, 2020).

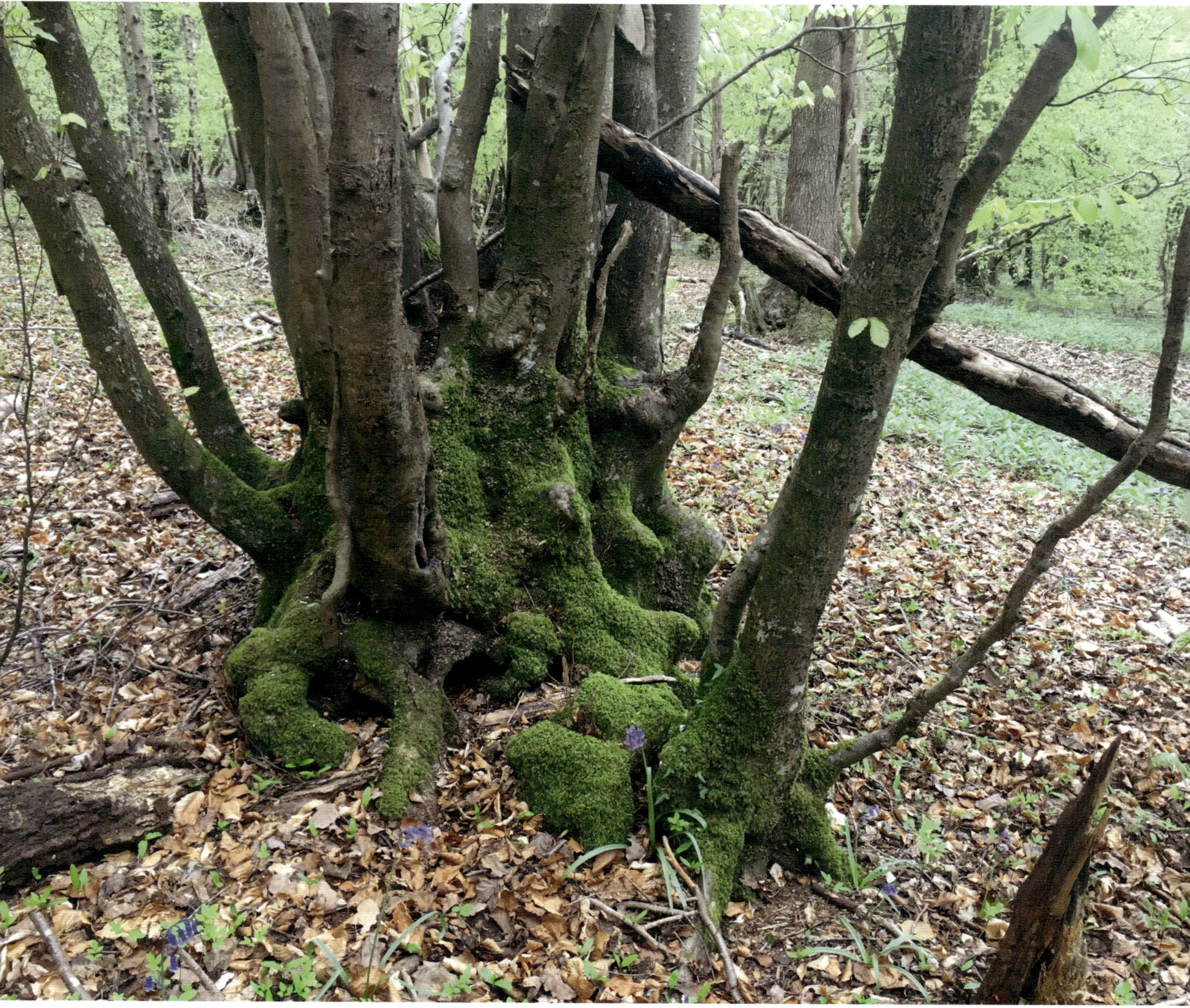

Lady Park Wood in spring.
Photographed by Fiona McIntyre,
April 2017.

LADY PARK WOOD AS A NATURAL RESERVE

GEORGE PETERKEN

In 1944, when the V2 rockets were raining down on London, the Forestry Commission and Oxford University agreed that Lady Park Wood should be set aside from commercial forestry to allow ecologists to study the natural, long-term development of unmanaged, indigenous woodland, and remarkably this study has been continued to the present day. The wood not only behaves naturally and looks primaeval, but we also have an unparalleled record of how individual trees have fared and how the wood as a whole has changed.

Lady Park is a mature stand of beech, sessile oak, ash, small-leaved lime, large-leaved lime, hazel, yew and many other native tree and shrub species. It occupies a spectacular position on the steep sides of the Wye gorge downstream from Symonds Yat. Historically, it is part of the ancient Hadnock Woods which stretch to the village of Staunton, all managed as coppice from the sixteenth century onwards, supplying wood for the colliers and thence charcoal for the local metal industries. The colliers have long gone (though their hearths remain) and it is now difficult to imagine this as an industrial wood. It was last coppiced in 1870, then allowed to grow tall, but in 1942, part was felled for the War effort. Shortly after, in 1944, the Forestry Commission set it aside as a research reserve for the study of natural ecological processes.

Starting in 1944, three kinds of change have been recognised. One is the slow, relentless and moderately predictable consequences of growth and competition, in which the largest trees usually prosper and the smallest trees die. The second is what Prime Minister Harold Macmillan called 'events', unpredictable disturbances to the status quo, which at their most extreme can transform a wood overnight: witness the 1987 storm across south-east England. In Lady Park, the main events have been the arrival of elm disease in 1971 and the great drought of 1976, but there have been others. The third is regeneration, the renewal of the wood as seedlings grow into saplings and trees, or new shoots spring from old trees. Our observations have been reported in a succession of articles and recently in a book.[1]

Nature reserve administrators would love to be able to say how the wood will develop in the future, but this is not possible. The 'events', which represent an unpredictable element in the wood's dynamics, prevent anyone knowing how the wood will develop in the future. It could be blown flat one night, or it might grow serenely on as a mature, undisturbed stand of trees.

Thus, after observing for three-quarters of a century, ecologists think they understand a good deal about the wood and how it works in the absence of human control. We have also noted how wild plants and animals have responded and can draw some conclusions

Note

[1] George Peterken and Edward Mountford, *Woodland Development: A Long-term Study of Lady Park Wood* (Wallingford: Commonwealth Agricultural Bureau International, 2017).

for nature conservation. Since 1944, foresters have revived their interest in managing woods by near-to-nature means, so Lady Park can provide some hints on how this might be achieved. Lately, a new interest has developed in (re-)wilding as an extensive nature conservation measure and a refreshing antidote to the mostly urban environments in which we live, and here, too, Lady Park can yield useful lessons on the long-term implications of such strategies.

The Lady Park experiment has attracted a good deal of interest from ecologists, conservationists, woodland enthusiasts and land managers, and has even been featured briefly on the BBC's *Countryfile*, BBC Radio's *Today* programme and other media, but the audience for this and most other ecological research remains small. This is partly due to the nature of the experiment. The general public cannot be admitted to the wood in large numbers – the place would no longer be a 'natural' experiment if they were – so there are inherent limitations on how the wood, the experiment and the findings can be brought to a wider audience. But it is also, perhaps, because scientific ecologists have not found a way to reach beyond like-minded specialists in a way that commands general interest.

Fortunately, there are other ways of understanding woods and communicating their value and interest. In recent years, widespread interest has been generated in the history of woods, how they have been used, and how their past has influenced the present, and this has contributed to the public support shown for the protection of ancient woodland. Lady Park has a long history which visitors certainly find interesting, but this is of limited use in explaining the Lady Park project, for the signs of how people have used the wood are fading. It is deliberately being allowed to become more natural each year.

But woods can also be understood aesthetically, artistically and even in human terms. In the eighteenth and nineteenth centuries, tourists who boated down the Wye seeking picturesque scenery regarded the woods as side-screens to the main features along the river. Visually, they provide a variety of form, colour and scale that changes with the seasons. We can see the violence in the fall of large trees and the quiet struggle of one tree trying to outgrow its neighbours. We know the stories behind the dead trees and the fallen, rotting logs, and much else. In Lady Park we have a community of trees that in some respects acts like human communities, with individual trees that have been lucky, others that have been unlucky and many that demand respect for their strength or resilience. We can also characterise woodland processes and each species in human terms.

With Lady Park we have the paradoxical need to make human connections to an experiment that is designed to eliminate people, in so far as this is possible. We look to minimise human influence in order to measure the impact people make on the environment, which also sounds paradoxical, but is consistent with scientific methodology. Perhaps, by inviting artists to see the wood for themselves and presenting their interests and interpretation in tandem with the ecological interest and understanding, we can together reach a wider audience than either ecologists or artists would reach alone.

Any ecologist who studies a wood over many years comes to know it in all its moods: bright and fresh in May, sombre and dark in November and totally transformed in January when snow lies on the ground under an overcast sky. He or she also comes to know each of the trees: their individual stories and how they co-exist, the accidents that have befallen them and how collectively they have developed into the woodland we see today. The wood is perceived as a constantly changing community with strong and weak individuals mixing together and different classes or species – each competing for its position.

The paintings, prints and drawings, and the artists who created them, speak for themselves. The following commentaries set out what I as an ecologist see in the artworks and what trains of thought they generate. In doing this, I will attempt to bring out the nature of the wood, how it works, how it evolved and what it is like to be there. Each artwork should have its own commentary, but most are grouped to avoid repetition and enable general points to be made. The groups, however, are far from watertight – many individual artworks could be placed elsewhere – but together they try to tell a story and focus perceptions.

At the outset I was simply keen to discover what features attracted the artists' attention. For two weekends and individually at other times, they ranged far and wide within Lady Park, though some found all they needed near the entrances at the top of the slope. None, however, penetrated to the steepest slopes below the cliff – reasonably enough, given that this is dangerous ground – but distinctive below-the-cliff niches and features have thus not featured in this collection.

My commentaries blatantly use the artworks as an excuse to explain some ecological and conservation points about natural woodlands. These points have been made in considerable detail in specialist publications and brought together in a book about Lady Park (see 'Lady Park Wood as a Natural Reserve' essay), but these were addressed to other ecologists, foresters and environmentalists and were not written in a form or place that would reach the general public. Today, however, ecologists need to reach a much wider audience in a way that makes the subject interesting and digestible. My hope is that the artists will help us reach people who would never think of picking a scientific ecology book off the shelves.

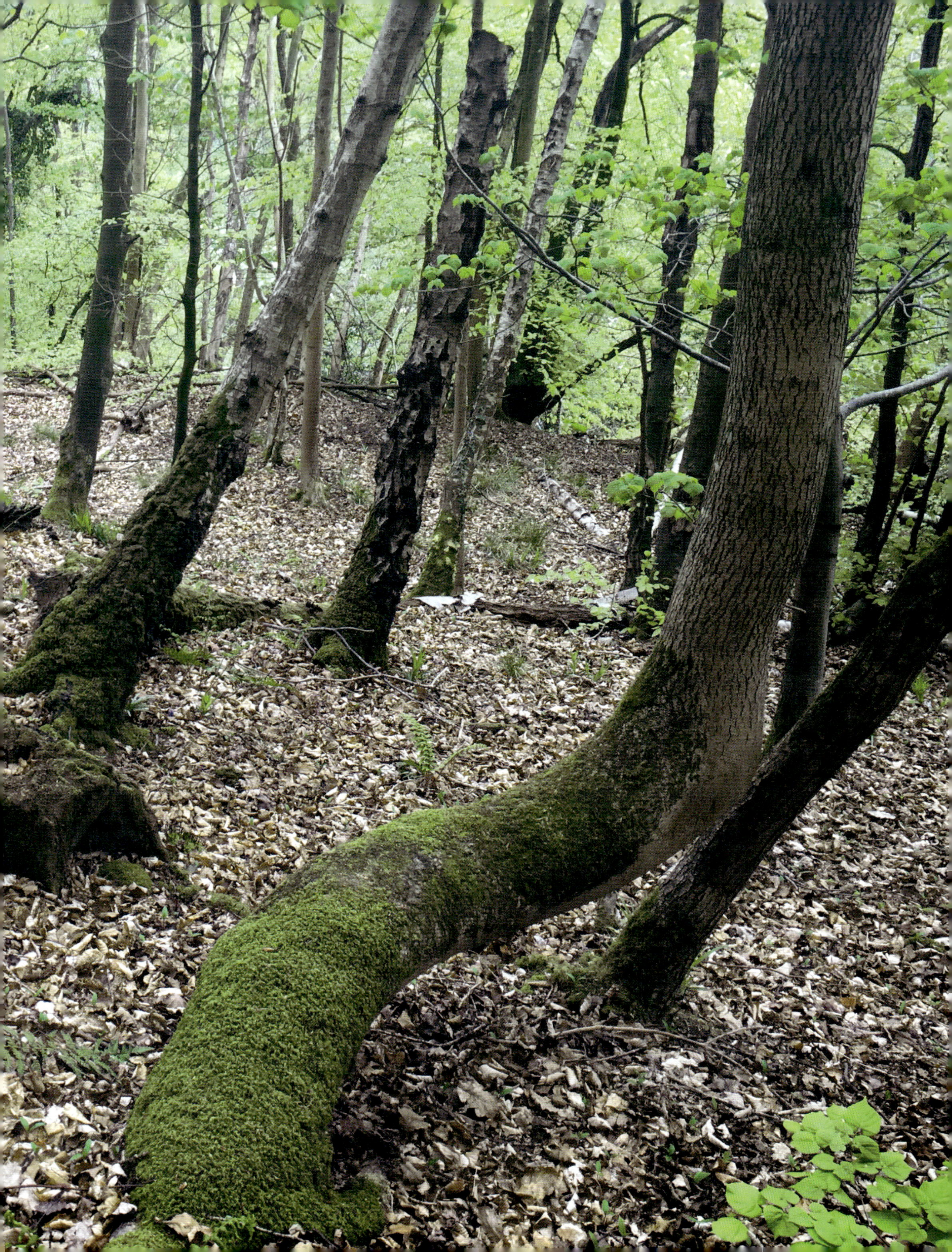

THE PAINTINGS AND DRAWINGS

WITH AN ECOLOGICAL COMMENTARY
GEORGE PETERKEN

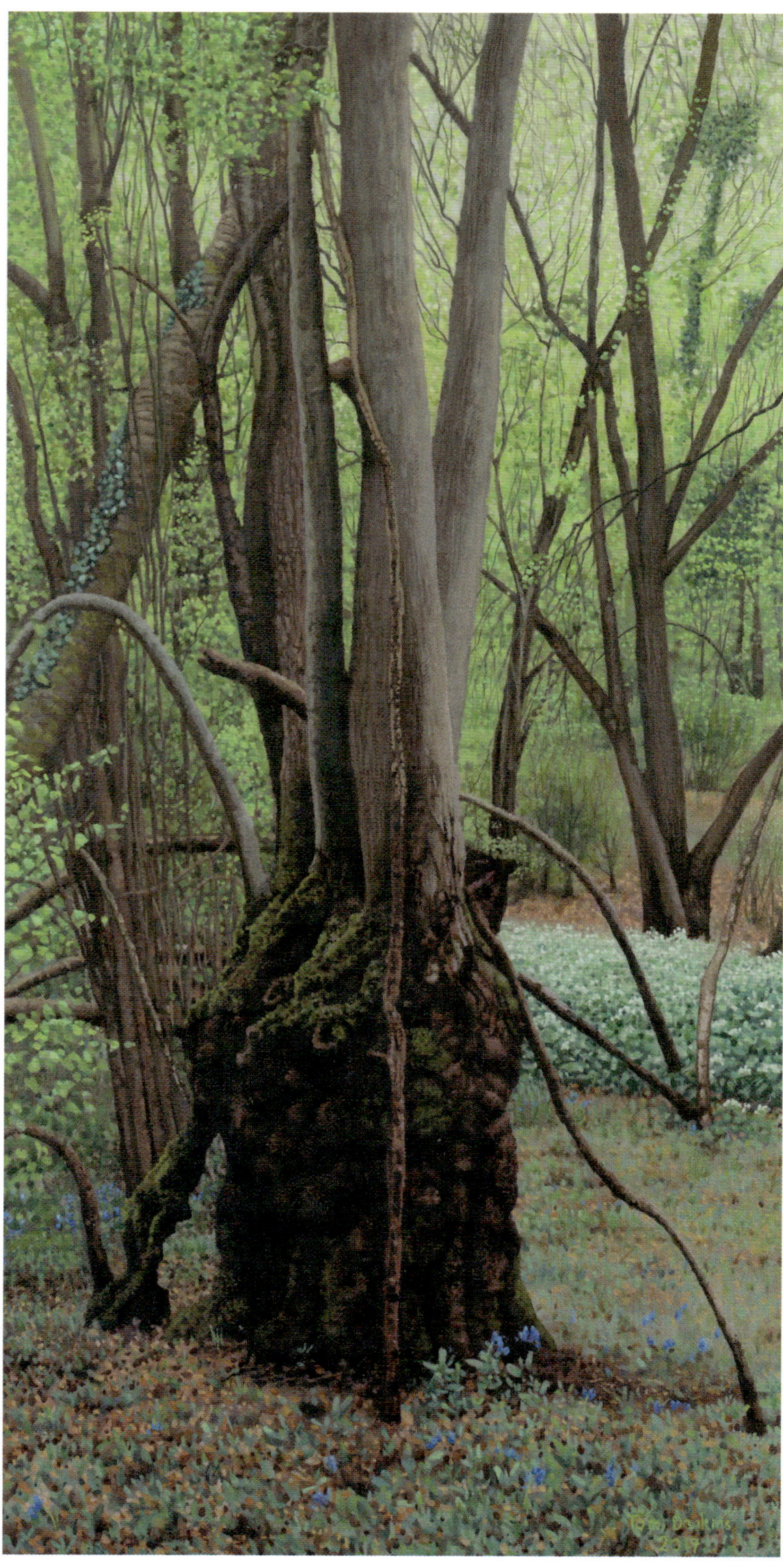

(fig 1)
TOM DEAKINS
The Green Man, 2018
Oil on panel
46 x 23 cm
Artist's collection

RELICTS OF THE PAST

TIM CRAVEN, TOM DEAKINS

Ecologists have several reasons for allowing a few woods to develop naturally. They learn how woodlands work by themselves; they observe the conditions under which much of our wildlife must have evolved; they use them as scientific baselines against which to measure the impact of people elsewhere; they restore habitats that are in short supply in managed woods; and they generate wild environments which can refresh visitors with the contrast they offer to the built environments in which most of us live our lives. However, it is never possible to eliminate the influences of people completely, and impossible to erase the former presence of people in the woods that we try to restore to a natural state. In the case of Lady Park, we cannot erase the mining spoil, the charcoal hearths and the old roads, all of which have changed the land form permanently.

Tom Deakins' *The Green Man* (fig 1) records what is now an alien presence in a natural wood, but one that would have been familiar to woodmen throughout the lower Wye Valley until the early twentieth century. It is a high-cut small-leaved lime stool (or just possibly a beech), the result of repeatedly coppicing, or cutting the tree at his height. Like the charcoal hearths and other features, it reminds us for the time being that people worked here for centuries and probably for millennia.

This tree's history is clear in its form. It was last cut in 1942 in order to allow access to larger timber trees. Previously, it had been cut in 1870 as part of an ordinary coppicing operation, and possibly again in 1902 when the 32-year-old regrowth was thinned to allow the best young trees to grow quickly into timber. Since 1942, it has been allowed to grow freely, so the eight trees growing from the stool are now 75 years old. The expanded trunk, or stub, on which they grow will be hollow, however sound it may look, and eventually the trees will become so heavy that they will wrench the stub apart.

Ancient pollards and stub trees possess the individuality of great age, but they also embody mysteries. How old, for example, is the expanded base of The Green Man? If it had been coppiced, say, 10 times at intervals of 25 years up to 1370, that would make it roughly 400 years old, which is far from impossible, for limes are potentially immortal. Further, why did the woodmen cut so high? After all, high-cutting wastes a metre of wood on every stem and most coppice cuts were made close to the ground. Sometimes, high-cut stubs were created as distinctive trees to mark boundaries between the felling compartments, but in the Wye Valley such cutting was far too common and indiscriminate for this. Sometimes it was a response to rabbits and hares – cut high and they will not graze the regrowth – but that cannot be the explanation here because many other limes mixed in with the stubs were cut close to the ground. Perhaps there was some economic advantage, but that can't be so either, for the prevalence of high-cut stubs reduced the

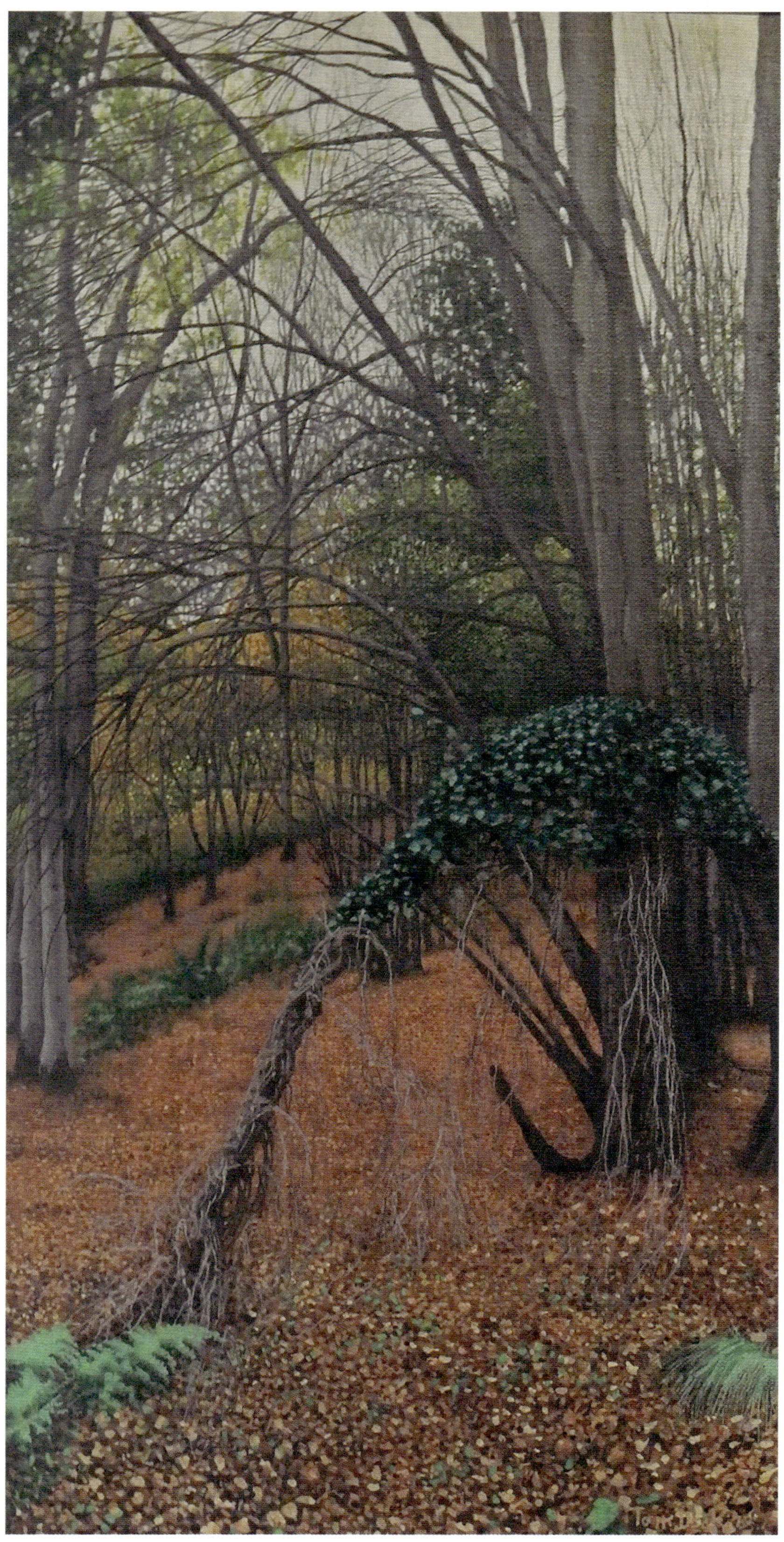

(fig 2)
TOM DEAKINS
Arches, 2018
Oil on panel
46 x 23 cm
Artist's collection

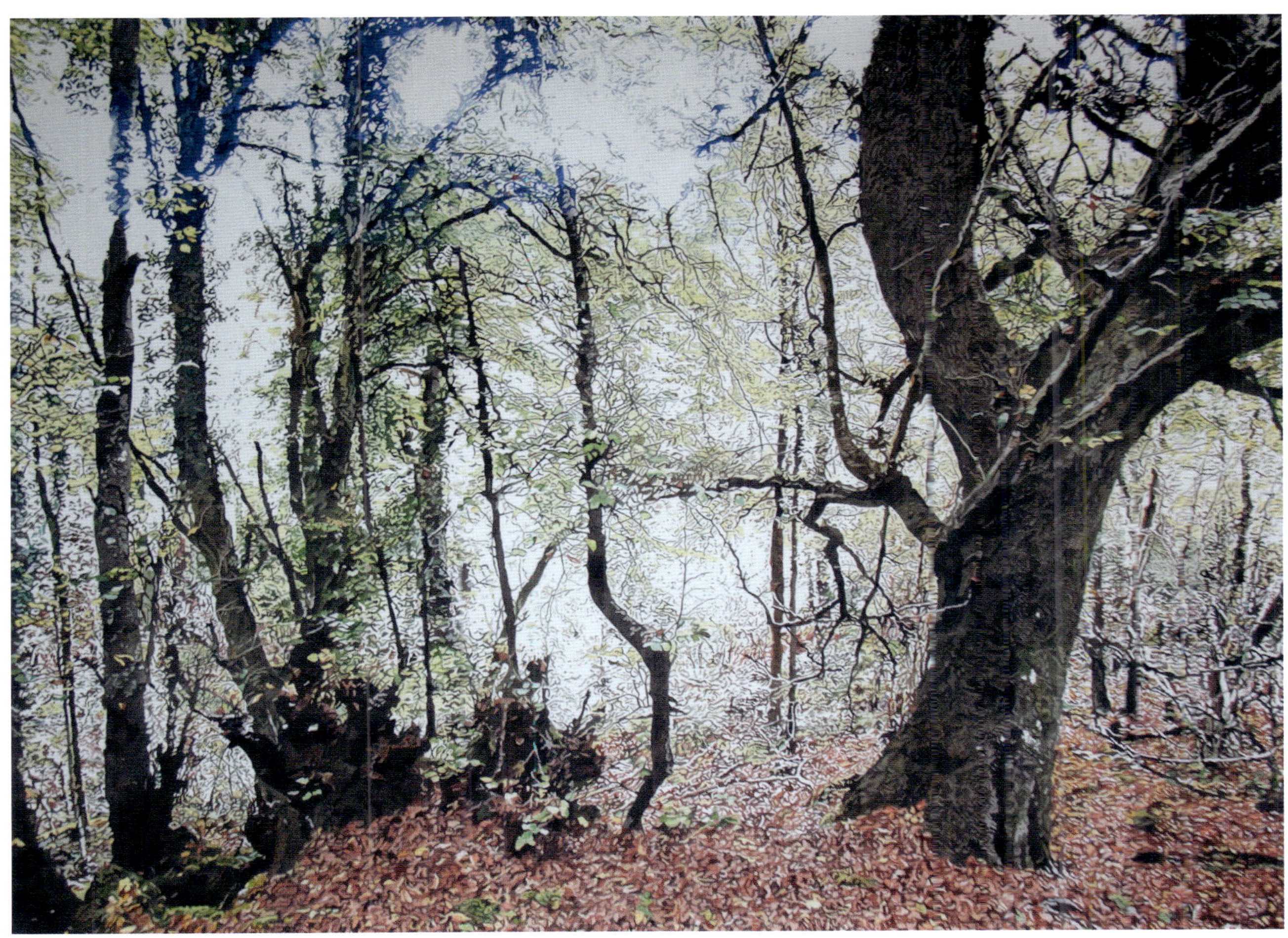

(fig 3)
TIM CRAVEN
October Frieze, 2018
Casein on linen
50 x 67.6 cm
Private collection

value of the woods, according to eighteenth-century records from woods further south in the Wye Valley. We are left with a mystery and a faint suspicion that the woodmen suffered from lumbago.

Tim Craven's *October Frieze* (fig 3) and Tom Deakins' *Arches* (fig 2) show beech and lime stools cut closer to the ground. Alongside the former's beech is a standard oak, the other component of traditionally managed woods. Both the coppice stools and *The Green Man* (fig 1) are much older than the large standard trees, probably several centuries old – they take us back to the Middle Ages. Each year, these and other relicts of pre-twentieth-century woodmanship, such as giant pollard trees, become fewer and will eventually vanish. Meanwhile, we enjoy the privilege of combining the new with the old.

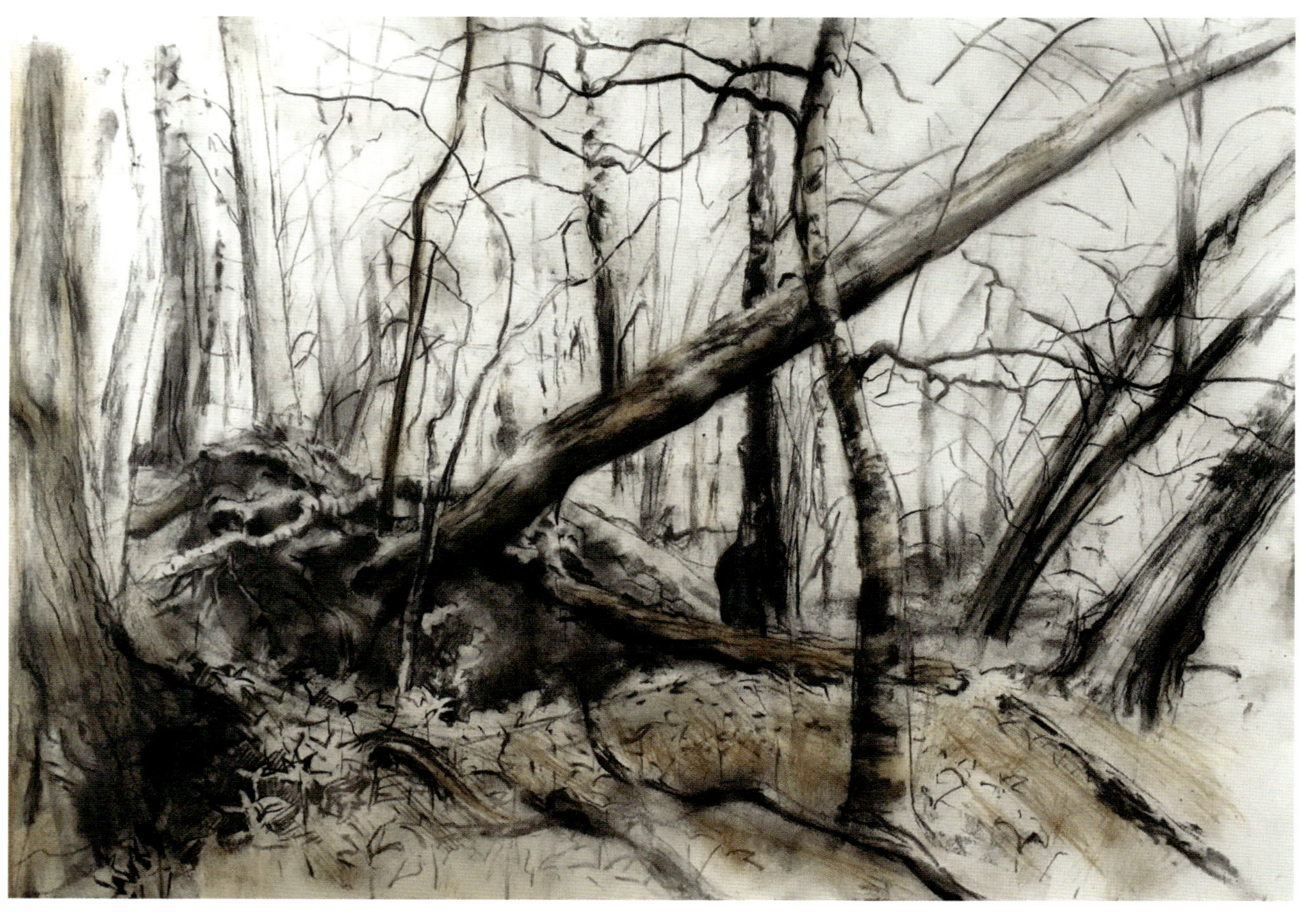

(fig 4)
FIONA McINTYRE
Rewilding, 2018
Charcoal and earth from the forest floor on paper
62 x 72 cm
Private collection

THE WILD WOOD

FIONA McINTYRE

The only wild woodland we will see now and in the future is woodland that has in the past been used, abused or managed by people, or has grown up on land that was once deforested. Kenneth Grahame got it right in *The Wind in the Willows*: Badger lived in the wildwood, but the wildwood had grown up on the foundations of places once inhabited by people.

So, too, Lady Park Wood. Much as we might like to find remnants of primaeva woodland lurking in remote corners of Britain, reconstructed wild woodland retaining the indelible marks of former human presence is all we can know, as McIntyre's *Rewilding* (fig 4) clearly highlights. Here, the ground is irregular, due to shallow ironstone mining in the nineteenth century and earlier, but the trees are unmistakably natural. The centrepiece is a leaning tree that lived for a while after it was uprooted, and may have generated a replacement stem from its base, whereas its near neighbour and contemporary fell to the ground, where it died, leaving a rotting trunk that eventually broke on the lip of the slope. To the right, other trees have merely leaned as they grew, and as their leans became pronounced, so one of them developed a new leader from the upper side of the trunk, which will eventually become the tree's new crown. The woodland of which they are part is characteristically disorderly, with trees of many sizes and species. The miners departed long ago, but they still influence events: hillocks and hollows ensure that trees are rooted on slopes and thus more likely to fall.

The drawing also indirectly illustrates an apparent contrast between artistic and ecological perceptions. For the artist, the frame defines the interest, but for the ecologist context is also important. In this case, we know that the leaning and fallen trees in the centre were blown over when the plantations beyond the limits of the natural reserve (to the left) were felled in the ordinary course of timber harvesting. The consequence was that the upper margins of the reserve were exposed to stronger gusts and several trees were unable to withstand the extra pressure. The general point is that no reserve can be entirely isolated from its surroundings. However much we may want a woodland to be totally free of human influence, we are unable to exclude the indirect effects of human activity elsewhere. Be a natural woodland reserve ever so large, it is still subject to the effects of climate change, wide-scale pollution and the absence of wolves and other large beasts that were once part of pre-Neolithic woodland.

It is also worth mentioning here a general point that applies to other paintings in this collection. Managed woodlands are orderly, because foresters salvage trees that have been blown over and fell trees that look unsafe, especially those that have died on their feet. This is because we use most woods to grow timber, or maintain them for the

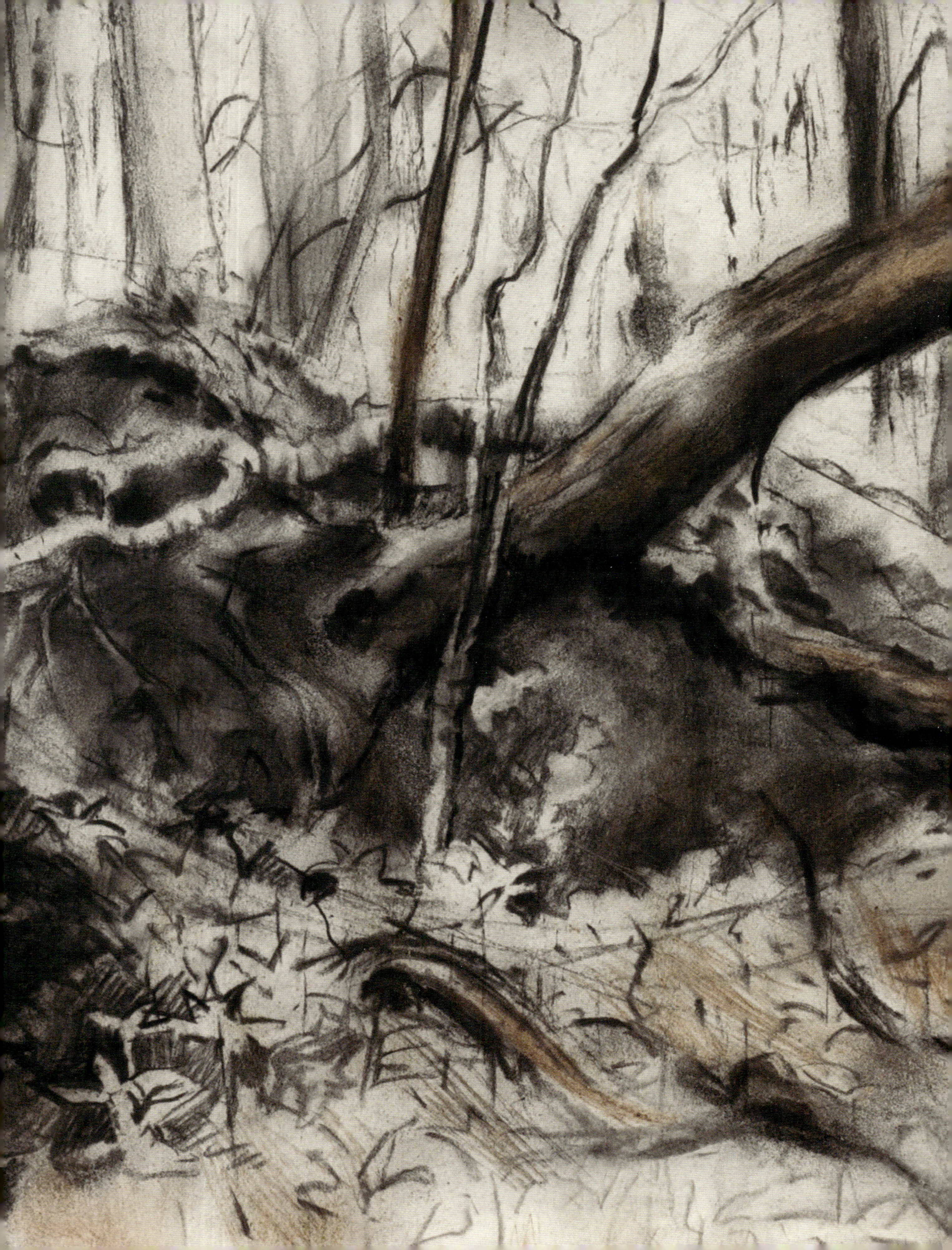

public to enjoy in safety. When those are the objectives, the trees tend to be upright and shaped like lollipops on a stick, simply because those that are not shaped like this are removed. They also tend to be roughly the same size and in straight lines, because they started life together as plantations. And, quite often, they are all the same kind, the species that the owner or forester liked best or which he – and, until recently, it was usually a he – deemed most profitable.

Natural woodlands, in contrast, seem untidy, even chaotic. They are mixtures of tree species which started life at different times, so they are irregularly distributed, of many sizes and form a variety of shapes. Moreover, leaning trees are part of the scene and they are not to be cleared up, because that would impose a human value-system in a place where natural processes should reign supreme. Trees lean if they are blown over or knocked aside by a falling neighbour, yet cannot fall to the ground because they lodge against another, stronger tree. Such partially fallen trees retain much of their root system, so there is a good chance they will live, but their crowns almost always come to rest under the crown of another tree – they suddenly become sub-canopy trees with a damaged root system – and the result is more often a lingering death. If they live and thrive, they often take the opportunity to right themselves by growing a new stem from the upside of the leaning trunk, which then takes over physiologically, leaving the former leader to live on as a subordinate branch – thus they are self-righting trees.

(fig 4)
FIONA McINTYRE
Detail: *Rewilding*, 2018
Charcoal and earth from
the forest floor on paper
62 x 72 cm
Private collection

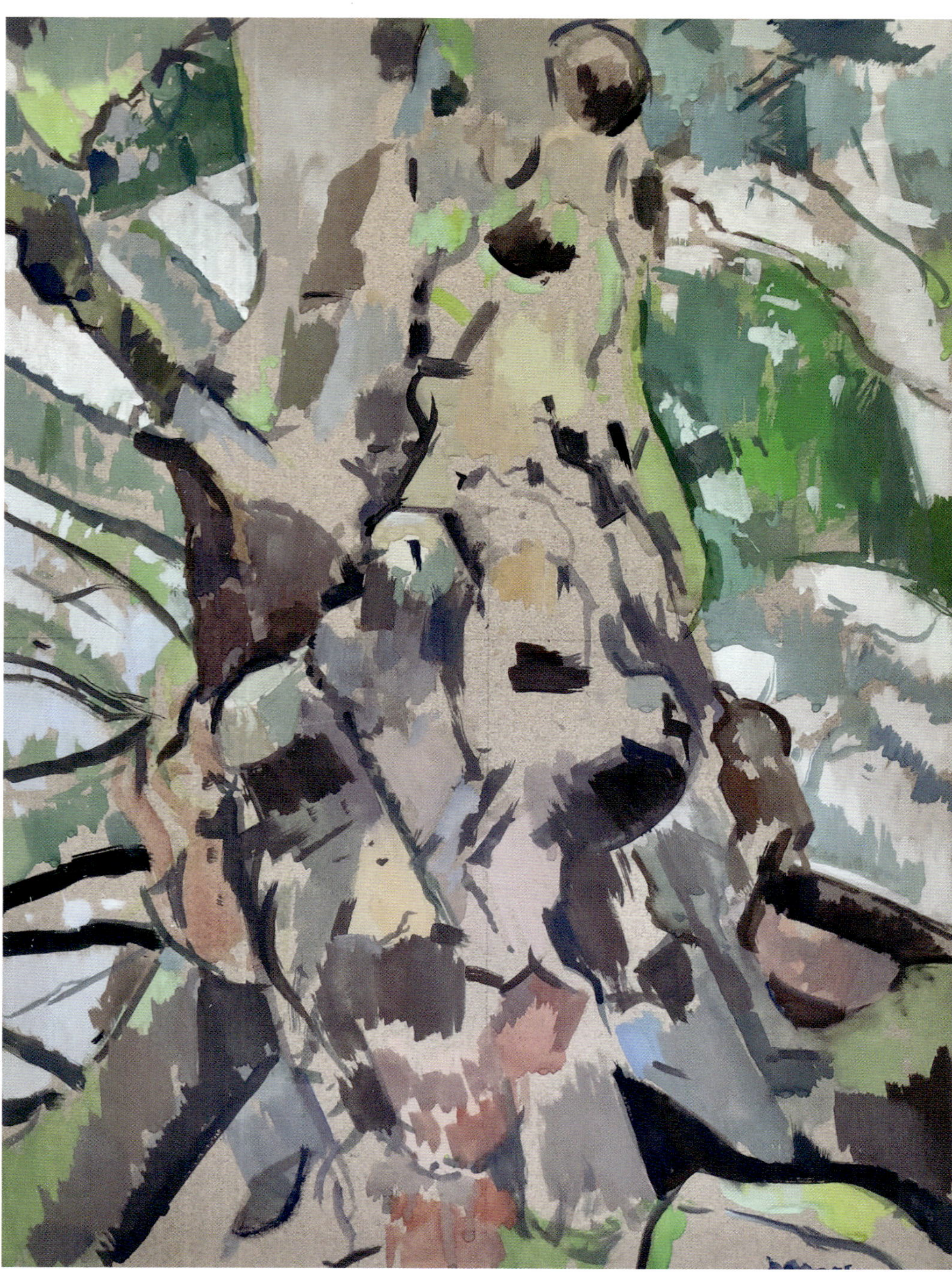

(fig 5)
ROBERT AMESBURY BROOKS
Large Tree Stump, 2018
Oil on canvas
77 x 58 cm
Private collection

TREES AS INDIVIDUALS

ROBERT AMESBURY BROOKS, STELLA CARR, ALEX EGAN

Trees become individuals as they grow older. Anonymity belongs to trees planted in evenly spaced, straight lines – they are no more individual than a Grenadier Guardsman on parade. Truly ancient trees, such as the Major Oak in Sherwood Forest, the Ankerwycke Yew at Runnymede and the great Chestnut at Tortworth, acquire names through their size, distinctiveness and associations.

None of the Lady Park trees has a name, but several are distinctive – and they attracted the artists. Robert Amesbury Brooks gave his old beech such a matter-of-fact title – *Large Tree Stump* (fig 5) – that he could almost be a scientific ecologist, who is meant to be objective, dispassionate, seeing a spade as a spade. However, this is not a stump but a living ancient remnant from the time when Lady Park was managed, and of course this beech bears the marks of its past. Unlike oaks, which hang on to dead branches for decades, dead beech branches rot in a few years and the adjacent bark tries to grow round the stump to seal the tree's interior from passing fungal spores. Often, the seal is incomplete, leaving holes that, with rot, grow into holes that afford dens for forest mammals, hideaways for nesting birds and miniature pools in which insects can lay eggs. Eventually, the rot will advance so far that the tree may break in a storm – and then it really will be a stump.

The camouflage-like tinting of the trunk emphasises the wrinkles and warts of age. Beech trees in youth have smooth bark but, like people, their skin becomes characterful in old age. These colours also remind us that old trees are habitats for lichens and mosses, especially in the wet climate of western Britain, where trees can be so densely covered in variegated patches that the actual bark is invisible. In this case, however, the blotches are unlikely to be lichens, for the Wye Valley is down-wind of South Wales and did not escape the polluted, lichen-shrivelling air blown from nineteenth- and twentieth-century heavy industry. The air is cleaner today, but the lichens are only slowly recovering. Lady Park may have been placed beyond the direct influence of people, but it cannot escape its history, nor the nitrate-enhanced rain of today.

Alex Egan's spectral presence of a large, unmistakably distinctive oak tree, *Lady Park Wood – A Visitation* (fig 6), brings Middle Earth and its Ents to mind, if not triffids hiding in the undergrowth. It also reinforces the point that Lady Park is a wood in transit on from managed to natural, for the shape of that tree could only have developed in the open circumstances of a standard timber tree in a coppice that was cut regularly. It contrasts sharply with the smaller and younger trees amongst which it stands, which have grown slim and tall since that management ceased.

Most observers – ecologists included – only properly appreciate the individuality of a tree when it grows large and thus old. In Lady Park, however, some 10 per cent of all the trees in the wood have been individually recorded at intervals from 1945 onwards, so observers have collectively known the trees that were there from the outset for nearly 75 years. Between the careful measurements of the recording dates, we have watched how they grow and what happens to them, and in this way even the small trees have become individuals with their own particular history.

Inevitably, like people, trees become more individual with age: seedlings, like babies, look alike to casual observers, but tall saplings and youthful poles bear some marks of their 'upbringing'. By the time they are mature, trees have developed according to their circumstances and inherent vitality, and this is apparent in their form, just like the lines of a human face give some hint of that person's accumulated life experiences. Egan's tree must be an oak, for it has low spreading branches that were once vigorous but have now withered and died, surviving as dry reminders of a more spacious youth. The crown has regrown, which may show that it was previously pollarded, though in this instance it simply looks as if it was once shattered in an accident. But it grows on, a fit grandfather surviving from a former time. The irony here is that it is probably not a grandfather at all, for, as Lady Park has become more natural, not one single oakling has survived in 75 years to become a tree.

The combat camouflage patterning of Robert Amesbury Brooks' beech (fig 5) and the screen of smaller trees surrounding Alex Egan's oak (fig 6) both remind us again of the capacity of woodland to conceal. Large trees can be easily overlooked as one walks round a wood if there is a screen of small trees beside the path or the pattern of sun flecks breaks up the shapes and colours. The ecologist bent on woodland survey knows that he or she must step off the paths and into the body of the wood if the true character of the place is to be seen.

We expect trees to grow upright, either like the National Trust oak when they grow in the open, or like a huge lollipop if they grow in a wood, but the lesson of Lady Park and other mature natural woods is that they take on many other forms, not just leaning, but also lying on their side like a Roman emperor at a feast. Annabel Cullen's *Rejuvenated Beech* (fig 7), and Stella Carr's *Fagus Metanoia* (fig 8), have been attracted to perhaps the most distinctive individual tree in Lady Park, a beech that was blown over in a storm from the north-east many moons ago, but which fought back so strongly that it has become at least six trees – all but one now reaching the canopy – growing from the prostrate (and perfectly healthy) original trunk and crown branches. One can easily find the early stages of this response when, a few years after a tree has tipped over, new shoots grow from the fallen trunk, but their ability to grow depends on how much of the original root system survived the fall. Remarkably, sub-canopy trees with no more than a third of their root system intact have generated new trees successfully – like flying a jet to its destination on one engine.

Success in rejuvenation also depends on where they fall. If they come to rest under a tree that casts deep shade, they will have difficulty surviving. If they fall with other trees and end up at the bottom of the pile, they are the most likely to be 'hurt', much like the rugby player at the bottom of a collapsed scrum. If, as they fall, the trunk hits another fallen tree or a ridge or rock on the ground, their trunk may snap, and this does them no good at all. But the most important factor is the species of tree. Birch, gean and other

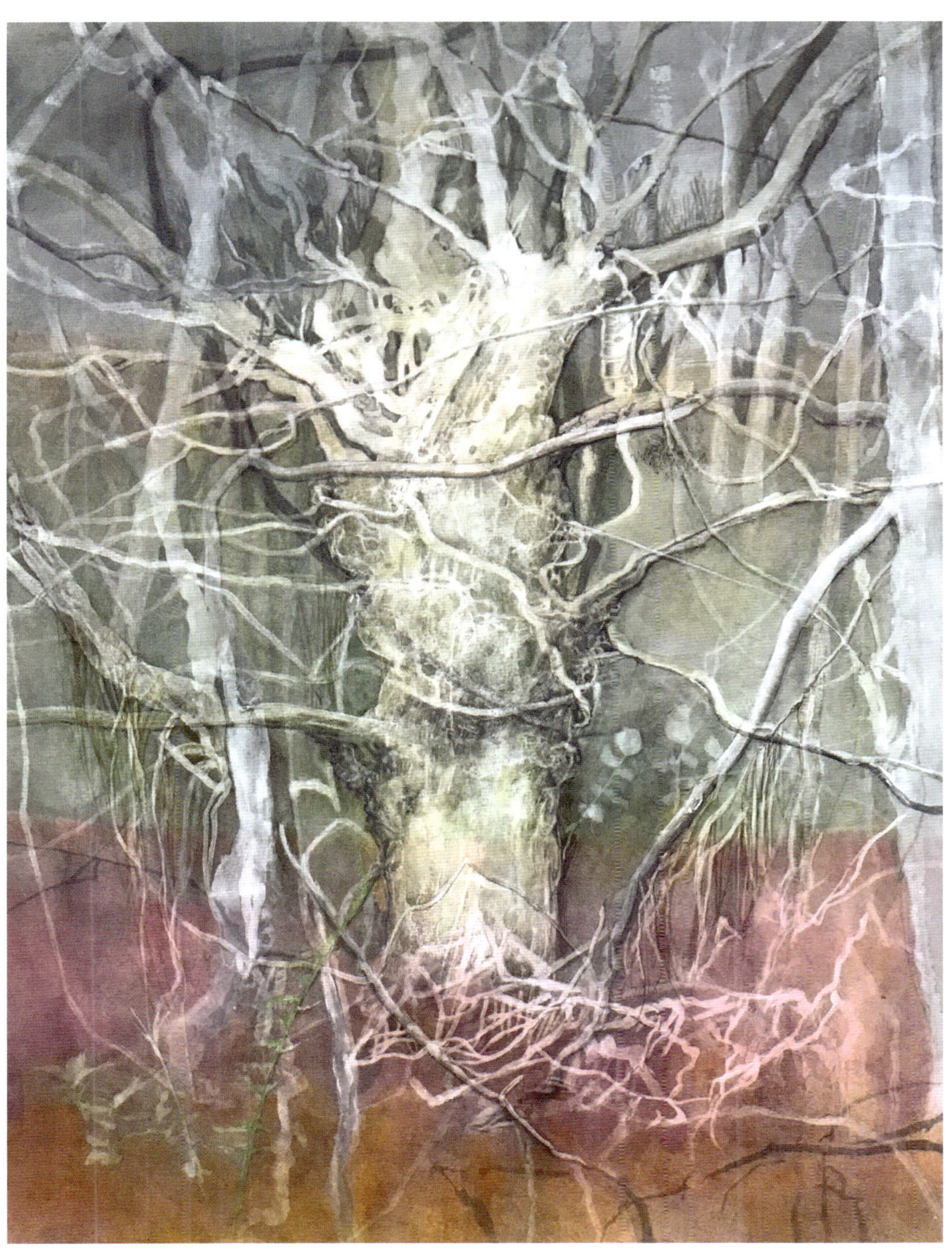

(fig 6)
ALEX EGAN
Lady Park Wood – A Visitation, 2018
Watercolour on paper
53 x 45 cm
Private collection

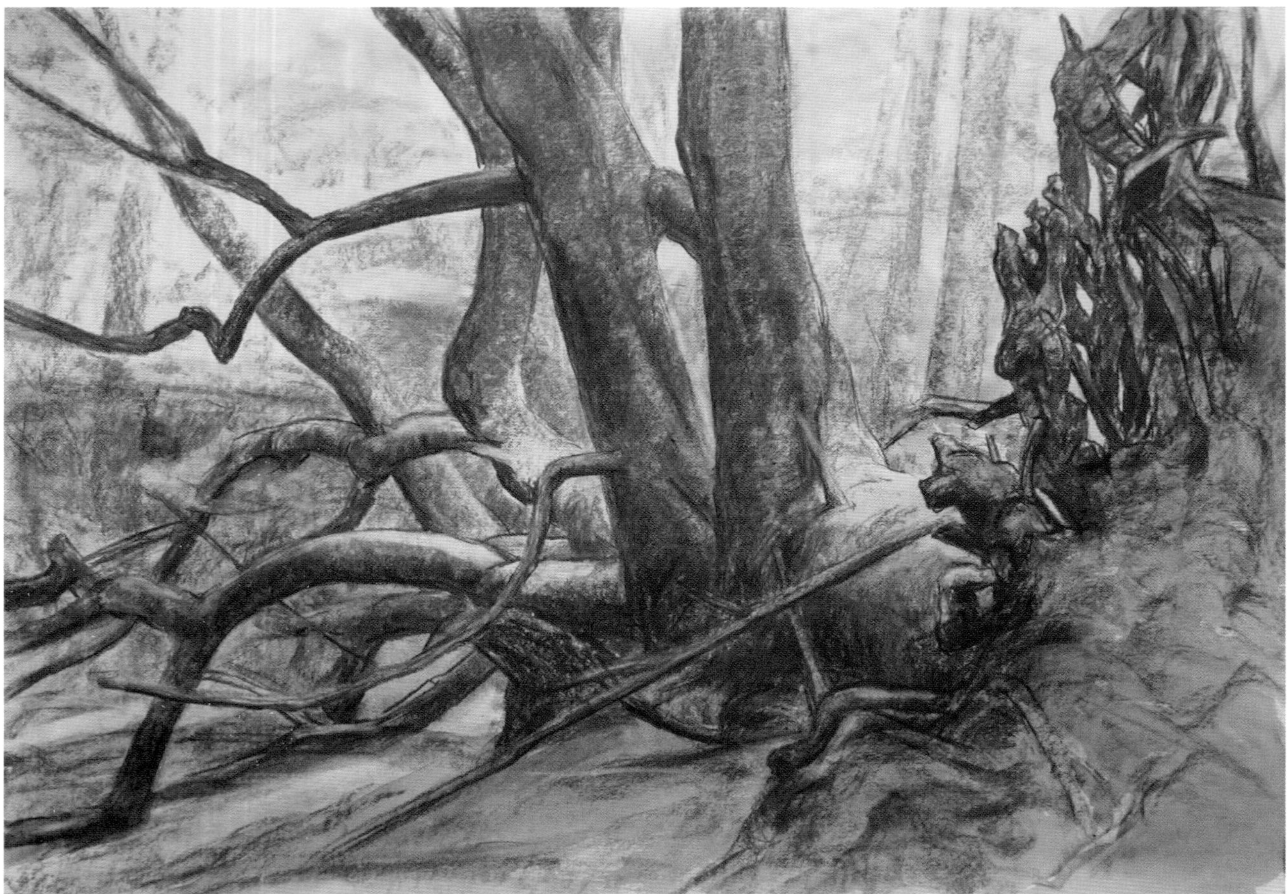

pioneers invariably die, for they cannot bear shade. Oaks usually try to resprout, but within three years or so their new shoots wither and die, and that's it. Ash is a moderate shade-bearer as an adult, and often survives: Lady Park contains groups of ash trees grown from a single, prostrate tree, almost as remarkable as the beech in this painting. Wych elms grow well from fallen trees, but currently their progress is limited by disease.

This leaves the two limes as the species that really prosper in the knock-about conditions of natural woodland. Both can generate a copious fuzz of new growth from their original rootstock to the proximal ends of their crown branches. Indeed, they are capable of rooting from near the tips of small branches if these are pressed firmly and securely to the ground by, say, another fallen tree or large branch – just like wild strawberries, in fact. And there are several instances in Lady Park where fallen limes have generated a colonnade of new stems along their entire trunk. Combining these capabilities allows lime to migrate through the wood. Below the cliff there is one large-leaved lime that grew tall, then leaned and rooted at the tip. From this new plant a new tree was generated which also leaned, rooted and generated another new tree. It grows just like an extremely slow looper caterpillar moves, making its way at sub-glacial pace across the wood. Deer form the only serious barrier to this happening more often, for the new shoots from fallen trunks or rooting branches are readily browsed.

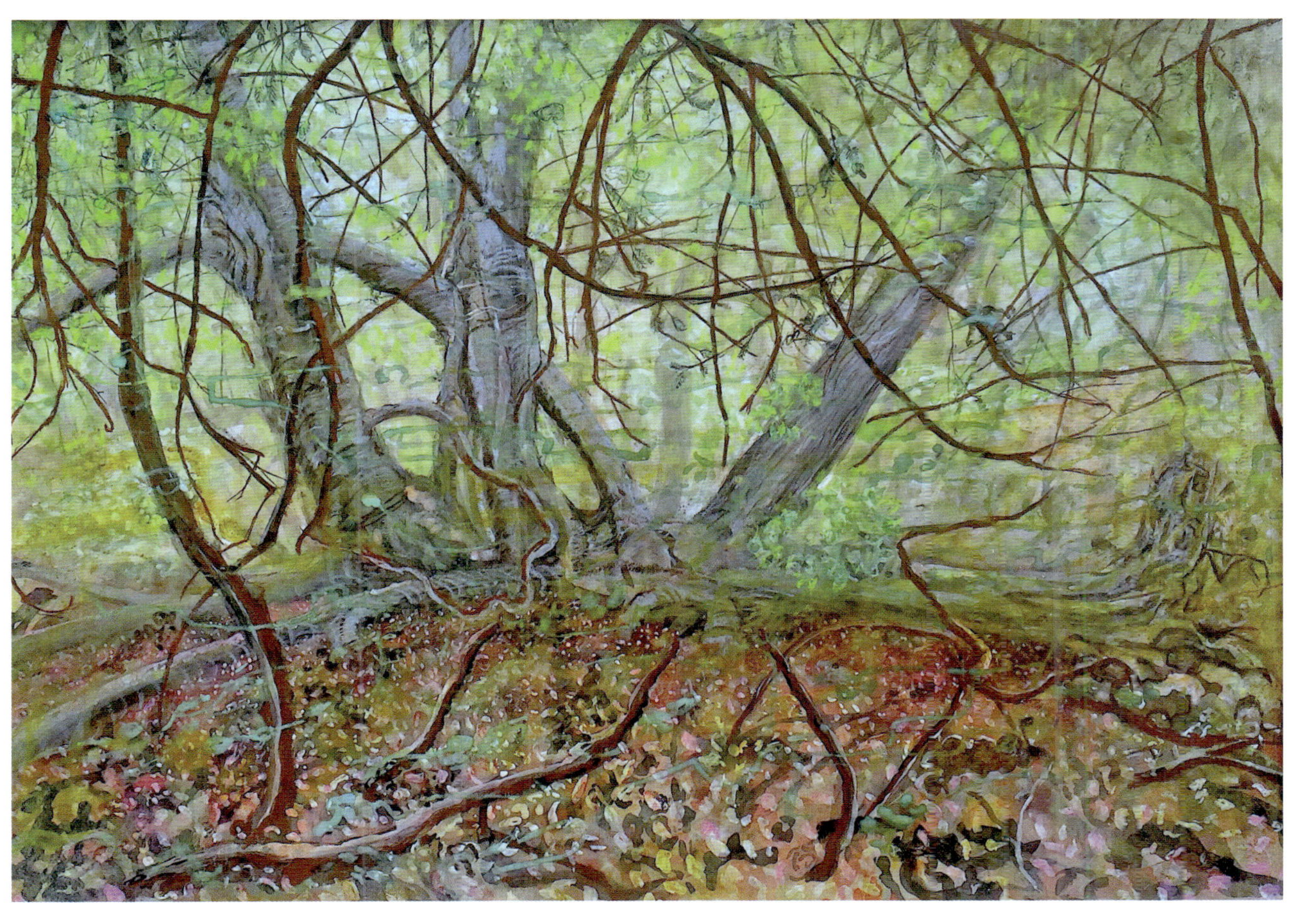

(fig 7) Left:
ANNABEL CULLEN
Rejuvenated Beech, 2019
Charcoal and ink on paper
59 x 84 cm
Artist's collection

(fig 8)
STELLA CARR
Fagus Metanoia, 2019
Ink, gouache and raw pigment on paper
42.5 x 68 cm
Private collection

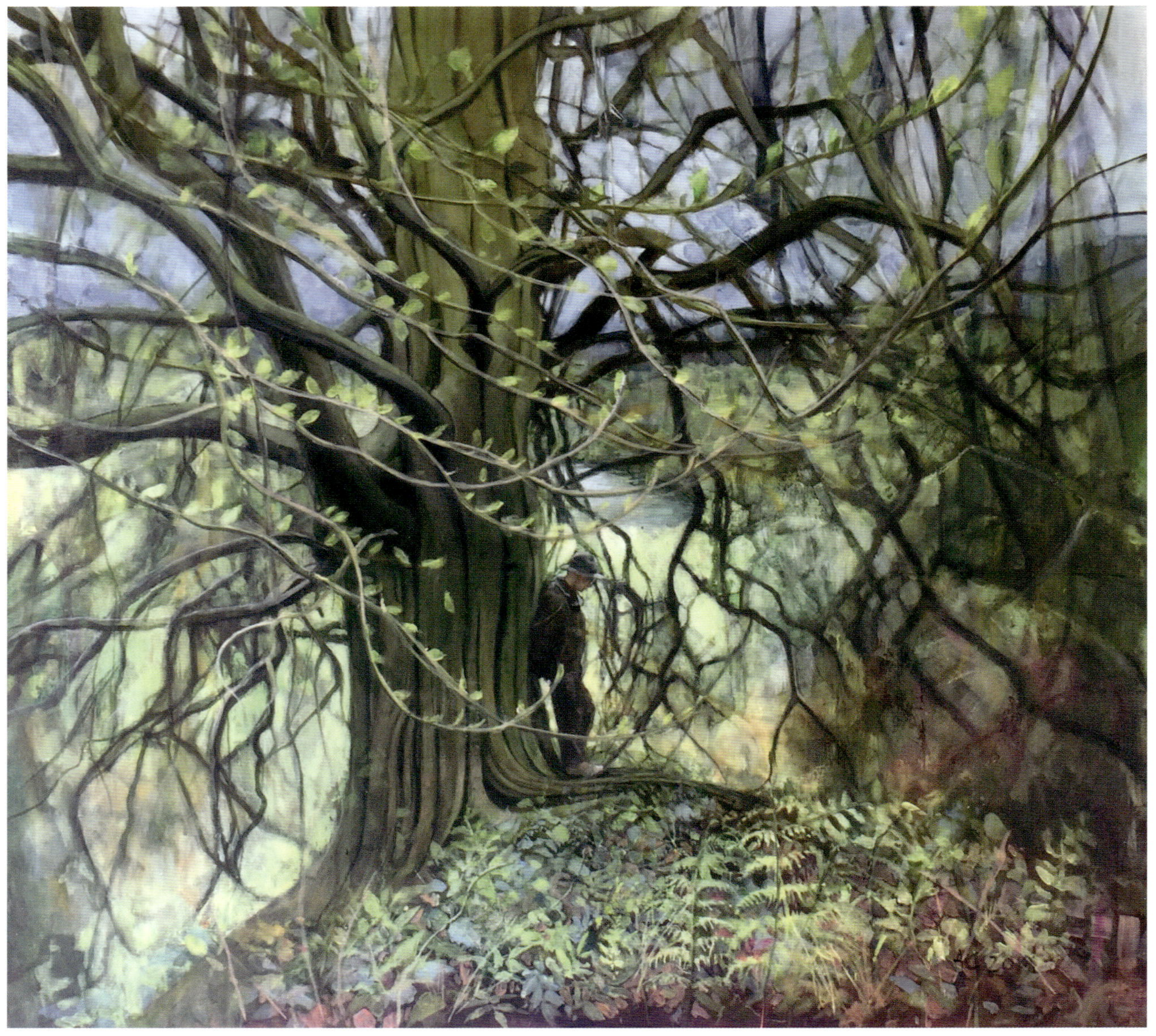

(fig 9)
ALEX EGAN
The Forester, 2018
Oil on canvas
58 x 55 cm
Private collection

LARGE YEW TREES

BLAZE CYAN, ALEX EGAN, ANNABEL CULLEN,
ROBERT AMESBURY BROOKS

Large yews are second only to great oaks in individuality and attracting fame. Lady Park has many yews clinging tenaciously to cliffs, but few are large. That's typical of yews, which only really grow large and very old in full sunlight. Within natural woodland they stay small and, notwithstanding their evergreen character, can be shaded to death by beech. Blaze Cyan (*The Yew, Lady Park Wood*, fig 12), Robert Amesbury Brooks (*Trunk of the Yew*, fig 11) and Alex Egan (*The Forester*, fig 9), all show the same tree, clinging precariously to a limestone outcrop, where their clasping roots are as distinctive as the tree itself. Annabel Cullen (*Large Yew*, fig 10) sets the yew against a background of woodland, which brings out the gloom and foreboding associated with yew-rich woodlands. The soil surface in some of the yew-beech woods on chalkland scarps and in the ravine woods of Castle Eden Dene, in the north-east, must be amongst the darkest places in any British wood.

These yews and other distinctive trees are clearly recognisable individuals and for most people they stand in a matrix of anonymity, but, for the ecologist studying the wood tree-by-tree over decades, the feeling of trees as individuals goes much further. In Lady Park we have followed the fortunes of some 20,000 trees over 75 years from transient saplings to giants that have scarcely changed in that time and many others that have grown and changed in form. Over the years, some trees have been lucky; others, such as trees that happen to be crushed when a neighbour falls, have been unlucky. Some generate respect, simply because we know they have recovered from repeated setbacks, or they have survived in adverse circumstances, such as under the shade of a particularly vigorous beech. Others impress with their perfect growth form or because we know that they took quick advantage of the space vacated by a falling neighbour. Some of this is clear to a first-time visitor, but much more is apparent to the person who has known the trees for years, especially if he or she inherits the records of people who knew the trees before them. Objective and dispassionate though the scientific ecologist is meant to be, anthropomorphism and subjectivity easily intrude when the individual trees of a wood have been well known for decades.

Could this yew ever grow as large as the great churchyard yews? The quick answer is: not any time soon. At some risk to our safety, we measured it in 2015 and recorded its girth at 1.3m from the ground as 297cm. This is nowhere near comparable with, say, the famous Ankerwyke Yew, which stands just over the Thames from Runnymede and was therefore a likely witness to the signing of Magna Carta. At 8-9m girth it could easily have been a large tree nine hundred years ago. Even this falls far short of the once monstrous yew in the churchyard at Fortingall, Perthshire, which in the eighteenth century was measured at a girth of 16m. Whilst estimates abound, nobody really knows how old these trees are, but informed speculation suggests that they are older than the churchyards in which they stand, and indeed older than Christianity. The Lady Park yew will have to grow beyond the year 3000 to achieve these sizes, and by that time the rock face will have eroded to the point where its one-sided crown will have brought it crashing to the base of the cliff.

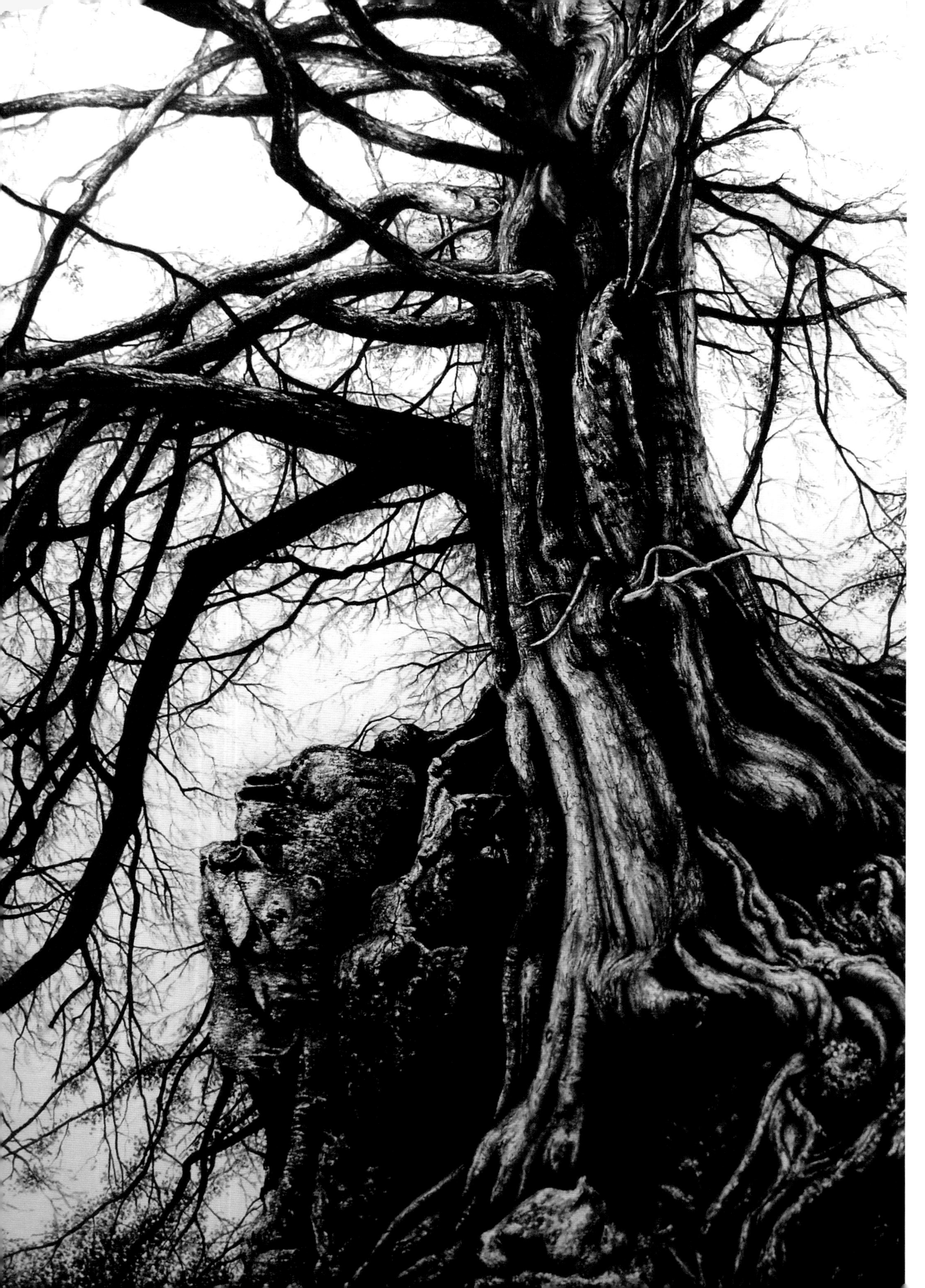

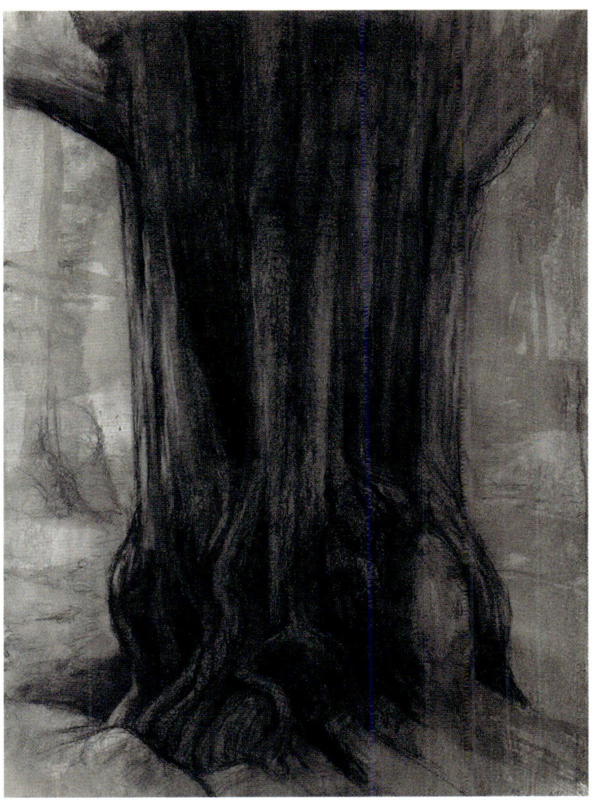

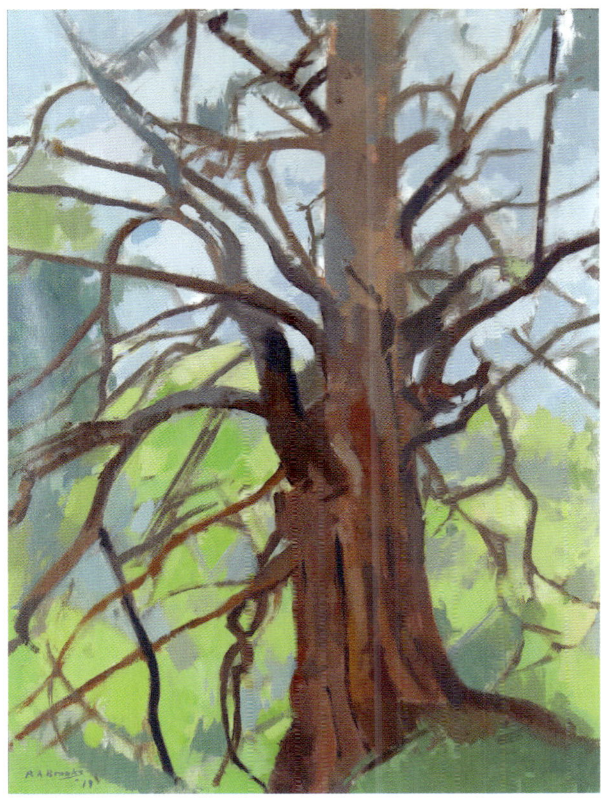

(fig 10)
ANNABEL CULLEN
Large Yew, 2019
Charcoal and ink on paper
76 x 56 cm
Private collection

(fig 11)
ROBERT AMESBURY BROOKS
Trunk of the Yew, 2018
Oil on canvas
61 x 46 cm
Private collection

(fig 12) Left:
BLAZE CYAN
The Yew, Lady Park Wood, 2018
Charcoal and conté on paper
47 x 32 cm
Private collection

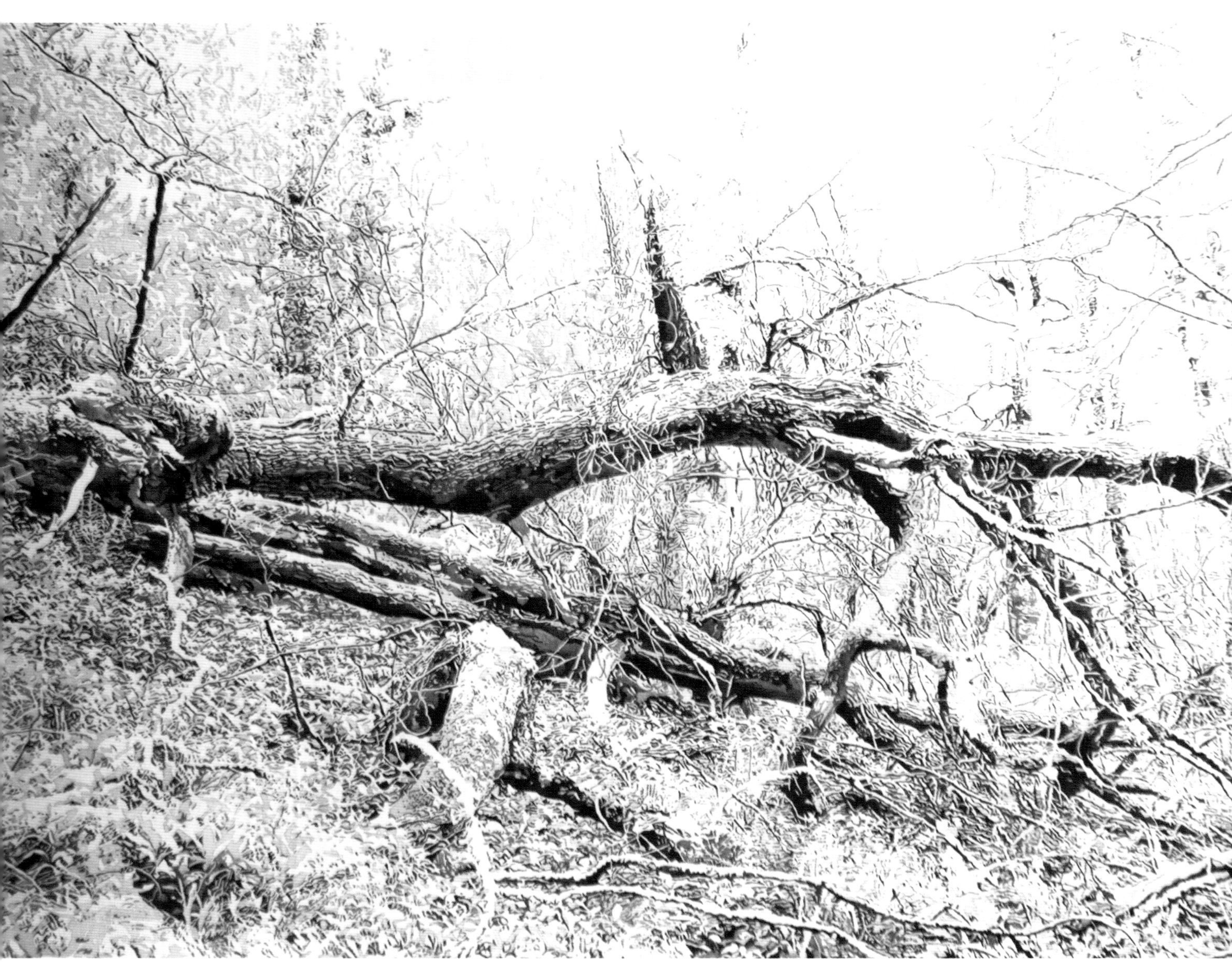

(fig 13)
TIM CRAVEN
Crash! (Lady Park Wood), 2018
Casein on canvas
61 x 91.5 cm
Private collection

TREE FALLS

TIM CRAVEN, ANNABEL CULLEN

In natural woodland, twigs, ousted saplings and small branches are falling all the time, something one discovers when one has to keep a driveway amongst trees clear of debris, but the fall of large-canopy trees is an 'event' – irregular, unpredictable, often spectacular and accompanied by the sound of a large crash (unless, like the great blowdown in October 1987, the sound of falling trees is lost amongst the howls of a hurricane). Sensible people avoid Lady Park in high winds so big-tree falls are rarely witnessed, except on one occasion when a large and apparently healthy beech fell without warning on a calm, sunny day one October: the two of us who were in the wood at the time looked at each other and simply asked 'What was that?'

Tim Craven's images show freshly fallen trees that dominated their part of the wood until they fell. *Crash! (Lady Park Wood)* (fig 13) shows a fallen oak against a background of seemingly shattered trees, strongly reminiscent of sepia-tinted black-and-white images of shell-shattered woods from the Great War. In sober reality, Lady Park tree falls are rarely like this: with few exceptions, trees left standing on the margins of gaps retain their crowns. Rather, this is a reflection of the great contrast in light between the open sky and the dark woodland interior. It is a reminder that when trees fall, the light regime for all plants below the canopy is totally transformed.

A recently fallen majestic tree that has grown for centuries shatters in seconds, leaving raw wounds, a scene of chaos and confusion. Crown branches that grew wide to intercept as much light as possible are shockingly flattened, crushed and scattered. Topmost twigs and their delicate coating of lichens are suddenly exposed to our gaze and touch, as if the convulsion has brought the private parts of the tree to public inspection. Hazels and other underwood growth are broken, crushed and flattened – the co lateral damage. Majestic trees that inspired awe and respect lie gruesomely broken. Everything is wrong: branches that reached for the sky now point meaninglessly towards the ground. Not only is it difficult to penetrate the fallen remains, but one must always be alive to aftershocks, the possibility that great trunks and branches have not yet come completely to rest.

Tim Craven's *Twin Pillars* (fig 15) also reminds us that large trees rarely fall alone. Their sheer size and weight, combined with their accelerating momentum as they fall, place their neighbours at risk – so much so, that tree falls are often like skittle alleys. At one point in Lady Park, a splitting beech knocked over a tall beech, which knocked over another beech, which (astonishingly and sadly) felled a large oak, which then crushed a multi-stemmed lime, which ... but you get the idea. Both trees in this image hit the ground (where they sometimes leave a dent), but on other occasions a tree is left

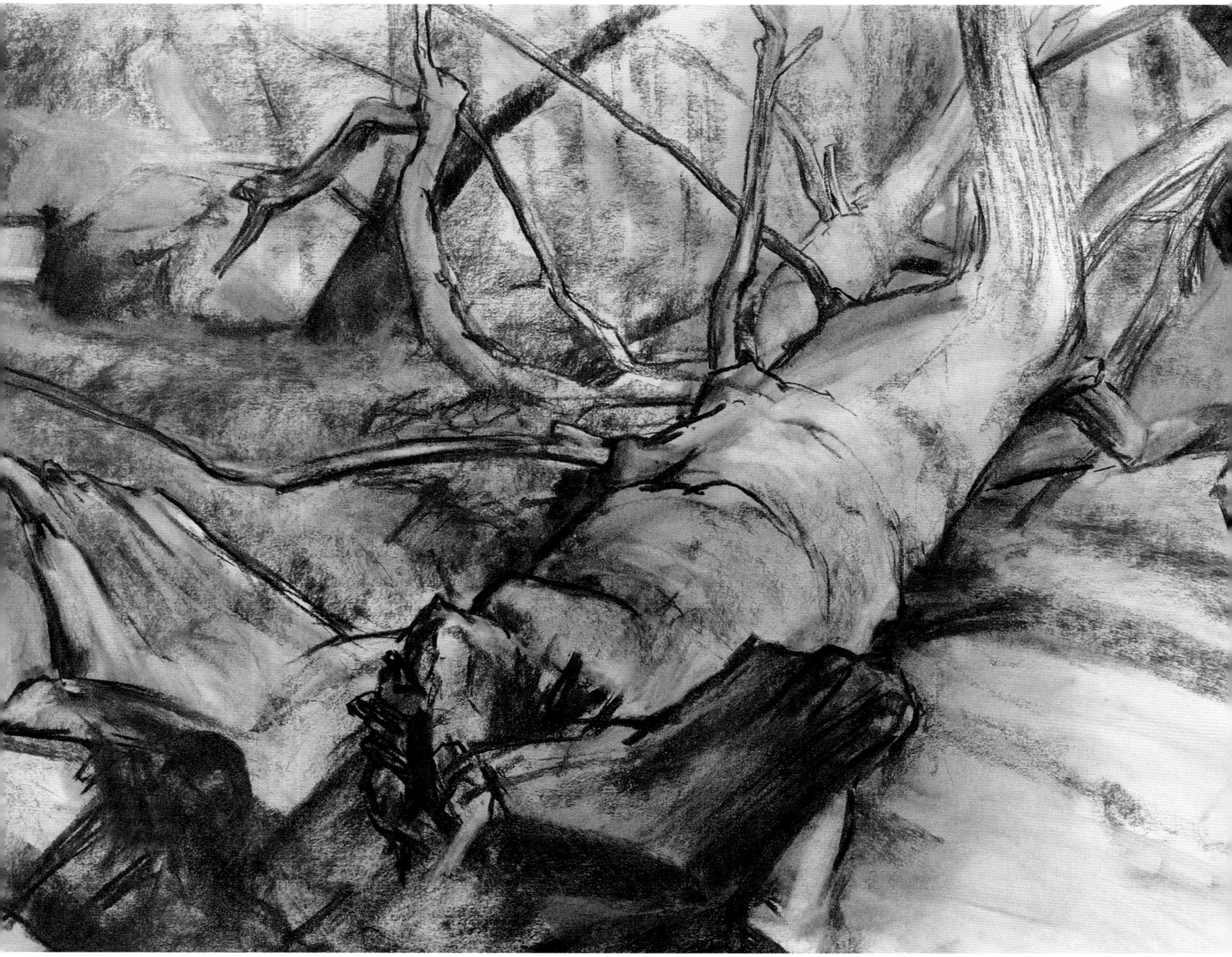

leaning on another – a classic feature of natural woodland. We once found a beech that had fallen into the crotch of a neighbour that stood its ground so well that the falling beech pivoted over the neighbour and came to rest with its crown branches on the ground, but its roots in a neighbour's sub-canopy.

Annabel Cullen's *The Crash* is a tree fall in close-up. Most people stay clear of the tangles, but, if we venture in, we enter the minotaur's labyrinth, vaulting over trunks, squeezing between branches that are now pressed together at different angles, losing any sense of the world outside and wishing one had a thread to guide our return. Wild boar, which have recently broken in to Lady Park, are the modern minotaurs. I have met a large sow hiding in the branches of a fallen beech with six striped piglets in tow: we were both disconcerted.

Time, of course, is a great healer. Detached twigs and branches will die and rot away, so penetration through the debris becomes easier – or it does until the brambles react and drape themselves over the climbing frame that the fallen trees have provided. Hazels resprout from shattered ends, often with great vigour, and may root from branches pinned to the ground by fallen trunks. The fallen tree itself may not die, for it can rejuvenate new shoots from the upper side of the trunk if enough roots remain in the ground. Herbs, too, will respond to the disturbance and the light and warmth from the increased sunshine by germinating, growing, flowering and renewing the seed bank in the soil. The human metaphors proliferate.

While it lasts the gap created by tree falls is a microcosm of woodland ecology. It is not just a hole in the canopy, but an array of niches each one of which will be experienced by wild plants and animals as quite different habitats. A small part is bare ground, but most is well vegetated or covered in woody debris. If a plant prefers a lot of light, it will find it mainly on the margins where the falling trees do not lie. If an insect prefers warm sunshine, it will find it on the north side of the gap, because the south side remains shaded by trees on the margin. If it needs warmth early in the day, it will find it towards the west side, for the sun rises in the east. Conversely, the driest, least humid spot will be on the north-east margin, where the afternoon sunshine is most likely to strike. This is the essence of woodland for wildlife. It is not one habitat but a mosaic of niches, each contributing to the diversity of the whole.

(fig 14)
ANNABEL CULLEN
The Crash, 2019
Charcoal on paper
59 x 84 cm
Private collection

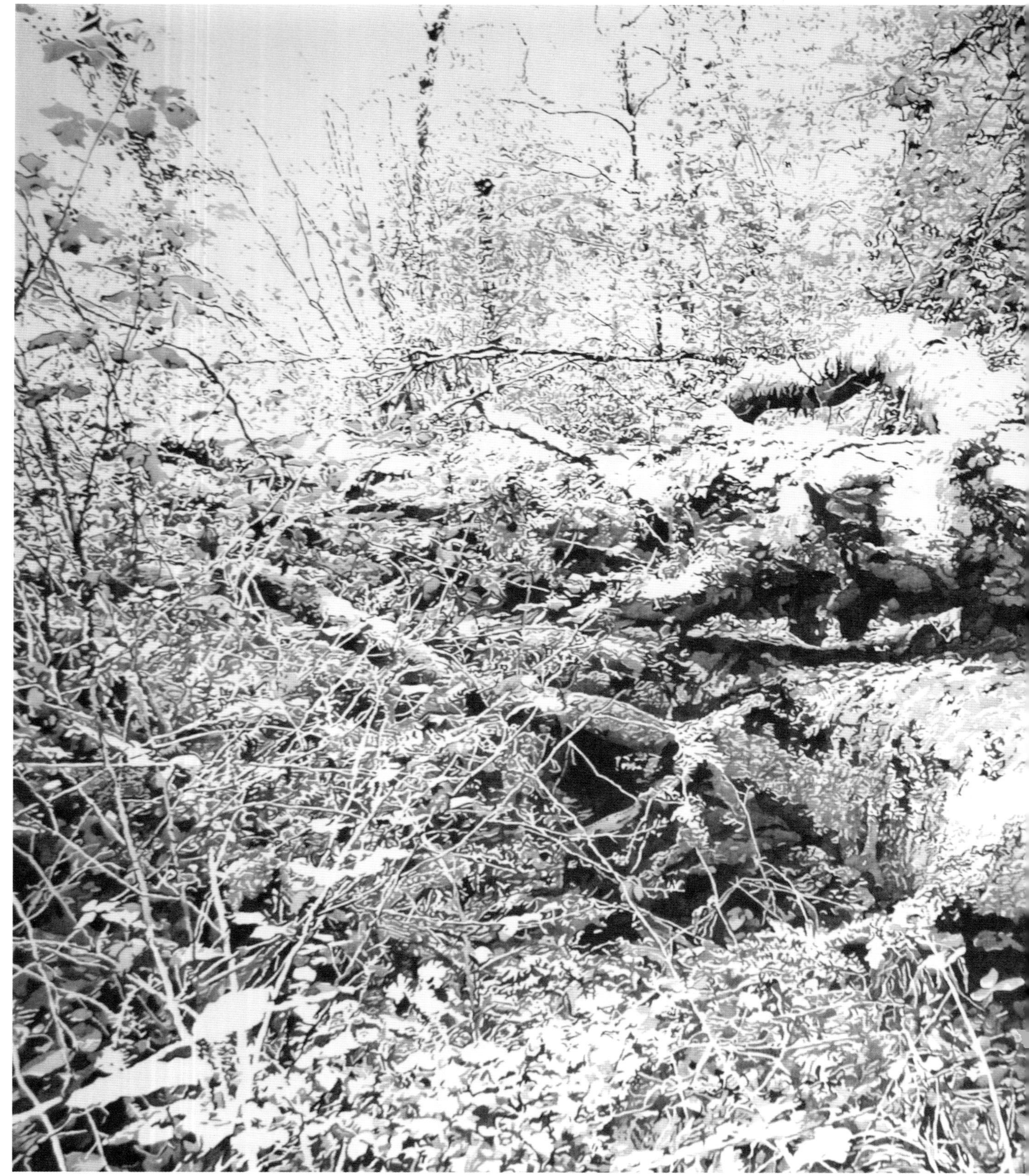

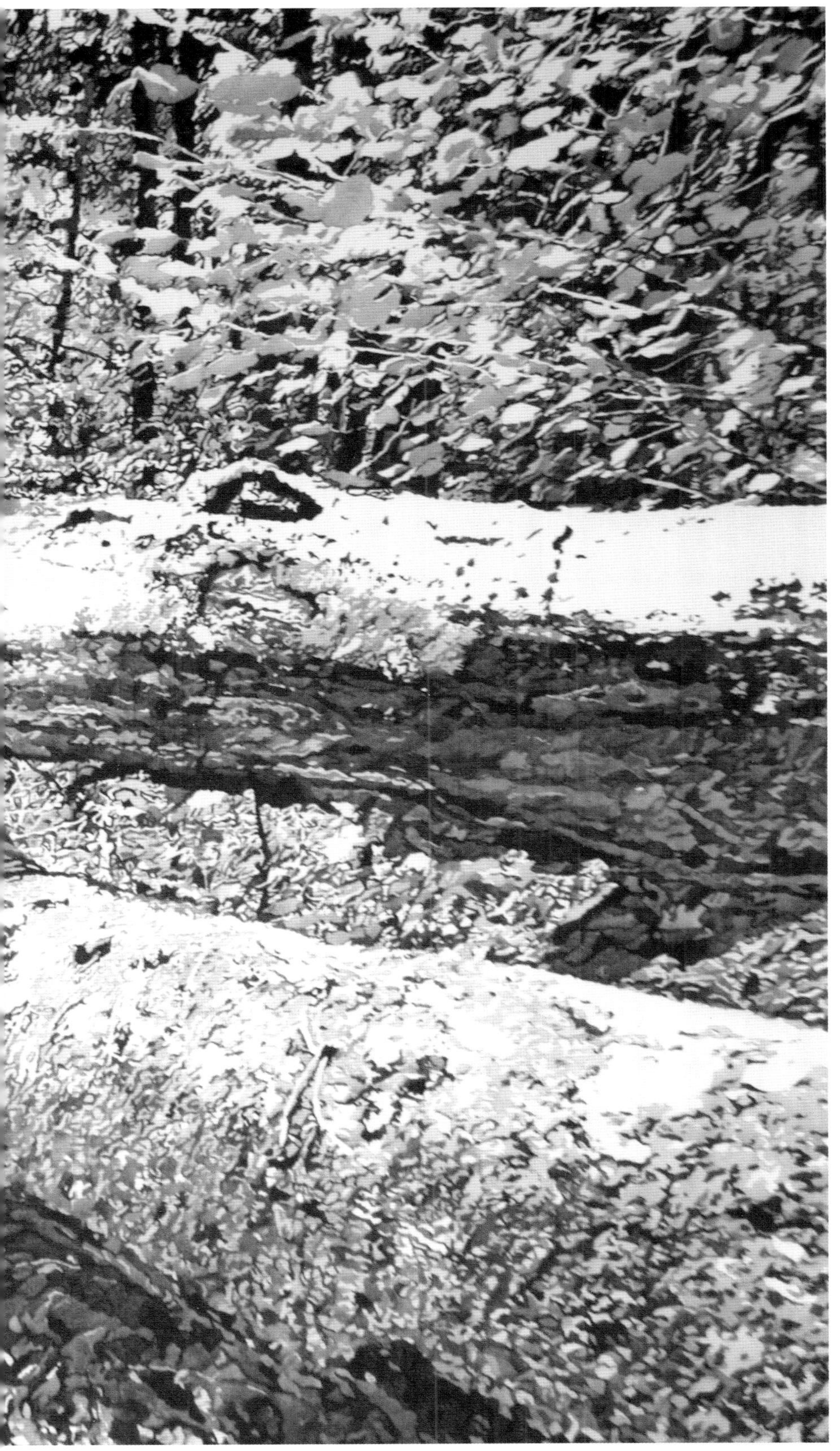

(fig 15)
TIM CRAVEN
Twin Pillars, 2018
Casein on canvas
61 x 91.5 cm
Private collection

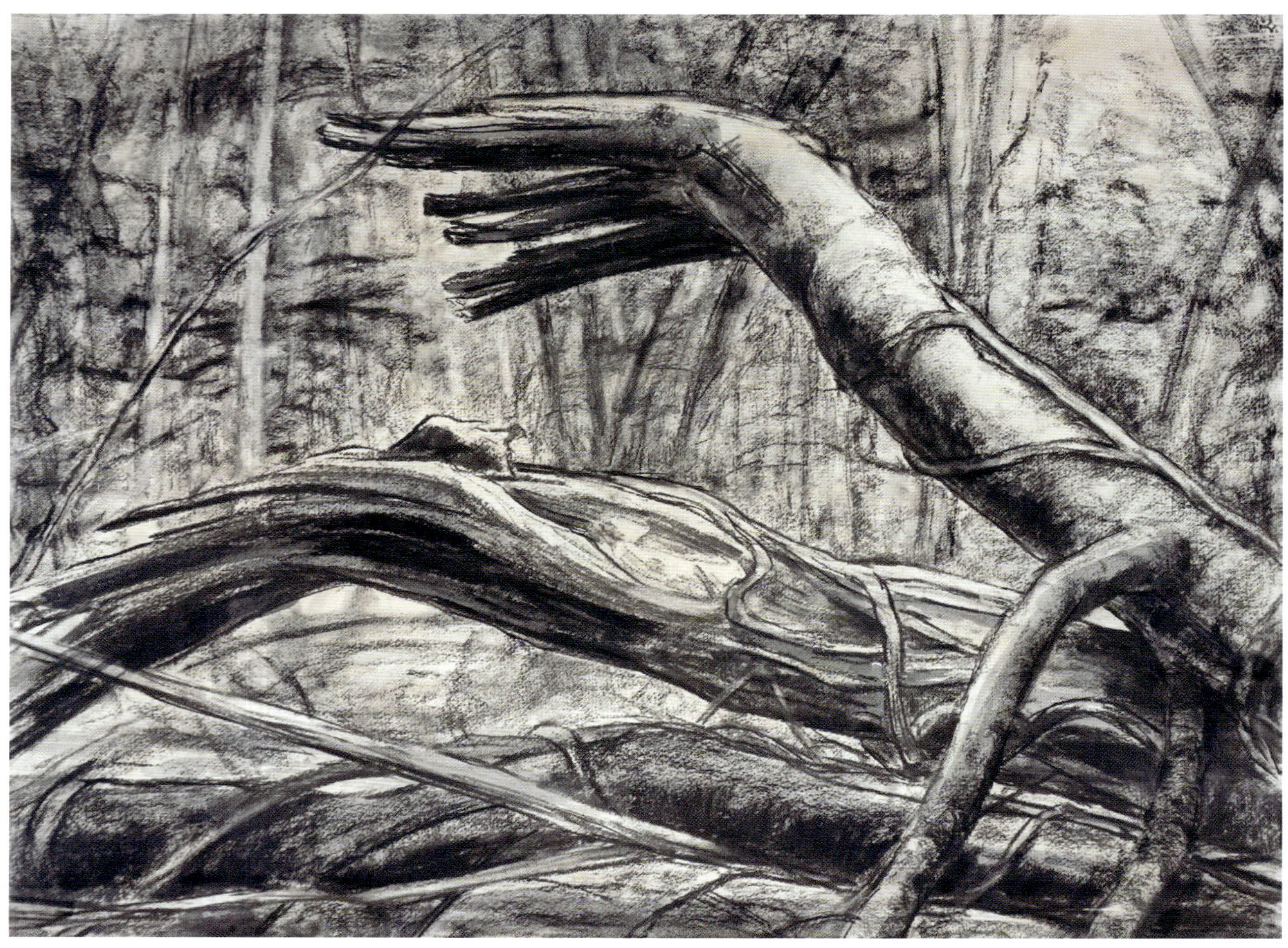

(fig 16)
ANNABEL CULLEN
Split Tree, 2019
Charcoal and ink on paper
56 x 76 cm
Private collection

THE FORCES OF NATURE

ANNABEL CULLEN

Have you ever tried to break a large branch off a tree? You make no impression – the forces required are well beyond even 'the world's strongest man'. Or, have you ever tried to wedge-split an oak or beech log containing a branch junction, and found that it is far harder than an ordinary, branch-free log, a mass of twisted grain of great density and strength?

This strength at the junction is necessary because the stretch forces exerted on the top side of a large, lateral branch are simply enormous, and any weakness would ensure that the tree fell apart. One can appreciate this when sawing off a small spreading branch. Saw across the top and the gap soon widens, the branch eases downwards and then cracks. But keep the saw blade vertical and saw from the sides and such is the strength of the wood that the branch will hold in position with just a narrow vertical flange of intact wood keeping it attached.

By zooming in close, Annabel Cullen's drawing, *Forces of Nature* (fig 17), dramatises the force required to wrench branches from hitherto undamaged trees. In a natural wood, force on this scale is generated by a falling tree as it brushes past a neighbour; or by the weight of wet snow lying on spreading branches, especially if, like the one drawn, it supports the additional weight of an ivy liana; or by large trees leaning out from a slope, where all the weight of the crown and upper trunk is to one side. We do well to remember, as we walk through a peaceful wood, that great forces could be unleashed at any moment.

In Lady Park, now that it has become more natural, these forces will be encountered more often than in a managed wood. Partly this is our fault for allowing grey squirrels to damage branches by bark-stripping their upper sides, thereby introducing rot just where the branch should be strong. Mostly it is because natural woodland includes old trees bearing the scars of age and history, in this case the damage caused to beech by the great drought of 1976. Add to that the fact that Lady Park grows on a steep slope where many trees lean out, and this is a genuinely dangerous place.

This danger is real. Big trees and large branches fall every year and not just in high winds as one might expect. As I mentioned in 'Tree Falls', a large, healthy and apparently well-balanced beech crashed down on a calm, sunny October day. Recently, I was measuring trees at the top of the wood when I heard a groan and watched a large ash split its trunk to a height of four metres and slump to the ground. The heavy snows of December 2018 brought down a lot of beech branches: the wood must have sounded like an artillery range. In 2019, one of a pair of great large-leaved limes splintered at the base and leaned to the ground, where it lives on. The most dramatic instance came when a group from Natural Resources Wales visited: standing there discussing dead wood, a large chunk of the subject matter fell from the crown of an oak and landed just three metres away.

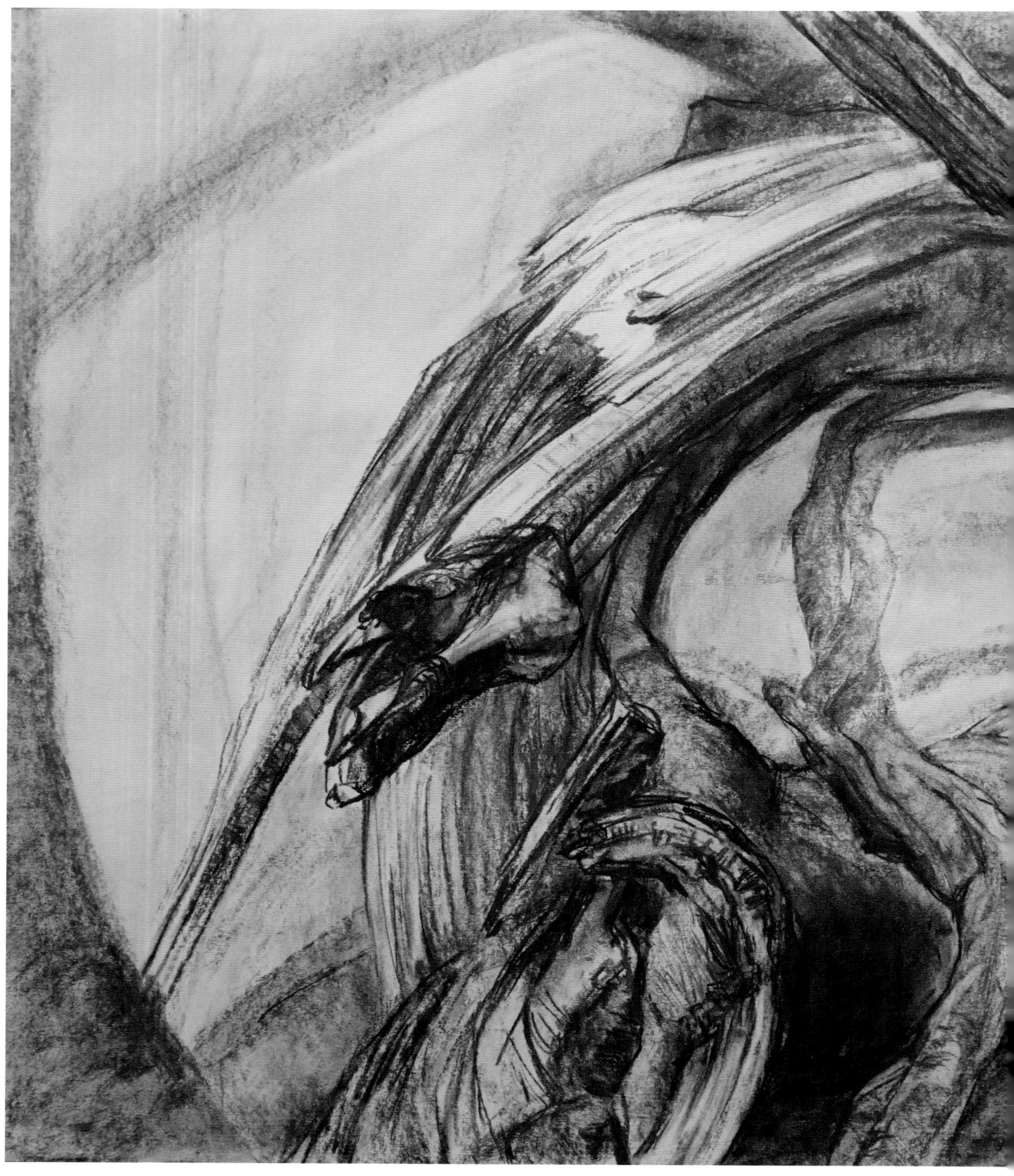

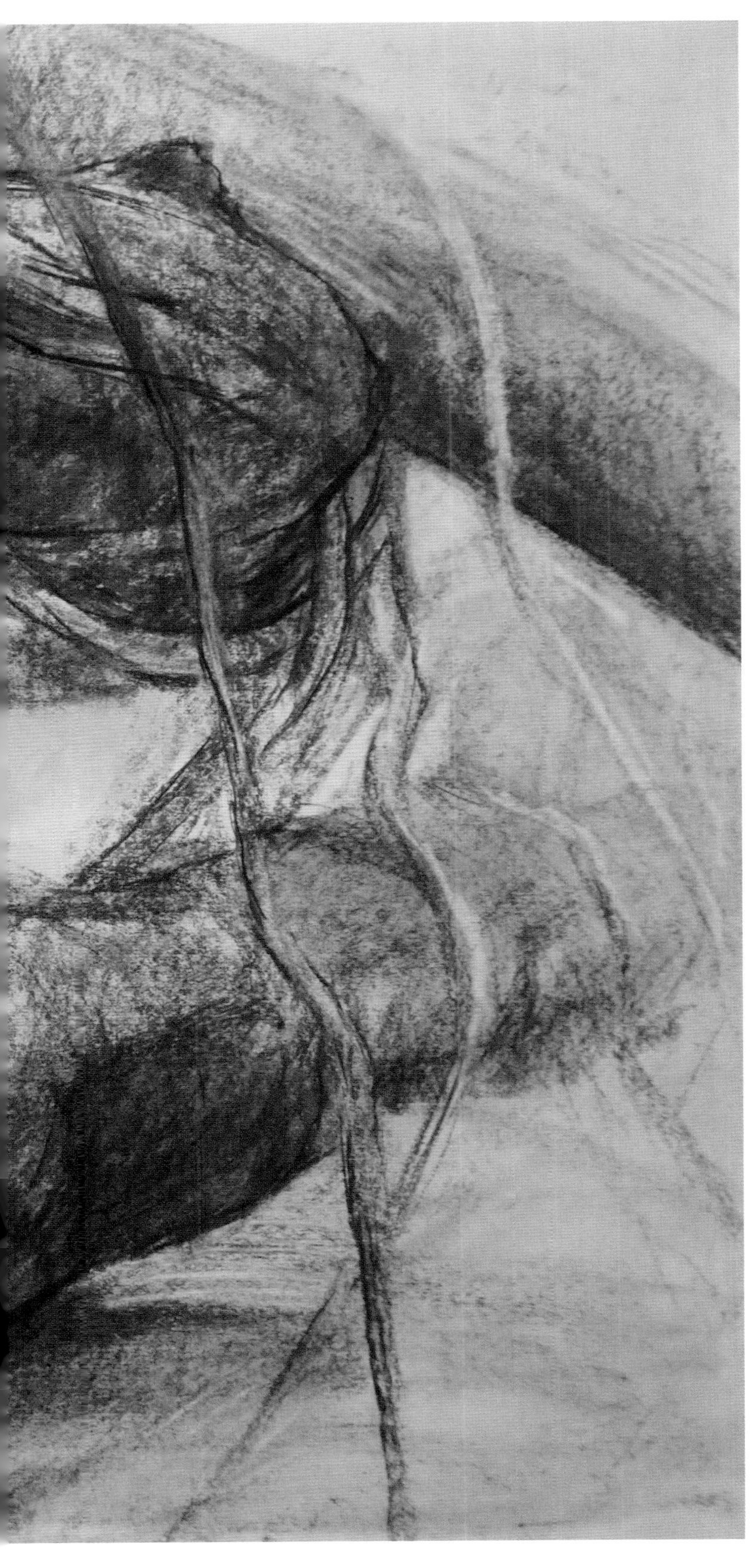

(fig 17)
ANNABEL CULLEN
Forces of Nature, 2017
Charcoal and ink on paper
59 x 84 cm
Private collection

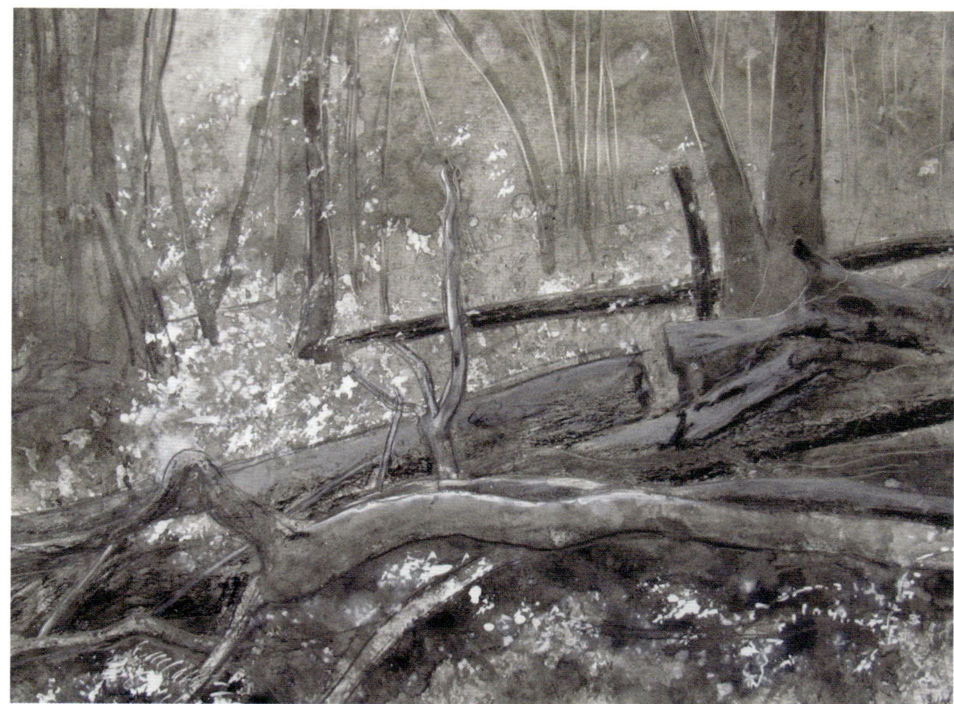

(fig 18)
RICHARD BAVIN
Study for Fallen, 2018
Charcoal, ink and
graphite on paper
30 x 42 cm
Artist's collection

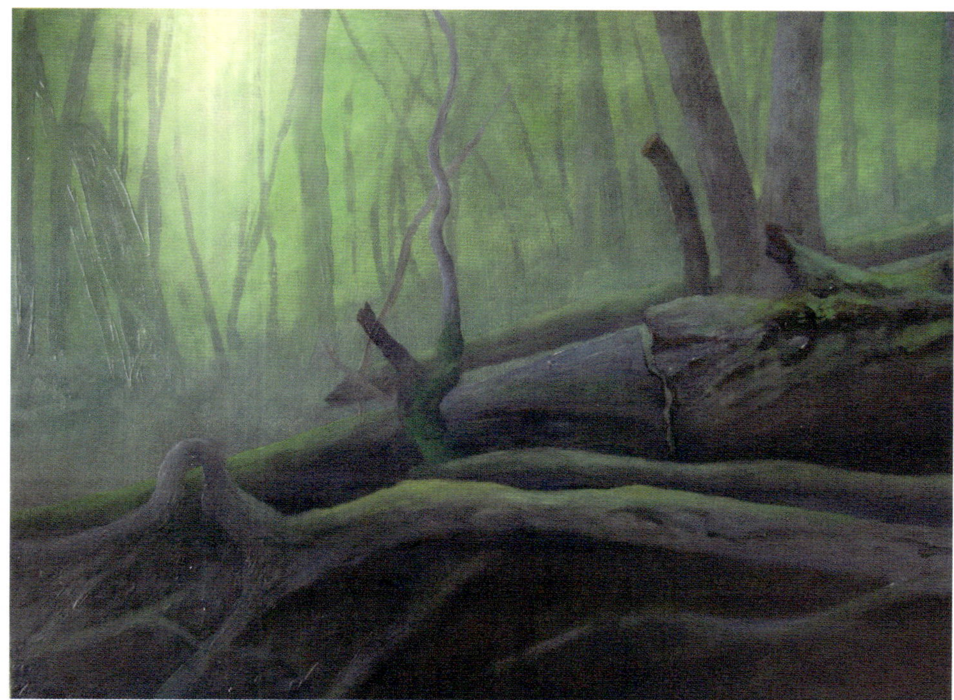

(fig 19)
RICHARD BAVIN
Fallen, 2018
Oil on panel
30 x 42 cm
Artist's collection

TREE-FALL GAPS

RICHARD BAVIN, LESLEY SLIGHT,
ABI KREMER

Ecologists have long studied how natural woodland renews itse f. At least in its modern, recreated incarnation, natural woodland takes the form of high fo-est – dense stands of tall trees with a distinct layering of canopy trees at the t∍p, sut-canopy be ow ∍hem and an underwood of shrubs, small trees and saplings further dcwn. The canopy trees inevitably shade the lower layers, which are thus usually dis:ontinuous and lack vigour – trees and shrubs just ticking over. The problem this represe∩ts is t∩at the sapl ngs that might replace th∍ canopy trees are also suppressed, grow sl∍wly and almost al∿ays die.

So, where do new trees come from? The answer is gaps, ∿here :anopy trees ha∿e died or fallen. Mortality of tall trees leaves a hole in the canopy - th∍ gap – that al ows in a flood of light to the ground. Suddenly saplings and underwc od that have not teen crushed in the fall have their chance. They grow rapidly and bid to jcin the canopy. They are still not assured of success, however, for the trees on the margin of th∍ gap now h∍ve a char∩e to extend their branches into the gap. So, the saplings face a race to grow tall before the marginal trees expand their crowns and close the gap. If th∈ gap is large, the saplings win, but if it is small, they lose.

Richard Bavin's *Fallen* (fig 19) is as evocative of Lady Park as any image could be. Technically, it depicts gap formation in natural high forest, but i∷ does so in a ∨ay that brings out the process by which gaps form, as well as the structure of gaps. It shows no regeneration of saplings in the foreground, which is often th e case in Lady Park, where, even if several trees fall together, the gap they create may be narr∍w, leaving ∍he crowns of trees on the margin to expand before saplings can grow t∍ll and strong enoцgh to survive in partial shade (a process that takes a decade, at least). In this case, with the glow of late afternoon sunshine in the background, there is a hint of l∍w growth, for this is a wide gap and in time it could well generate a clump of new cano∍y trees, which would all be the same age. Continue this process indefinitely and r atural woodland develops a pattern of small, even-aged groups of trees, each group representi∩g the rene∿al of the wood in a gap where enough trees went down together to enable the saplings to reach fcr the sky. Misquoting the Tate & Lyle treacle tin, out of the strong comes forth ife.

Richard's *Study for Fallen* adds significant detail to the ecological interpretation. Being more literal than the painting, we now see that a few beech saplings are struggling up in the foreground shade, and that the new growth in the distance is stronger than we thought. We can also see clearly in the foreground that a wide-branched oak, inherited from th∍ nineteenth-century coppice, was one of the trees that fell. Richard's

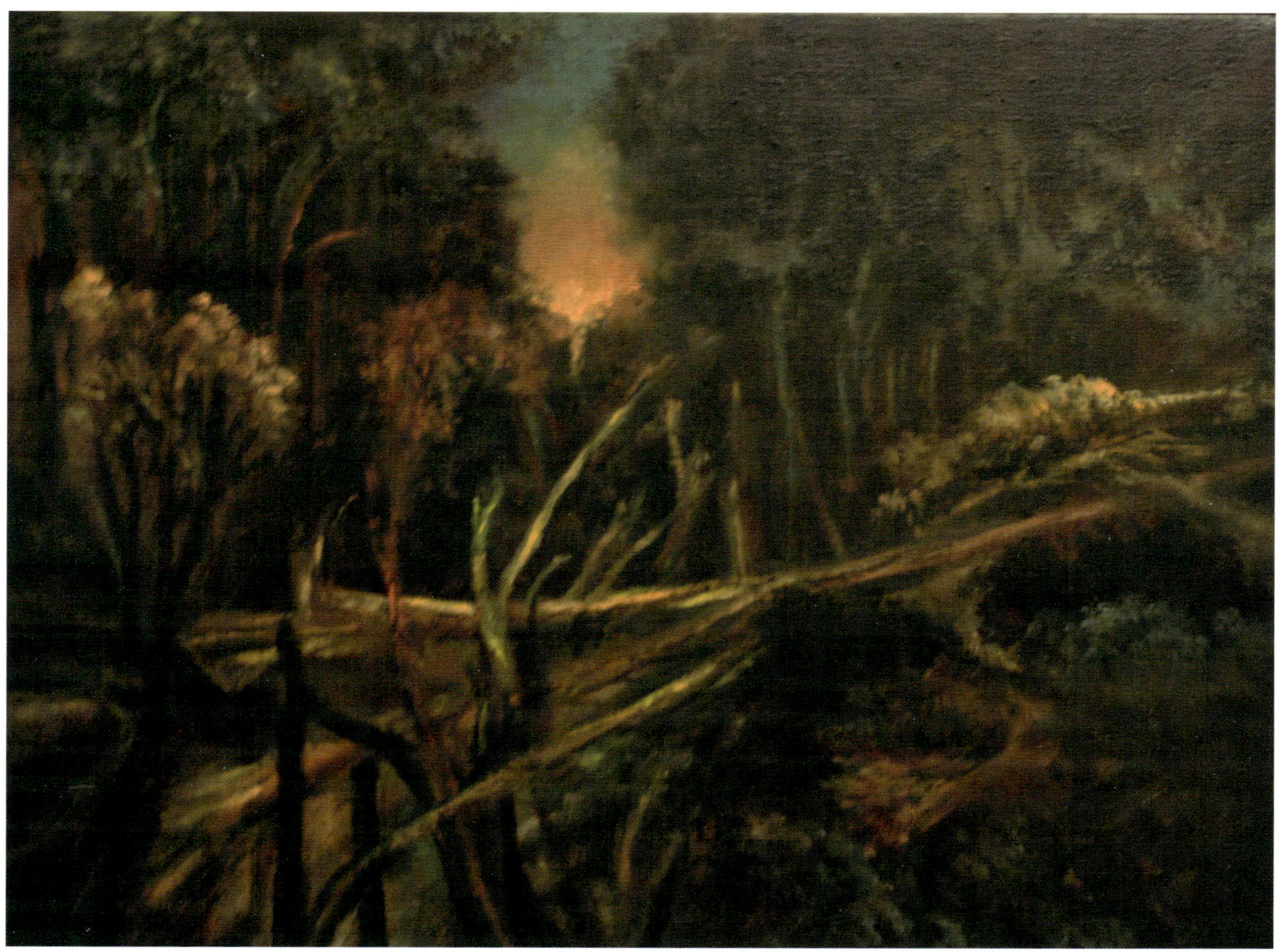

(fig 20)
LESLEY SLIGHT
Lady Park Wood – Late Afternoon, 2017
Oil on canvas
30 x 40 cm
Private collection

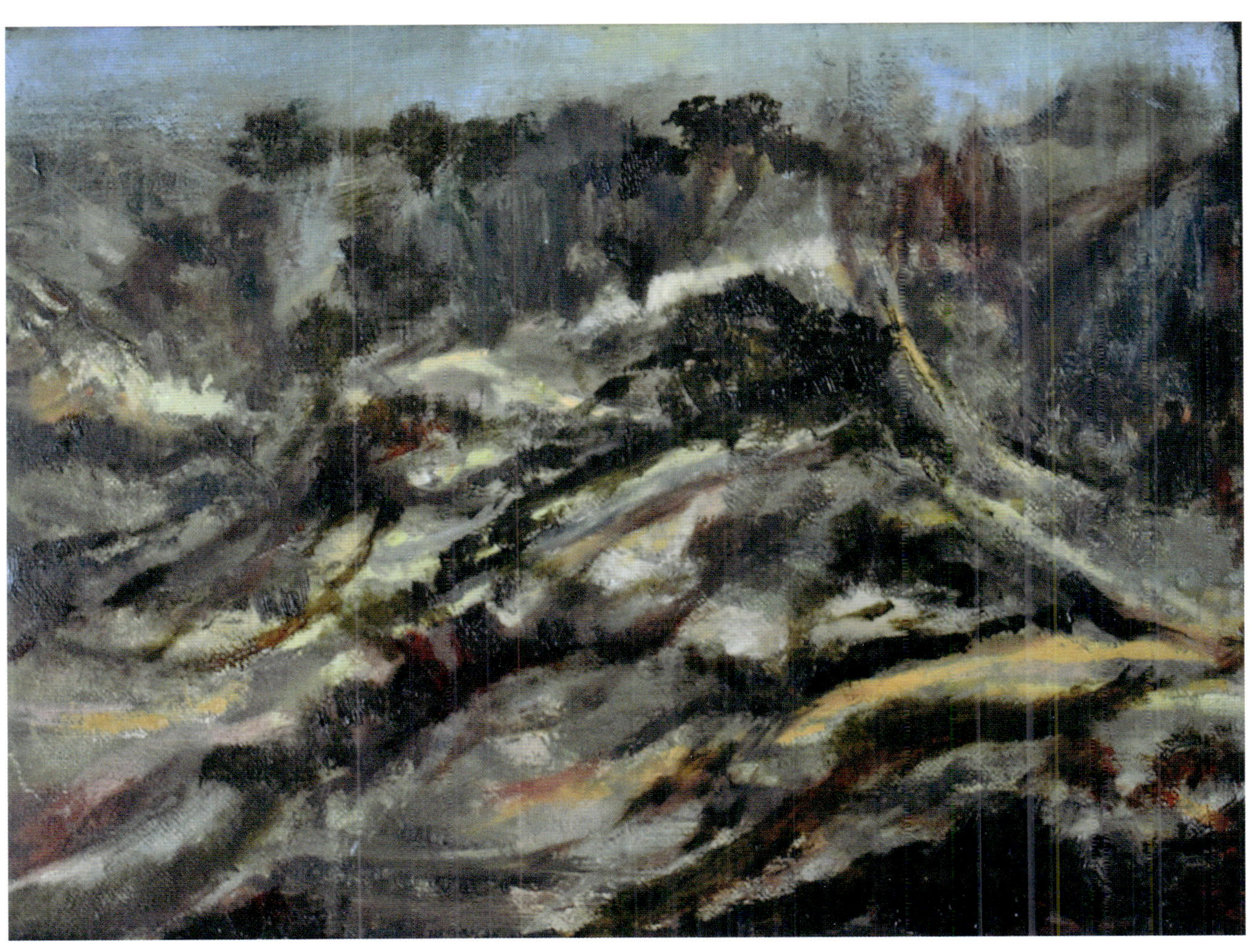

(fig 21)
LESLEY SLIGHT
Lady Park Study II, 2017
Oil on canvas
30 x 40 cm
Private collection

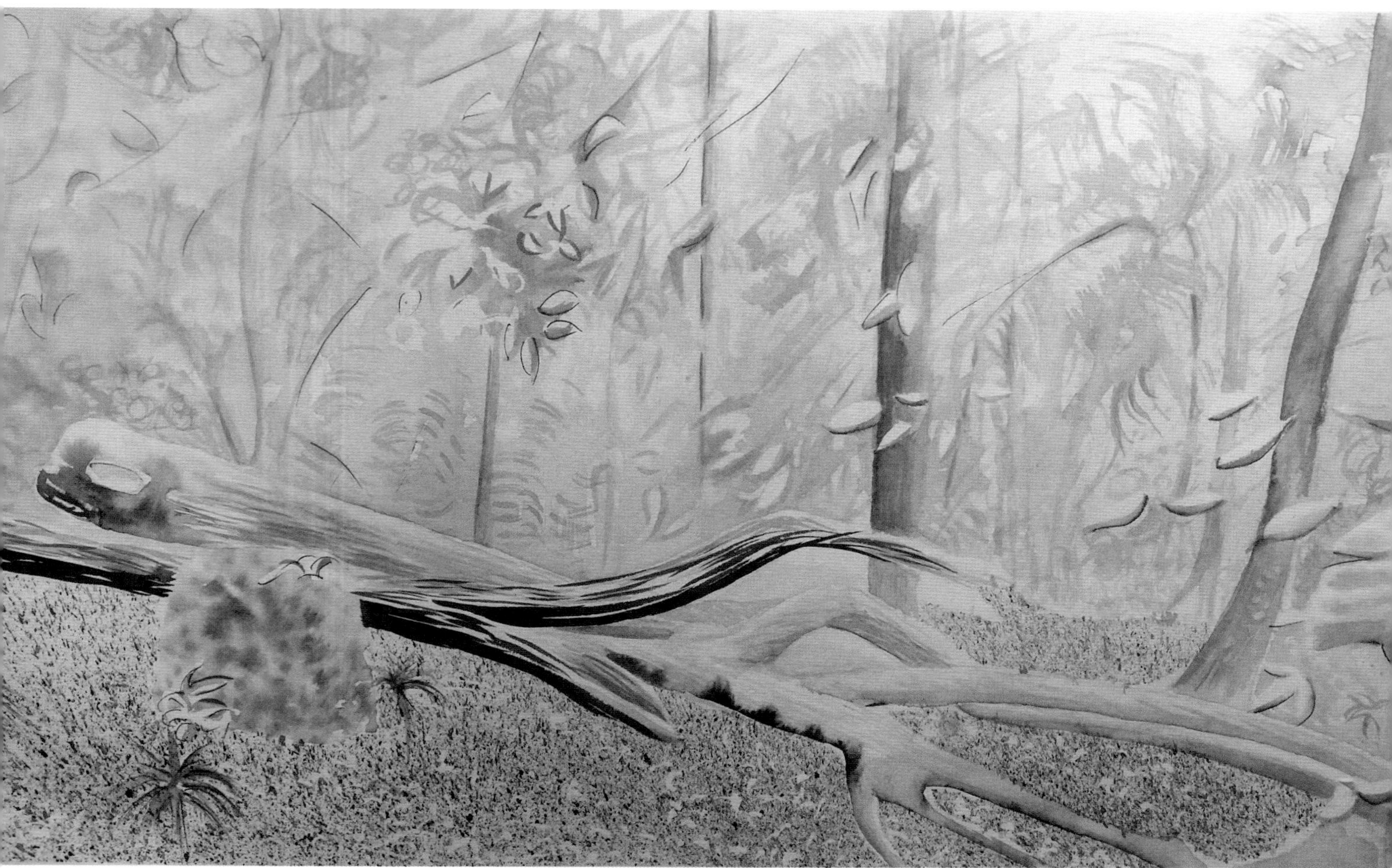

Regeneration (fig 24) (see 'Regeneration' section) does indicate a small cluster of saplings, which is often all one finds in a large gap. Together, these images show that the reality of regeneration in gaps is far from black-and-white, and also how the inheritance from the nineteenth-century managed woodland is slowly diluted by death and renewal.
It also incidentally reminds us that the ecologist has to be more literal than the artist.

The gap in Lesley Slight's *Lady Park Wood – Late Afternoon* (fig 20) is obviously elongated rather than circular, as is so often the case in Lady Park. The explanation is simple: Lady Park slopes; trees tend to fall down the slope and skittle the trees below, which are themselves prone to falls because the majority of their branches grow on the downslope side. From a distance, and on the steeper slopes, tree-fall gaps look like avalanche tracks, and that's roughly what they are. The image also shows that subordinate trees stand in the line of fire and suffer collateral damage. Some are also brought to the ground, but others are simply smashed, reduced to ragged shrubs with shattered branch ends. Responses depend on the species, but here we see that the smashed underwood trees have regenerated strongly, and well before any regeneration becomes apparent on the ground. In this case they are probably limes, which will regenerate with great vigour. Nevertheless, such trees will bear the marks of their 'accident' throughout their lives, which in the case of lime can be several centuries, and the point from which the new shoots grow will remain a relatively weak structure, so one day this may be where the tree breaks when the crown gets too heavy. But for a century or more after the event which brought down these trees, our artistic and ecological successors will be able to see that the event took place. Lesley's *Lady Park Study II* (fig 21) shows an appropriately confusing mountain of fallen timber across a broad tree-fall gap as it might confront a wanderer in natural woodland.

These and Abi Kremer's *Lady Park Wood 5* (fig 22) all show in their different styles a key visual feature of natural woodland: the contrast between the vertical, intact, orderly trees still standing and the horizontal, shattered, disorderly fallen trees. The first state takes a century or two to develop, but the second state forms abruptly from the first in less than five seconds, usually with no warning. Mathematicians would see this as an expression of catastrophe theory. Others might see it as a metaphor for political change, 1989-style.

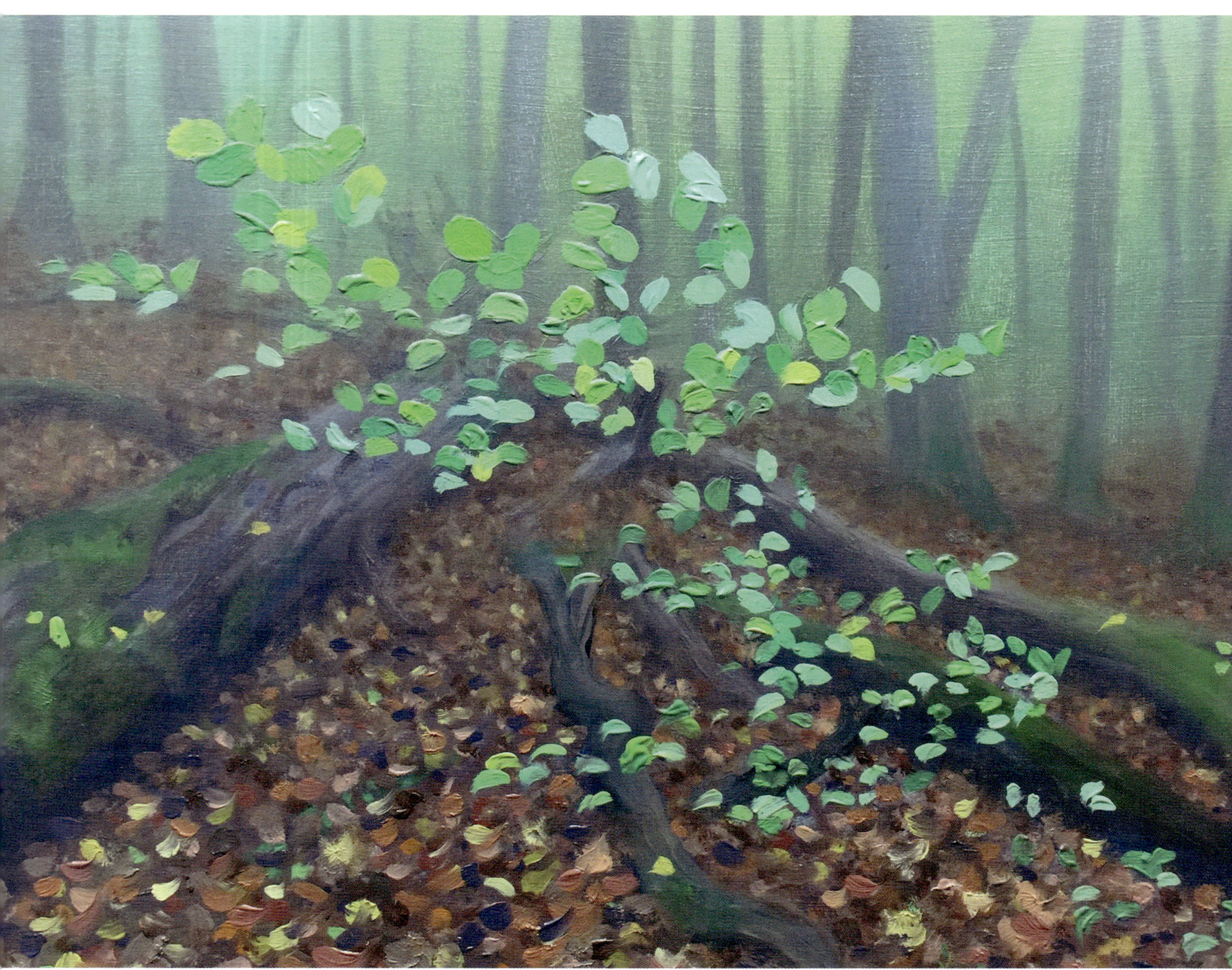

(fig 23)
RICHARD BAVIN
Renewal, 2017
Oil on panel
21 x 30 cm
Private collection

REGENERATION

RICHARD BAVIN

Individual oaks can live for 500 years in woods, but even they die eventually and must renew their kind. In their lifetimes, they will produce countless m llions of acorns, but only one need succeed in becoming a mature tree if the population is to be sustained. The pressure is slightly greater on birch, few of which will live beyond 80 years in woodland, but even they can be relaxed about reproducing Many trees and shrubs can also reproduce vegetatively by growing new shoots from mature plants that are capable of growing into trees themselves. In theory, individual trees can live forever by this means, but in practice only aspen and the two lime species may be immortal or nearly so. Aspens generate new trees from extensive root systems: the individual trees last only a few decades, but the root systems keep going indefinitely. The imes grow again from broken stumps, prostrate trunks and even from weak shoots that are pressed firmly to the ground by falling branches from taller trees.

Richard Bavin's two paintings draw attention to regeneration more than others in this collection. In both *Renewal* (fig 23) and *Regeneration* (fig 24) we see well-established beech saplings in gaps, though with the former only the title confirms that the disembodied foliage represents saplings rather than a freshly fallen branch. Beech is the most effective regenerant within woods because it bears shade and thus gets started before a gap has formed, and withstands levels of browsing that would reduce other tree species to bitten-down stumps. Even so, they only really grow vigorously if a gap opens up above them. Ash seedlings, too, can get started in shade and will grow fast once they are established and well lit, but these are now being killed off en masse by disease.

Artist cally, regeneration makes little impact until it develops into thickets, but in spring and autumn seed ings and saplings are briefly conspicuous against a background of leafless mature trees, for the former come into leaf slightly earlier than trees in the canopy and retain their leaves slightly longer. Like naughty children, they get up early and go to bed late.

Natural regeneration is always a hot topic amongst foresters and managers of woodland nature reserves. For foresters managing a wood for timber and profit, the possibility of natural regeneration represents new growing stock without the cost of replanting, but it comes with other costs in the form of uncertainty, delay and the inability to select which species will form the next crop. Nevertheless, there are stands of beech, oak, Sitka spruce, Douglas-fir and others in Britain which have been regenerated this way. For nature reserve managers, the concern is the long-term sustainability of the woodland they seek to protect and maintain. If a wood was acquired as a fine example of an oakwood, then the future of the oak must be secured, preferably by natural means. The problem here is that woods don't work that way. Beech regenerates under oak; oak comes up under birch; and so on. We must accept that there will be change and ensure that, on a larger scale, losses at one point are matched by gains elsewhere.

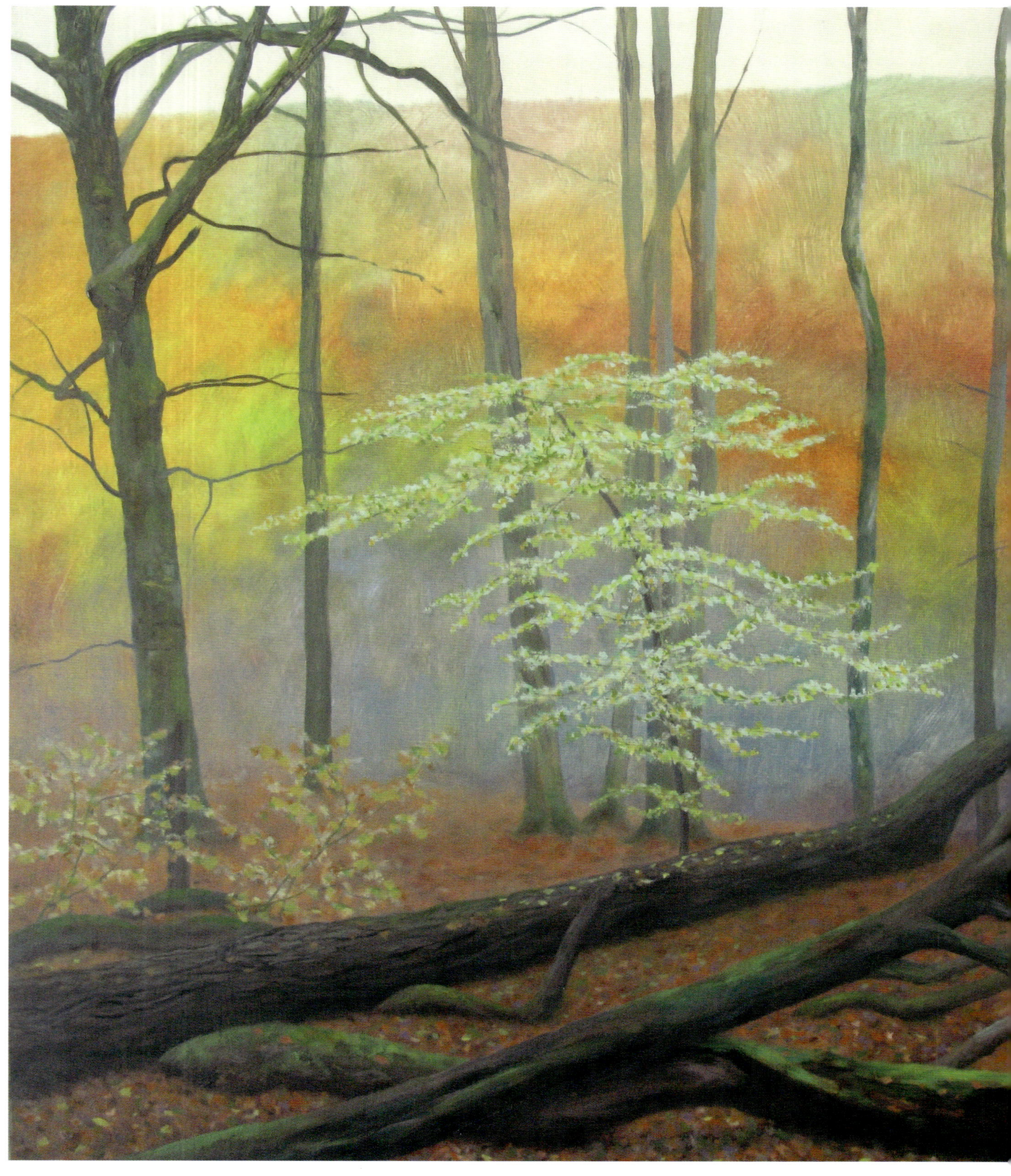

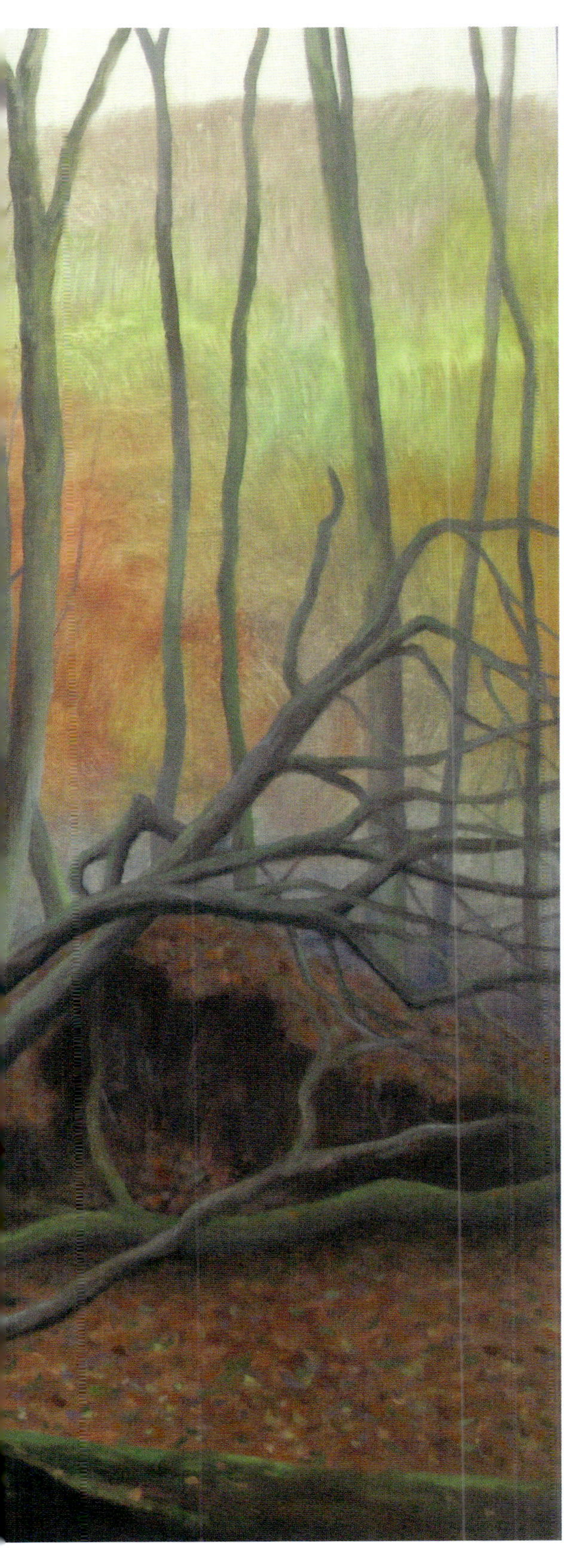

(fig 24)
RICHARD BAVIN
Regeneration, 2019
Oil on panel
40 x 50 cm
Private collection

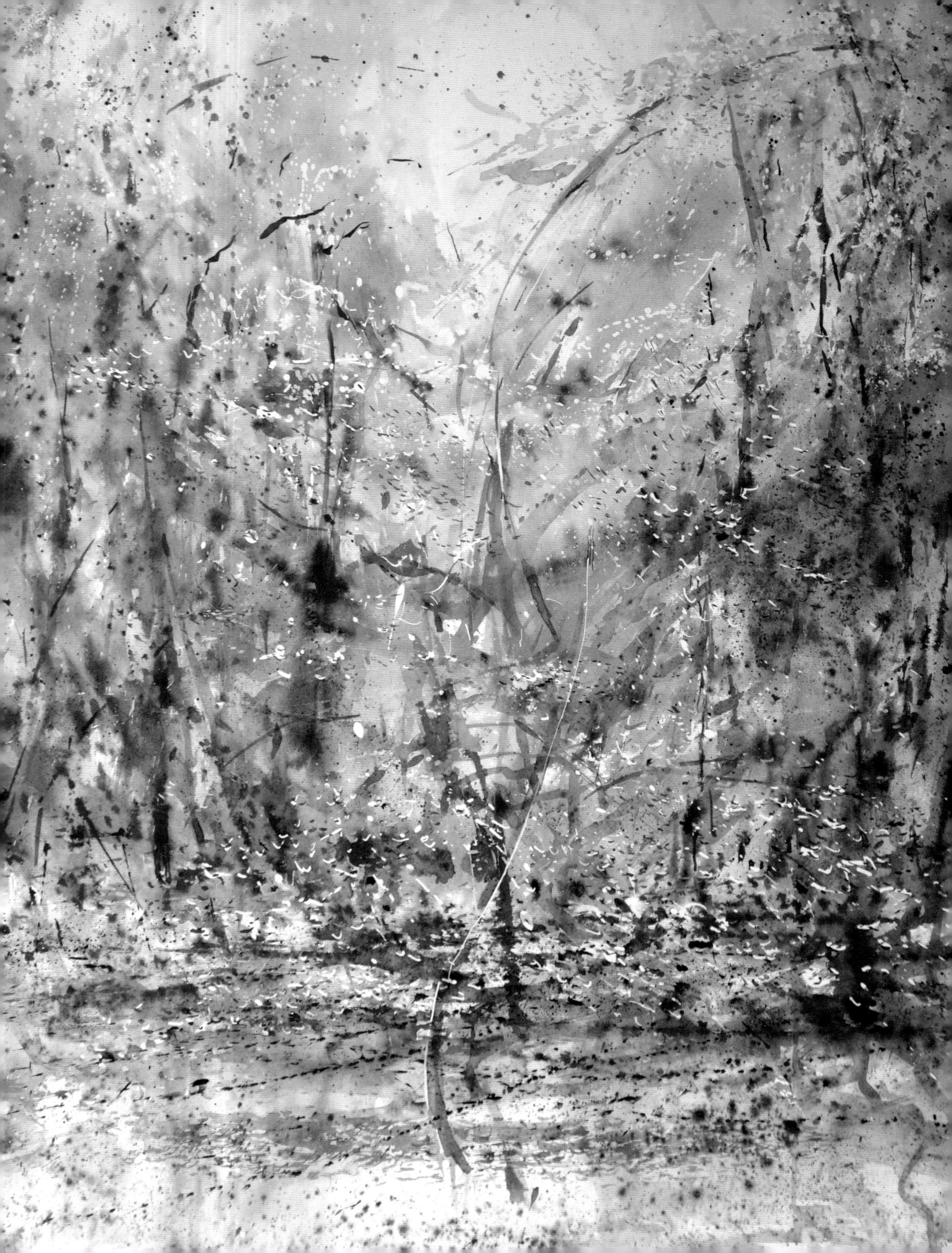

THICKETS

TOM DEAKINS, JANE EATON,
RICHARD HOARE, LESLEY SLIGHT

We have already seen from other paintings that natural woodland is far from uniform. It is a patchwork of different structures: mature groves of well-spaced giants, dense stands of middle-aged trees, graveyards of fallen trees in gaps, and thickets of saplings growing in what were, until recently, gaps. The temptation is to concentrate attention on the tall, mature stands, but these images in their various ways bring out the thickets and other congested patches that are also part of natural woodland.

By being impressionistic and scale-free, Richard Hoare's *Young Tree Breath of Light – Lady Park Wood* (fig 25) contrives to show two facets of natural woodland. It could easily be a thicket of young growth with a hint of the mature trees to left and right that were spared on the edge of the gap. Thickets such as this are dense and often impenetrable mixtures of saplings, regrowth from prostrate hazels, dead branches and vaulting brambles. They clear eventually as the saplings grow, branches rot and brambles die, but for 20 years or so they are no-go areas, just the places where deer and wild boar might lie up for the day. Or the image could represent tall trees surrounding a gap with a tangle of fallen limbs in the bright light admitted by their fall. From a distance and especially in summer, these too can appear to be dense, impenetrable mixtures.

This ambiguity can be a reminder that the processes in stands of different age are similar, except for the scale. As young thickets grow, the stronger (and usually taller) saplings prosper, while the weaker (and usually smaller) weaken and die, a process known as competitive thinning. In much older stands, exactly the same process takes place and at exactly the same proportionate rate. One can plot a graph of the logarithm of the density of trees against the age of the stand, and the result is a straight line. Scientific ecologists find this fascinating, but are self-aware enough not to try it on the general public. Perhaps a painting like this makes the point subliminally.

Jane Eaton's *Drawn to a Place* (fig 27) also combines the two facets, but without the ambiguity: the thicket is clearly viewed against a background of mature woodland. It evokes for me memories of laying out tapes to make visible the transect lines (sample strips) that are the basis of long-term ecological recording in the wood. Normally, in walking through a wood one simply steps round tangles, but ruler-straight transects inevitably pass through every structure available, including thickets. There is no alternative to an undignified scramble, trying all the time to leave the tangle undisturbed, for the ecologist does not want to become a factor in how this wood develops.

Tom Deakins' *Fallen* (fig 28) shows another aspect of the messy sub-structure of natural woodland, but in the background we can also see overgrown coppice of lime and other species – a useful reminder that managed woodlands pass through a thicket stage which is even more impenetrable and forbidding than any thicket generated by natural woodland. Leslie Slight's subject, seen in *Thicket*, is not a thicket now, but was one not so long ago. Thickets of brushwood, groves of saplings and clusters of bramble eventually grow out into dense, dark groves before they become the mature forest that we so often choose to photograph when we wish to represent natural woodland – just as butterflies are regarded by most people as colourful, flying things, forgetting that the egg, caterpillar and chrysalis are equal and more enduring precursors.

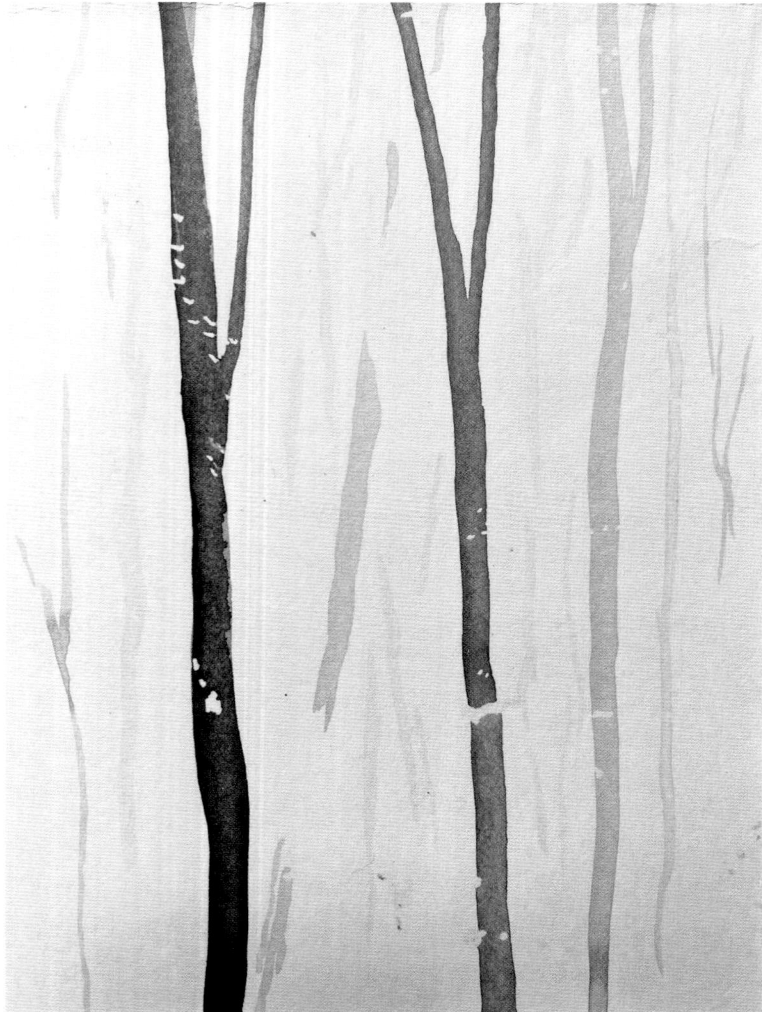

(fig 26)
RICHARD HOARE
Trees, Mist and First Leaves of Spring, Lady Park Wood, 2017
Ink on paper
17 x 12.5 cm
Artist's collection

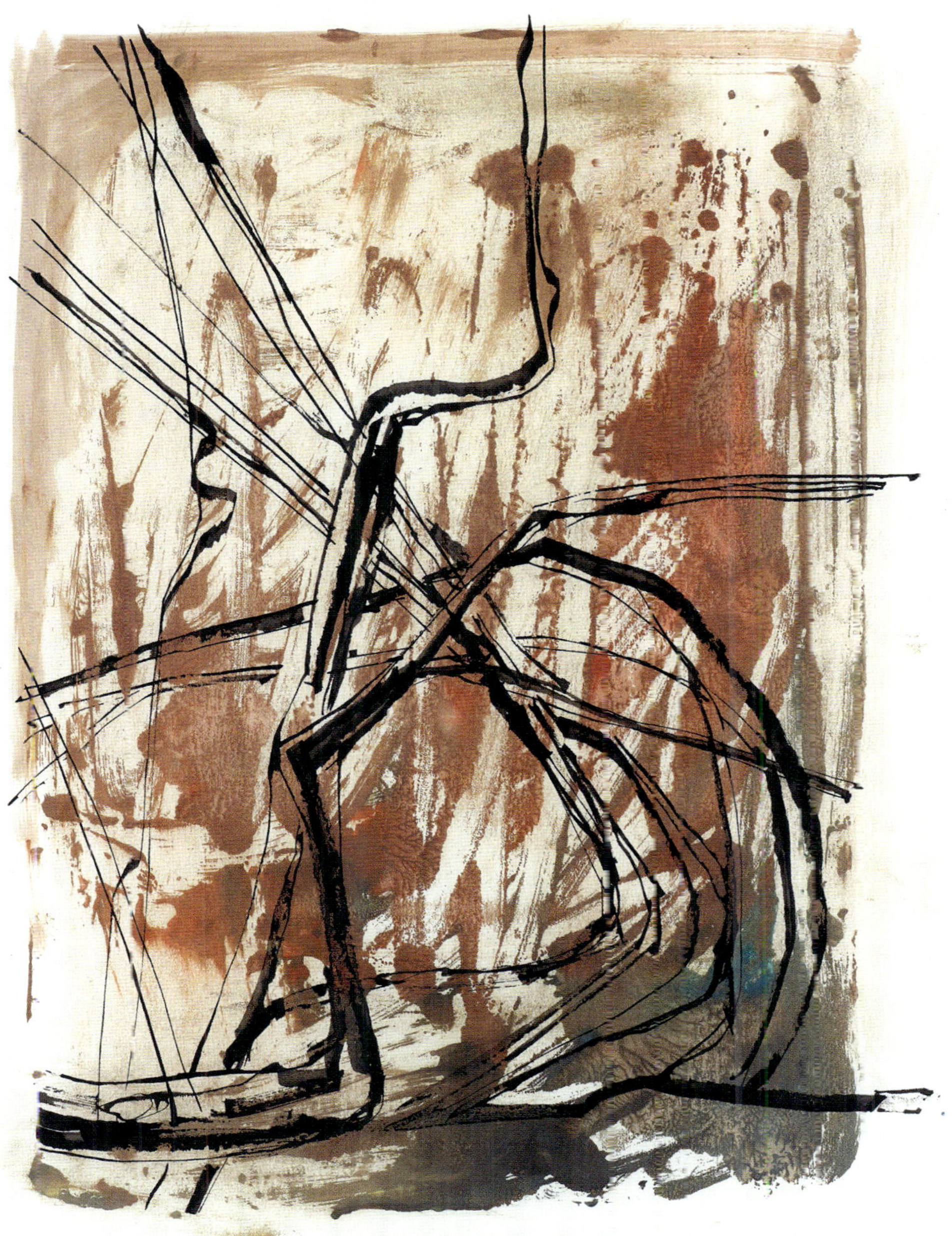

(fig 27)
JANE EATON
Drawn to a Place, 2019
Mixed media on paper
48 x 38 cm
Artist's collection

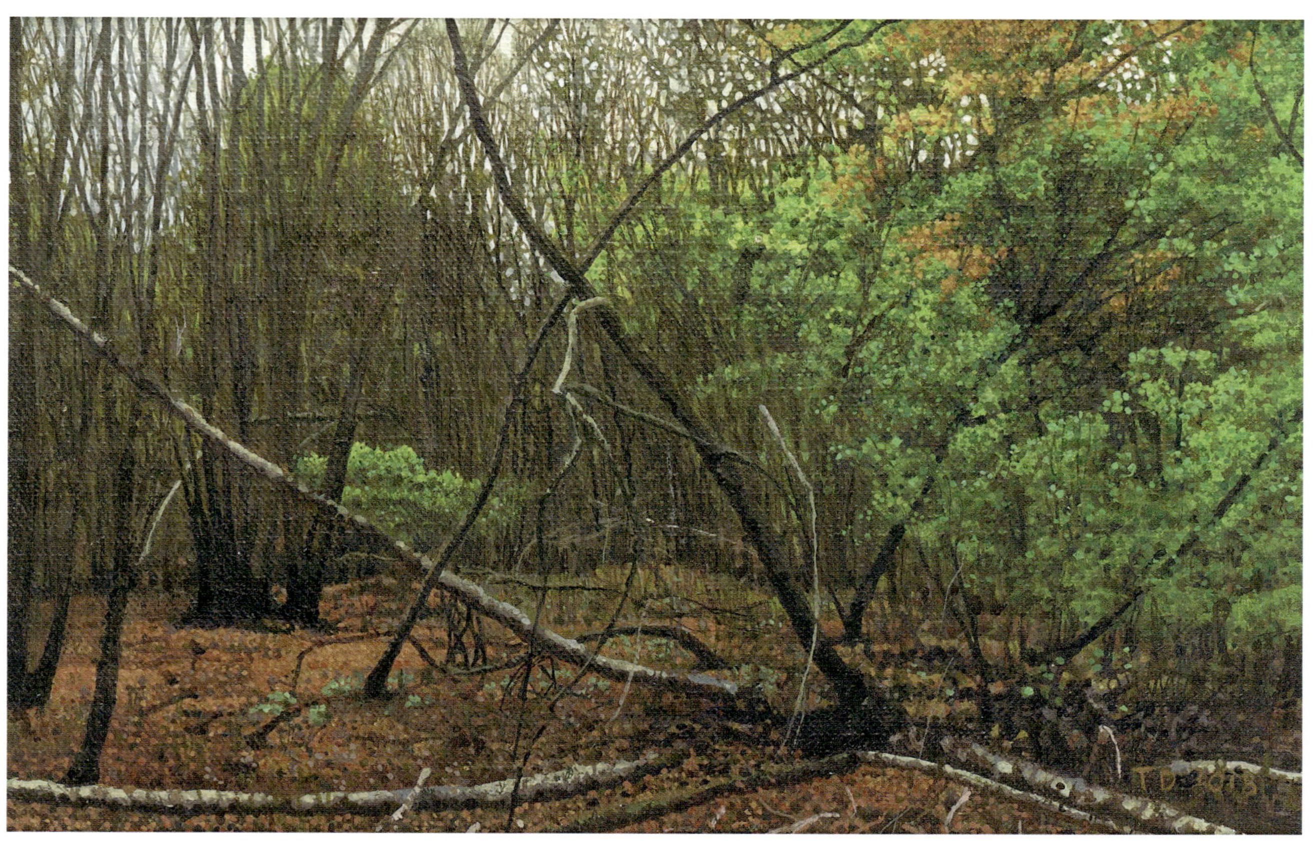

(fig 28)
TOM DEAKINS
Fallen, 2018
Oil on canvas
15 x 20 cm
Artist's collection

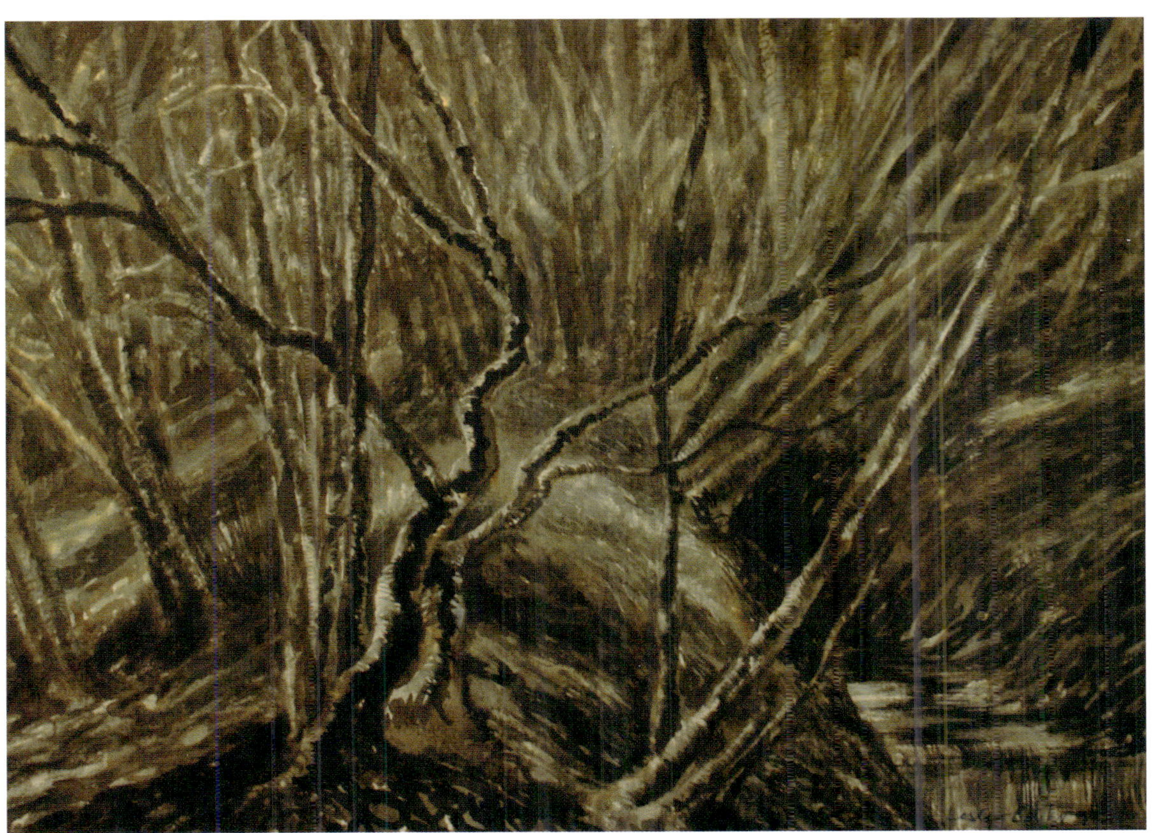

(fig 29)
LESLEY SLIGHT
Thicket, 2018
Ink on Arches Aquarelle 300-gsm paper
25 × 35 cm
Private collection

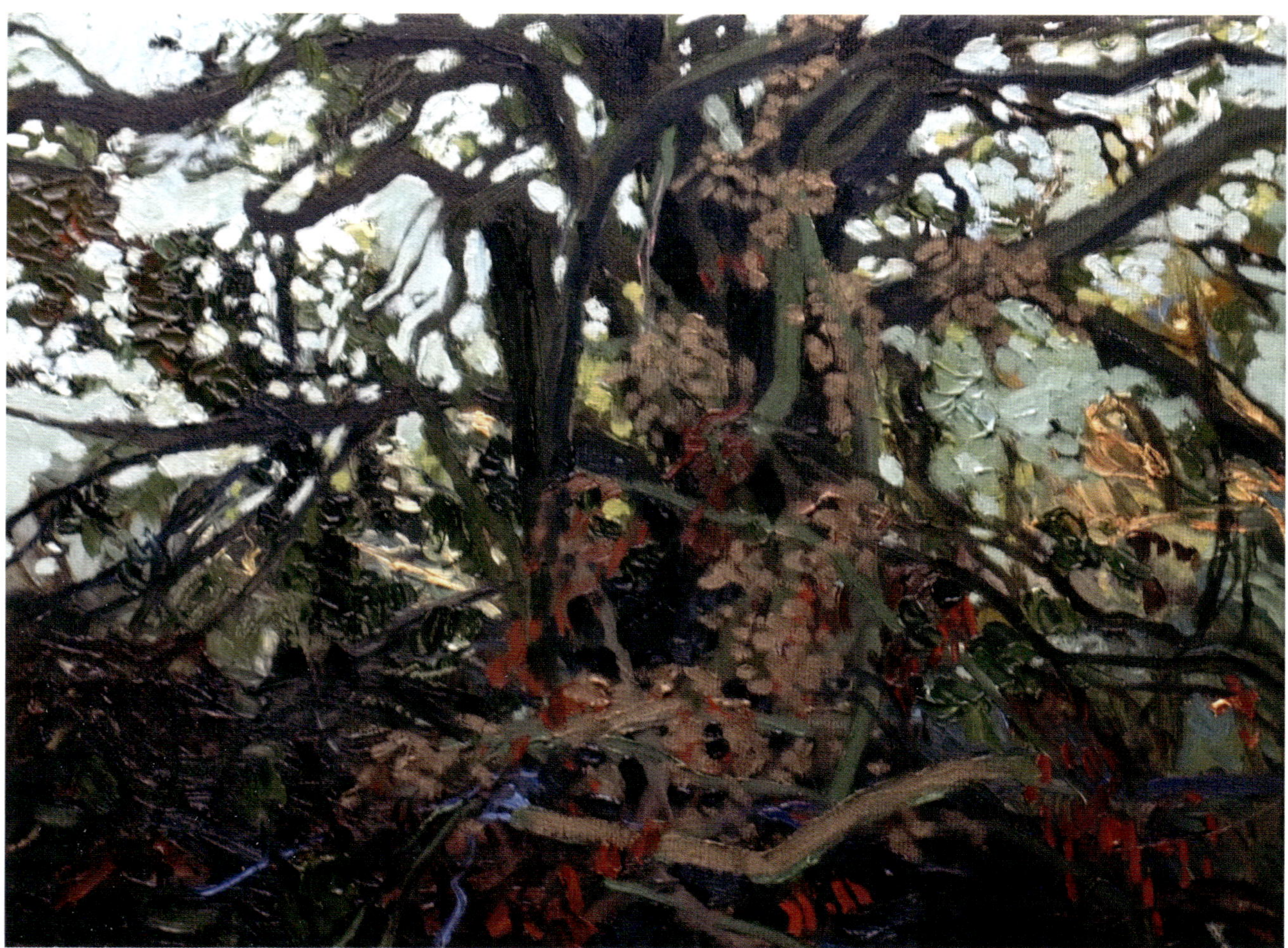

(fig 30)
JELLY GREEN
Broken Branches, Autumn, 2018
Oil on canvas
30 x 40 cm
Private collection

TANGLES

RICHARD BAVIN, STELLA CARR,
JELLY GREEN, JANE EATON

Thickets and tangles must be two sides of the one coin, but these disparate images add to the variety of confusion, disorder and impassibility that one expects to find in a natural woodland. Richard Bavin's eerie painting of a fallen tree, *Tangle* (fig 31), emphasises just how difficult it can be to walk round natural woodland. We have a measure of this in the form of the customary route taken to demonstrate the various aspects of Lacy Park Wood to visiting ecologists and foresters. Whereas 20 years ago groups could walk comfortably along the main path used when the wood was managed, now they have to hurdle over or limbo-dance under fallen trees and negotiate their way through branch wood, hoping to be able to find the way back. Jelly Green's spreading tree on the top of a slope – *Broken Branches, Autumn* (fig 30) – seems to be holding its arms wide to bar the way, and the mass of fallen branch wood and growing hazel reinforces the barrier. The out-of-focus main branches and the bright light from the open ground suggests the squint that one experiences walking out from the dark interior towards the light.

The overpowering tangle in Stella Carr's painting, combined with her title, *We Are All Connected* (fig 32), evokes my impatience and exasperation in an overgrown and collapsing maze of Old Man's Beard. Clematis is not a tree, but it tries hard to be one, scrambling over thickets of bramble and young hazel into the lower branches of fast-growing ash and emerging in their crowns. Unlike ivy, which clings to the trunks, Clematis loops and festoons at all levels in the stand. It can grow so heavy that it breaks its host. The tangle effect is also encountered by anyone who attempts to bring an overgrown hedge to order: if it contains a mixture with holly, blackthorn and ivy, it is easy to see the hedge as a metaphor for the universe – everything is connected to everything else.

Jane Eaton's title, *A Sense of Place* (fig 33), comes across as ironic. While the image includes the customary standing, fallen and leaning trees, the location could be anywhere in the wood. This aptly sums up a common experience of ecological surveyors looking for scattered plots or attempting to follow a pre-determined line through the wood. Even if you know exactly where you are, you have only to look around at something else, take a few paces, chase up another curio, then look back to discover that you are lost. Which is why ecological surveyors drive marker posts into important points and leave their anoraks conspicuously hanging on bushes – that way they can find their bearings again. Her 'concertina drawings', *Calligraphic Woods* (fig 34), reinforces the sense of disorientation and the means of reorientation. Whichever way one looks, there is just an array of sticks and branch wood, each different from the next, all undistinguished and unmemorable.

Just one image – the one with the huge swelling on the trunk – is recognisable, and it is that which forms the reference point around which one can fashion an escape.

Notwithstanding this array of thickets and tangles, jumbled confusion is remarkably localised in most natural woods. Most of the *Urwälder* – the so-called virgin forests – of mainland Europe are almost as easy to walk through as managed woodland. Each thicket and tangle comes from a localised circumstance or event. Jelly Green's tangle (fig 30) comes about because this tree has had enough room to spread out, but is old enough to start to break up. Further, another tree has fallen recently, breaking some of the beech's branches and adding the foreground piles of its own twigs and broken branches. In fact, the only really impenetrable spots in natural woods are where the crown branches of a canopy tree have smashed their way through branches of nearby trees, and even these tangles do not last more than a couple of years, for twigs and small branches rot rapidly and disintegrate.

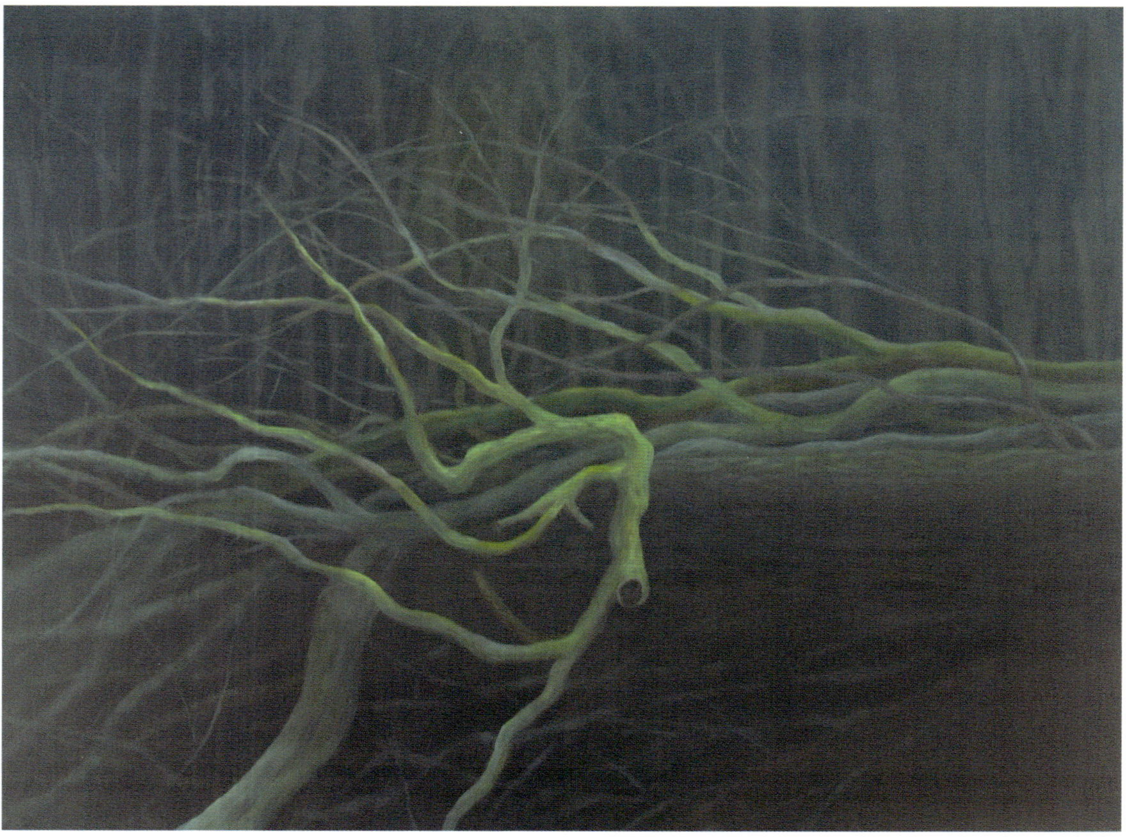

(fig 31)
RICHARD BAVIN
Tangle, 2019
Oil on panel
30 x 40 cm
Artist's collection

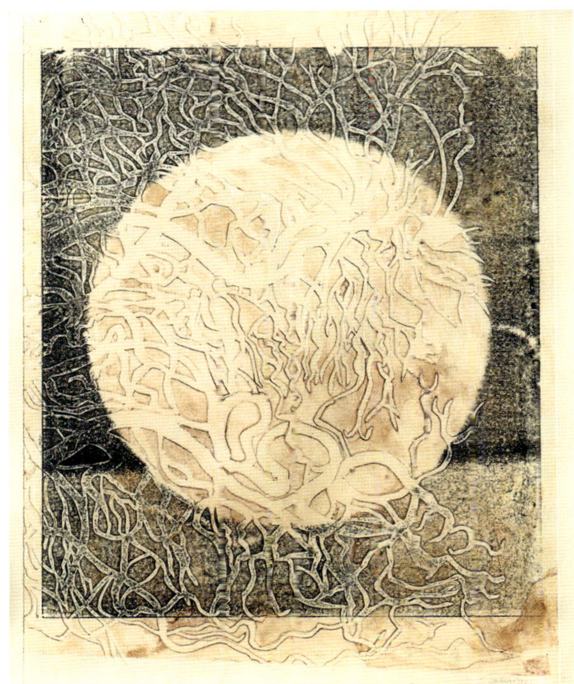

(fig 32)
STELLA CARR
We Are All Connected, 2019
Relief print on Fabriano paper
60 x 50 cm
Private collection

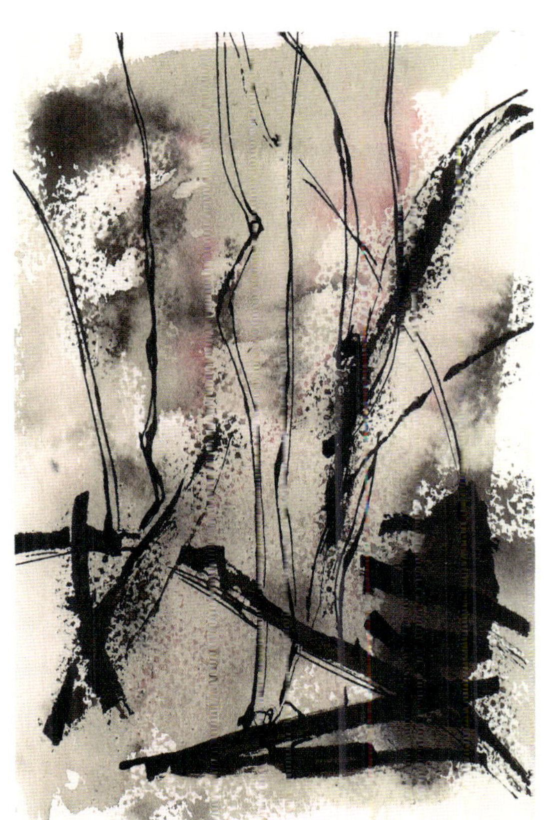

(fig 33)
JANE EATON
A Sense of Place, 2019
Fine art print from or ginal
sketch on paper
93 x 68 cm
Artist's collection

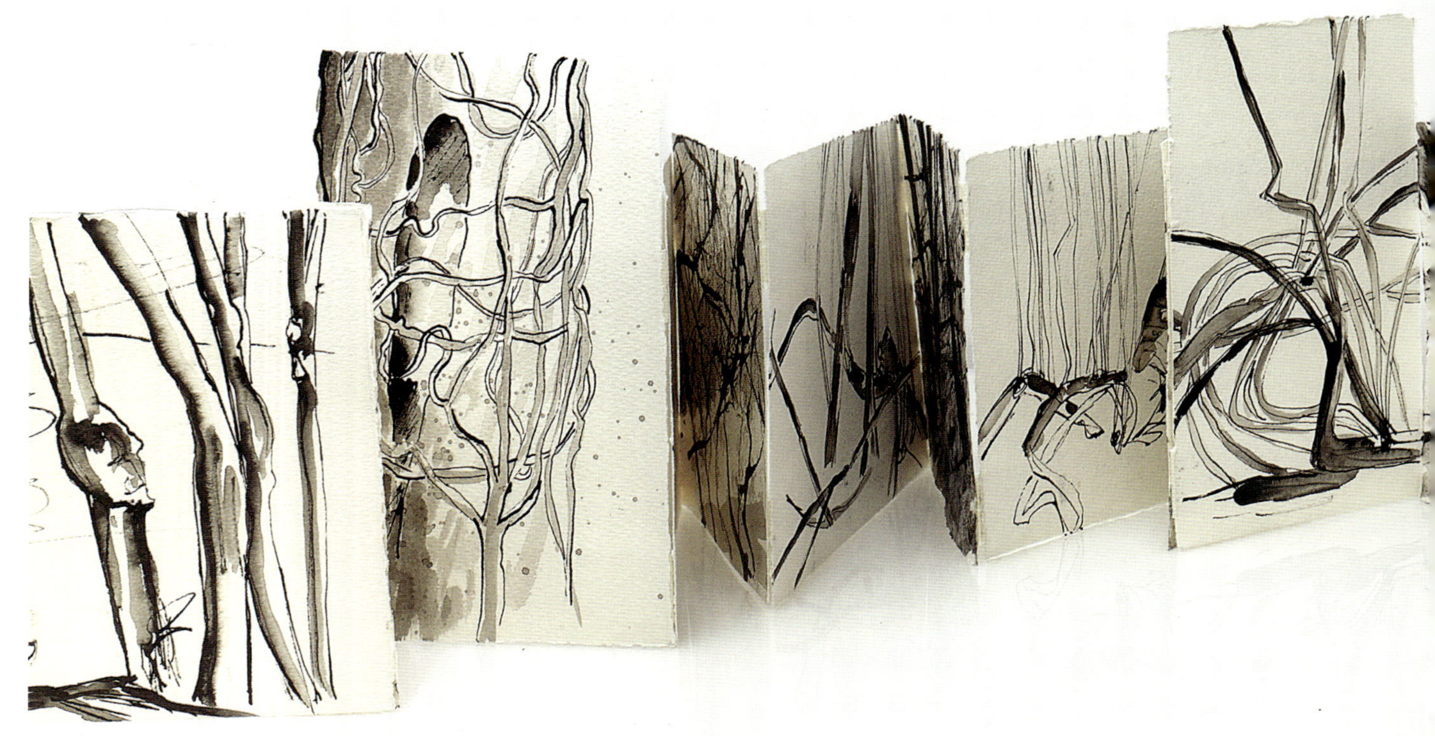

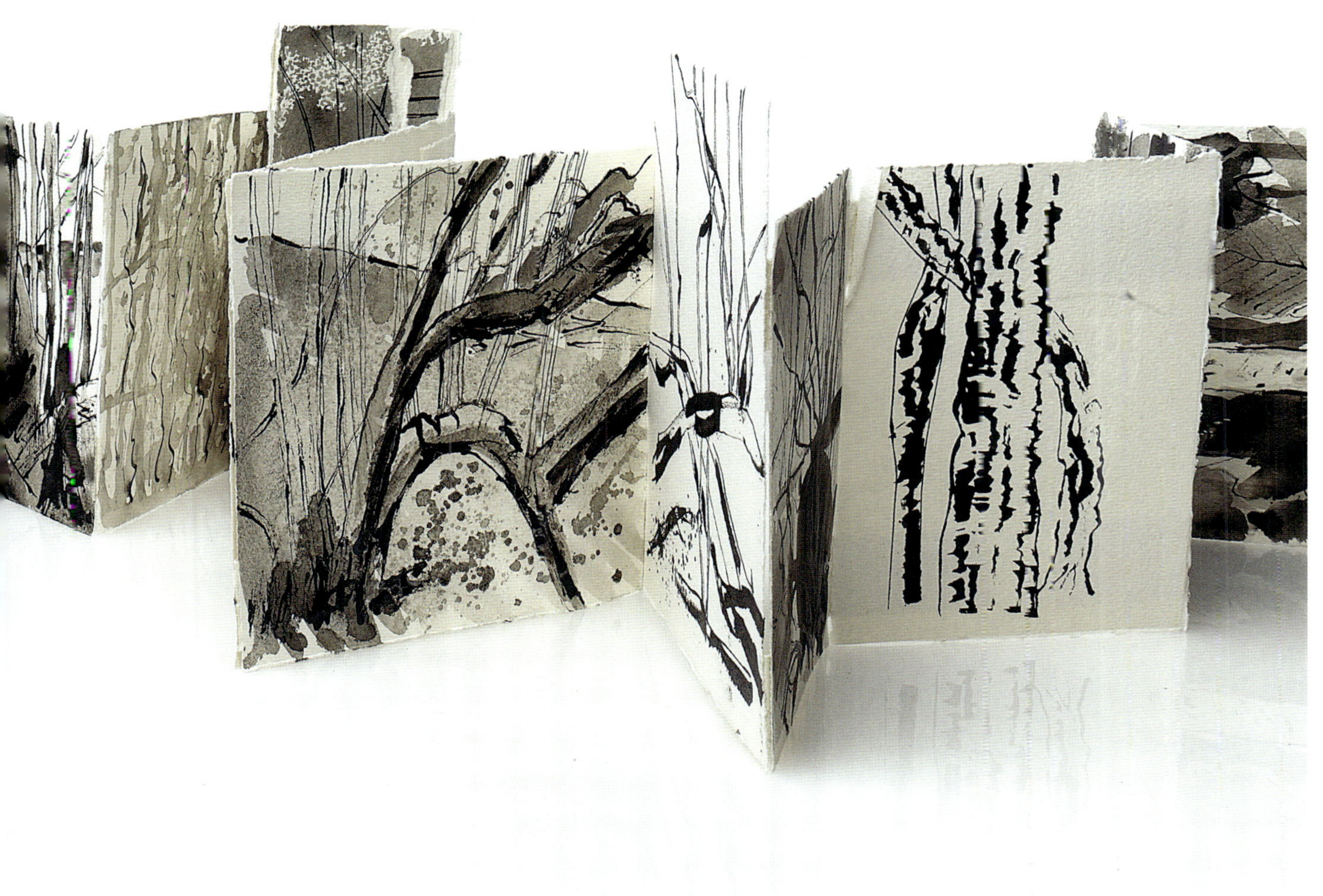

(fig 34)
JANE EATON
Calligraphic Woods, 2018
Ink on paper
Various dimensions
Private collection

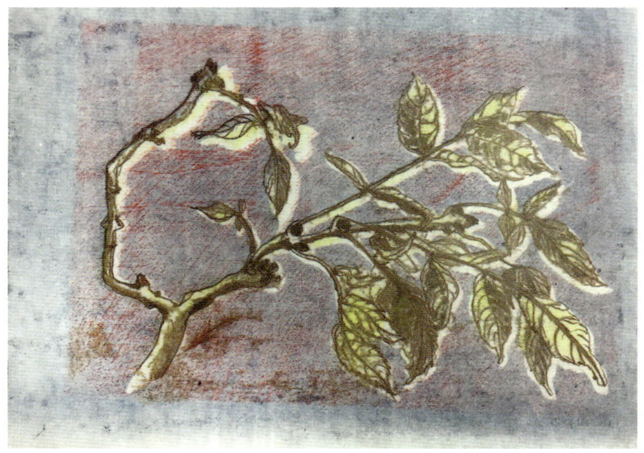

(fig 35)
STELLA CARR
Fraxinus, 2019
Relief print Washi
21 x 29 cm
Private collection

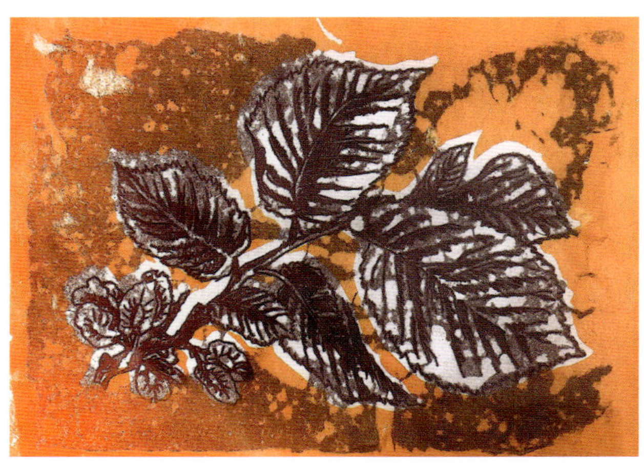

(fig 36)
STELLA CARR
Ulmus, 2019
Relief print Washi
21 x 29 cm
Private collection

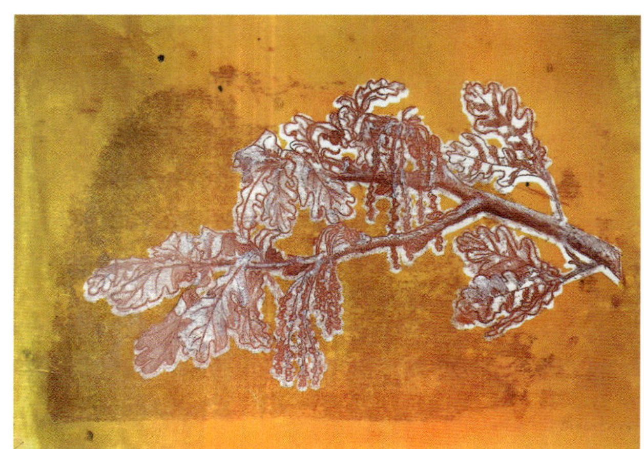

(fig 37)
STELLA CARR
Quercus, 2019
Relief print Washi
21 x 29 cm
Private collection

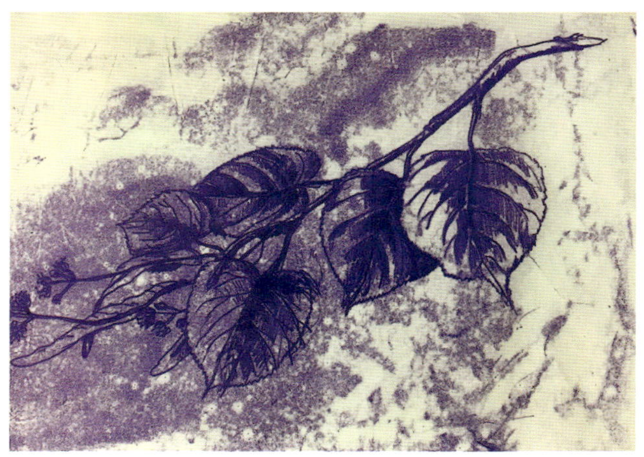

(fig 38)
STELLA CARR
Tillia, 2019
Relief print Washi
21 x 29 cm
Private collection

A DIVERSITY OF TREES

STELLA CARR

One of the features of Lady Park is the diversity of tree and species. Beech, ash, wych elm, sessile oak, large-leaved lime and small-leaved lime are the long-lived co-dominants (or were, in the case of wych elm); silver birch, downy birch, aspen, gean and alder are the short lived, opportunists that grow up after disturbance; field maple, hazel, holly, yew, hawthorn, service and whitebeam are smaller trees that must survive in shade or on the margins; and blackthorn, dogwood, wayfaring tree, guelder rose, spindle and dog rose are the shrubs. Most woods have a clearly dominant species – they are unambiguously 'oak woods', 'alder woods', and so on – but Lady Park not only has most of the native species, but maintains them as a mixture. One would imagine this is the natural state-of-affairs and that single-species dominance happens elsewhere because a past manager planted or favoured one species, but in fact many near-natural woods are dominated by one species; and, in the 75 years during which Lady Park has been allowed to become more natural, there has been a decrease in diversity, not an increase.

Stella Carr's foliage portraits – *Fraxinus* (fig 35), *Ulmus* (fig 36), *Quercus* (fig 37) and *Tillia* (fig 38) – show four of Lady Park's long-lived co-dominants: ash, wych elm, oak and one of the limes. Unlike the idealised tidy and usually simplified illustrations set against a plain background that typify plant identification books, these show examples of semi-ragged specimens against the kind of varied and often shadowy background one actually finds in woods. There is also a hint of the characteristic differences in form between species with the short, stiff shoot of wych elm contrasted with the laxer shoot of lime.

The oldest trees in Lady Park date from the mid-eighteenth century, but some grow from rootstocks that are very much older – but, how old? By studying pollen preserved in peat, environmental archaeologists have demonstrated that, more than 5,000 years ago, lime, oak and elm dominated the pre-Neolithic woodland with some ash, beech, pine and hazel in the underwood. There is every chance that the nomadic hunters, who then operated from the caves and rock shelters in the Wye gorge opposite Lady Park, would have chosen Stella Carr's four species if they had been in the habit of painting trees on cave walls.

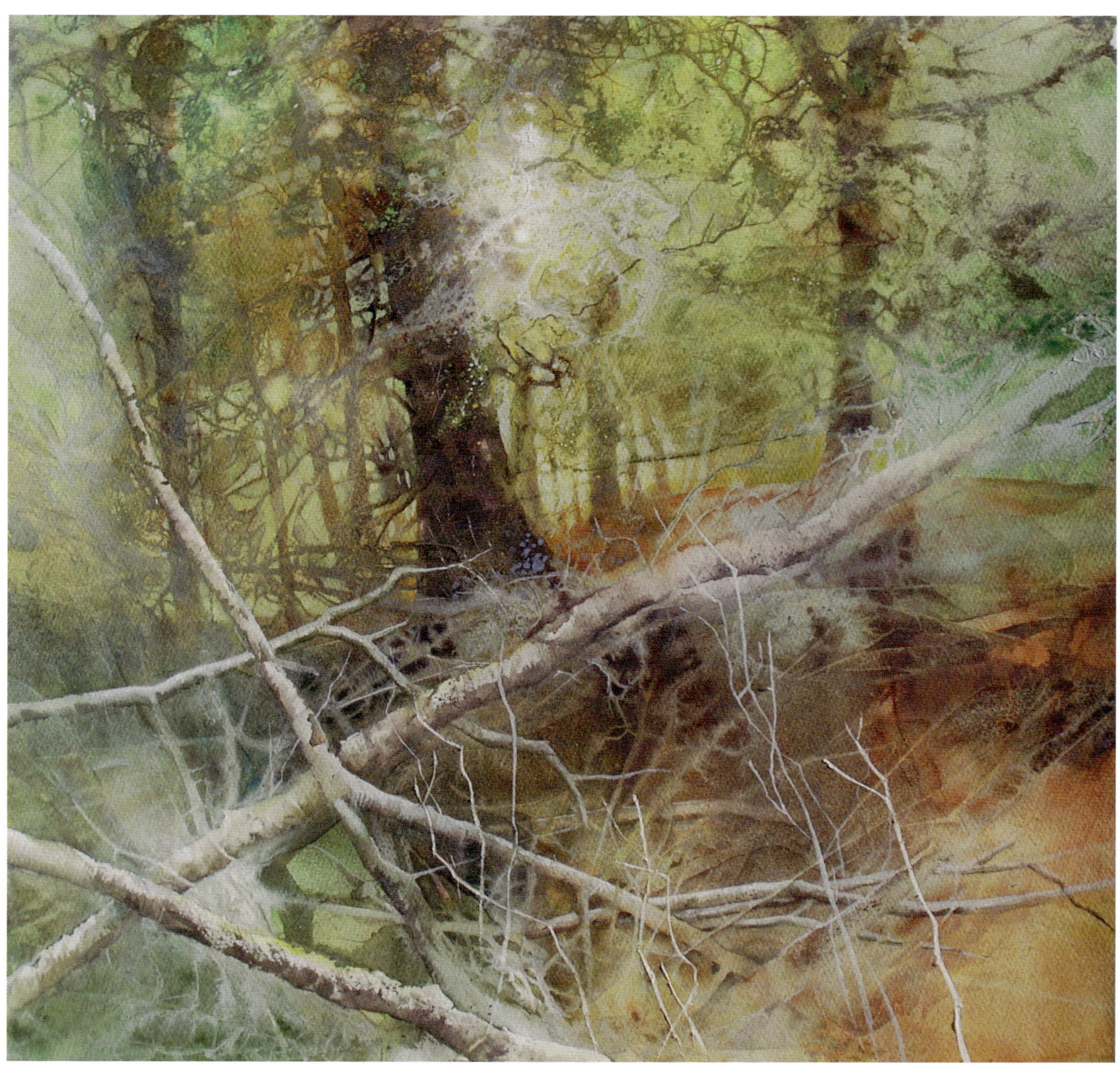

(fig 39)
ANN BLOCKLEY
The Standing and the Fallen, 2018
Water-based media on paper
73 x 69 cm
Private collection

WOODLAND AS A LAND OF VERTICALS

ANN BLOCKLEY, ALEX EGAN,
FIONA McINTYRE, SUSAN PETERKEN

Accustomed as we are to managed woodland from which fallen and leaning trees are speedily removed, natural woodland, which has lots of both, comes as a surprise. Nevertheless, our experience of natural woodland in Lady Park shows that most of the trees still grow upright, even though the woodland has nothing of the uniformity of a monoculture plantation and is everywhere littered with fallen limbs and failing saplings.

Ann Blockley's scene, *The Standing and the Fallen* (fig 39), could be formally described as 'standard trees growing in a thicket of younger growth'. At least four large trees can be seen, of which the one on the right clearly has, or had, branches spreading from the trunk from about 6 metres and upwards. This is a very familiar structure in Britain's formerly coppiced ancient woods, where, until the first half of the twentieth century, a scatter of oaks (standards) were grown for timber amongst a mixture of other species that were cut, or coppiced, every 5 to 20 years. The oaks could formerly spread their branches over the underwood with impunity, but as coppicing lapsed and the underwood grew taller than it had grown for centuries, the lower branches of the oaks became shaded and then died. Here, in Lady Park, the last coppicing was in 1870, but the wartime fellings in 1942 amounted to a de facto coppicing. By the time of this painting, the underwood had enjoyed 75 years of unrestricted growth, while the oaks have had much less to enjoy.

The foreground scatter of small branches lying at drunken angles hints at a process that ecologists know well, but of which most visitors may be unaware. Stands of trees thin themselves by competitive exclusion, an unrelenting battle between neighbours where the large trees almost always grow faster than smaller trees and live longer. The small trees become increasingly shaded, languish and die, and they do this to highly predictable thinning rules. We can easily appreciate the death of large trees when they fall and imagine the great crash as they rip past their neighbours and crash to the ground, but the great majority of trees die small, quietly and unnoticed. Or, rather, they are noticed only when one leaves the track to pick a way through the mortal remains of small trees such as these.

Lady Park Sketch 2 (fig 40) and *Sketch 1* (fig 41) by Alex Egan, show both the dominant verticality and the variety of form that trees will exhibit if they are not regulated by foresters. Traditional foresters in particular spent a great deal of time and expertise on thinning, a process whereby the most vigorous trees of good – that is, straight – form were selected and the rest cut out in stages, leaving only enough at each thinning to encourage the selected 'final crop' trees to continue growing up and straight. In Lady Park, the stands are not thinned, so there are many crooked and slow-growing trees, but there are also some beautifully straight, tall and fast-growing specimens. In the nearby managed woodland, thinning indirectly damaged the growth of the retained trees because it encouraged grey squirrels to strip bark from trunks and branches, thereby reducing some potentially fine beeches to inverted candelabras.

Alex Egan's *Sketch 1* (fig 41) shows a fine, python-like ivy climbing the great oak and another work, Susan Peterken's *Ivy Stranglehold* (fig 42), shows ivy trying to be a strangler fig. Ivy is capable of holding its own as ground cover, so carpeting some woods on lime-rich soils that it excludes herbs. Here it aspires to be a tree. It is well able to reach the crown of a mature oak, but it cannot support itself if the oak dies and rots. It lives as long as birches: we accept that the oak is over 200 years old, but how many realise that the ivies are probably approaching their 80th birthdays?

Drawn in a part of the wood that has been almost entirely left to nature for 150 years, Fiona McIntyre's *To the Edge* (fig 43) draws attention to an immense gall on the trunk of an oak. Thus embellished, this otherwise undistinguished tree is one of the wood's few unmistakable specimens, and it usually attracts comments from visitors. Fortunately, the 'eyes' are one above the other, not horizontal, or it would look like a face and nervous visitors might be seeing demons in the undergrowth. Ecologists are not prey to such imaginings, even when working alone in a wood, but they are often on high alert. Standing quietly looking in one direction making notes, oblivious to events elsewhere, it is easy to be startled when a deer barks or when a blackbird suddenly scuffs through dry leaf litter.

Trees grow vertically because they have evolved to grow away from gravity and towards the light. The two forces work together, especially in a wood where most trees start their growth in gaps. The interesting question is: why do some not grow straight up? In natural woodland where trees of different sizes grow side-by-side, small trees will grow at a slant to avoid large, shady neighbours. The anti-gravity impulse must be strong, for trees that start growing close to the base of a cliff still grow upright, even though light comes from one side: it is their branches that grow one-sided.

On slopes, as at Lady Park, trees have slants thrust upon them as soil erodes and as branches on the down side grow heavier than those on the up side. Small trees may be flattened or knocked aside when neighbours fall. The strangest non-verticality develops when a leaning small tree loses its leader, develops a new one, leaving a permanent kink in the trunk. Similar zigzag forms will develop when a tree that was growing at a lean in one direction seizes an opportunity to grow in another direction, when a falling tree nearby opens another gap. In Lady Park there is one place where this happened to a group of ash poles, which now remind me of the artist David Nash and his *Ash Dome*, which was planted as a circle of saplings on a plot in North Wales and has been seen regularly as an introductory image for programmes on BBC 4.

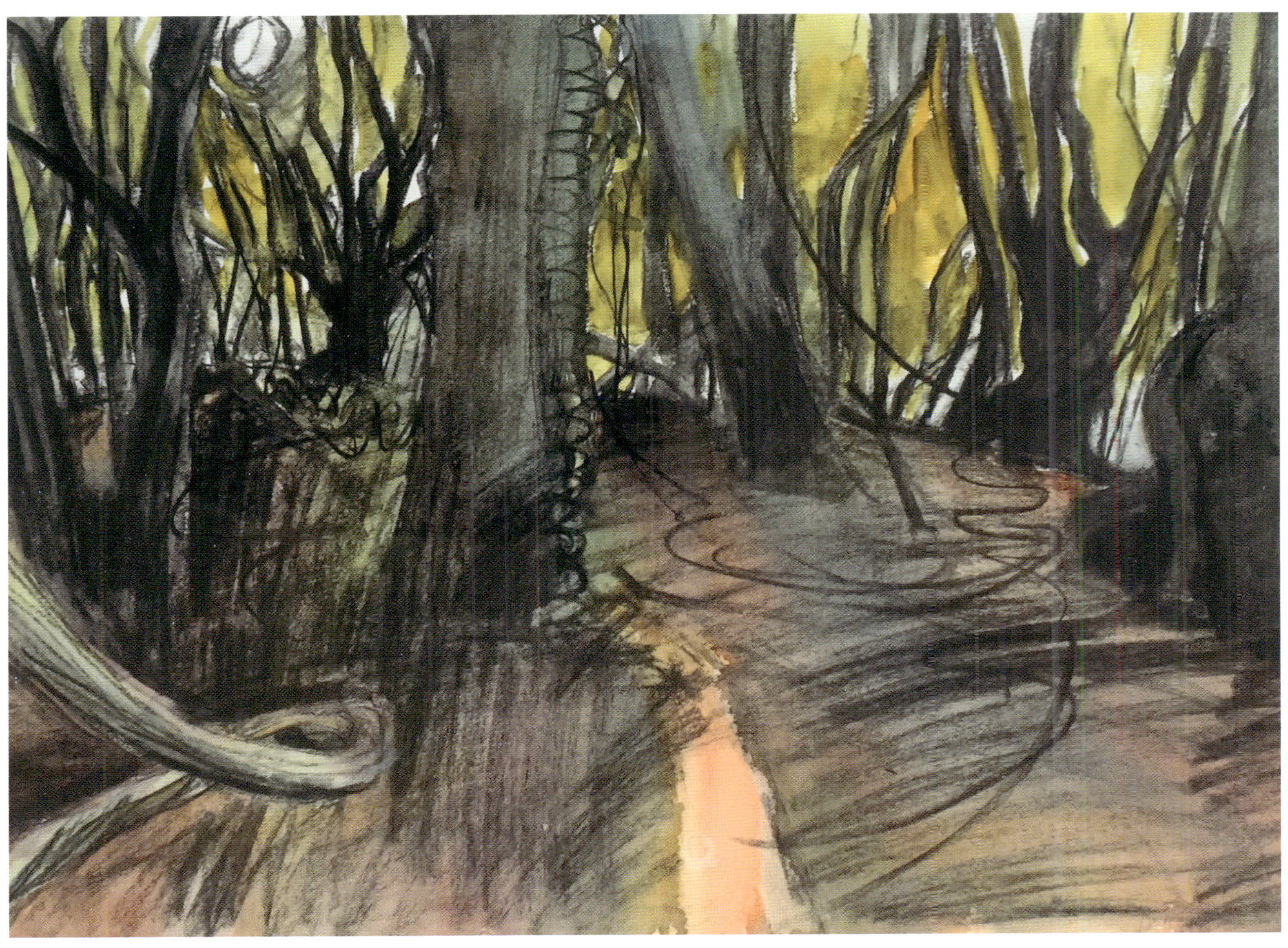

(fig 40)
ALEX EGAN
Lady Park Sketch 2, 2018
Drawing on paper
50 x 36 cm
Private collection

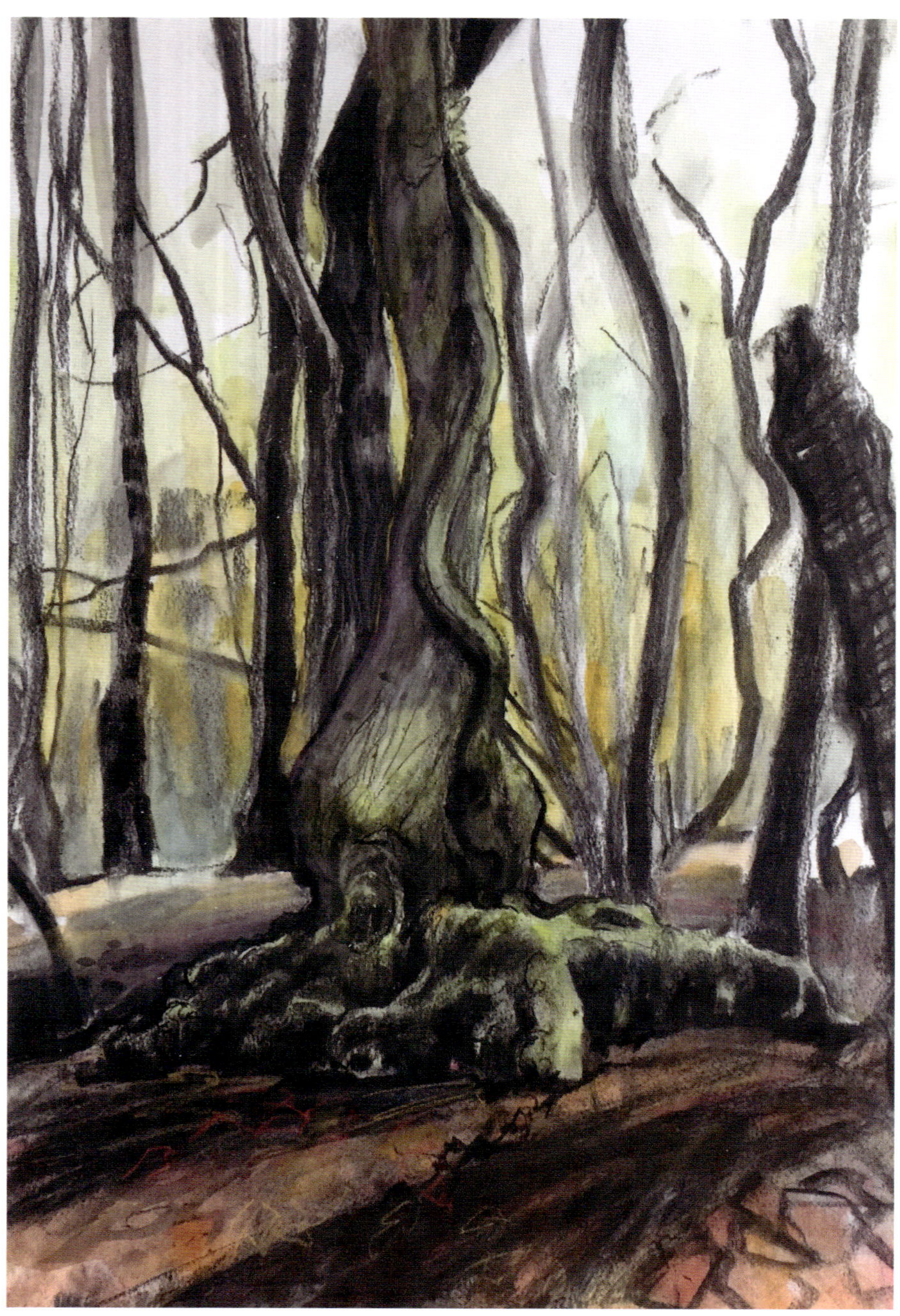

(fig 41)
ALEX EGAN
Sketch 1, 2018
Drawing on paper
50 x 36 cm
Private collection

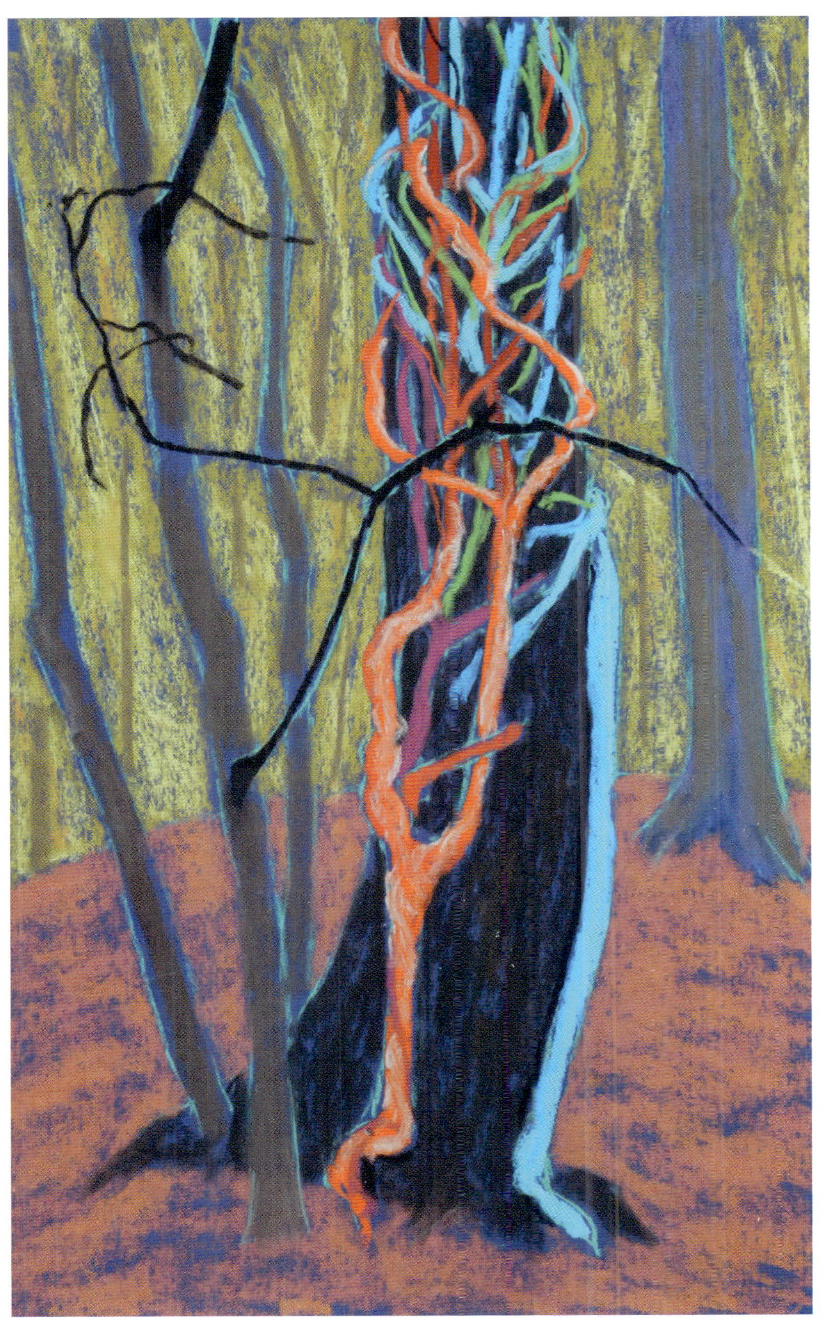

(fig 42)
SUSAN PETERKEN
Ivy Stranglehold, 2018
Pastel on paper
45.5 × 27 cm
Artist's collection

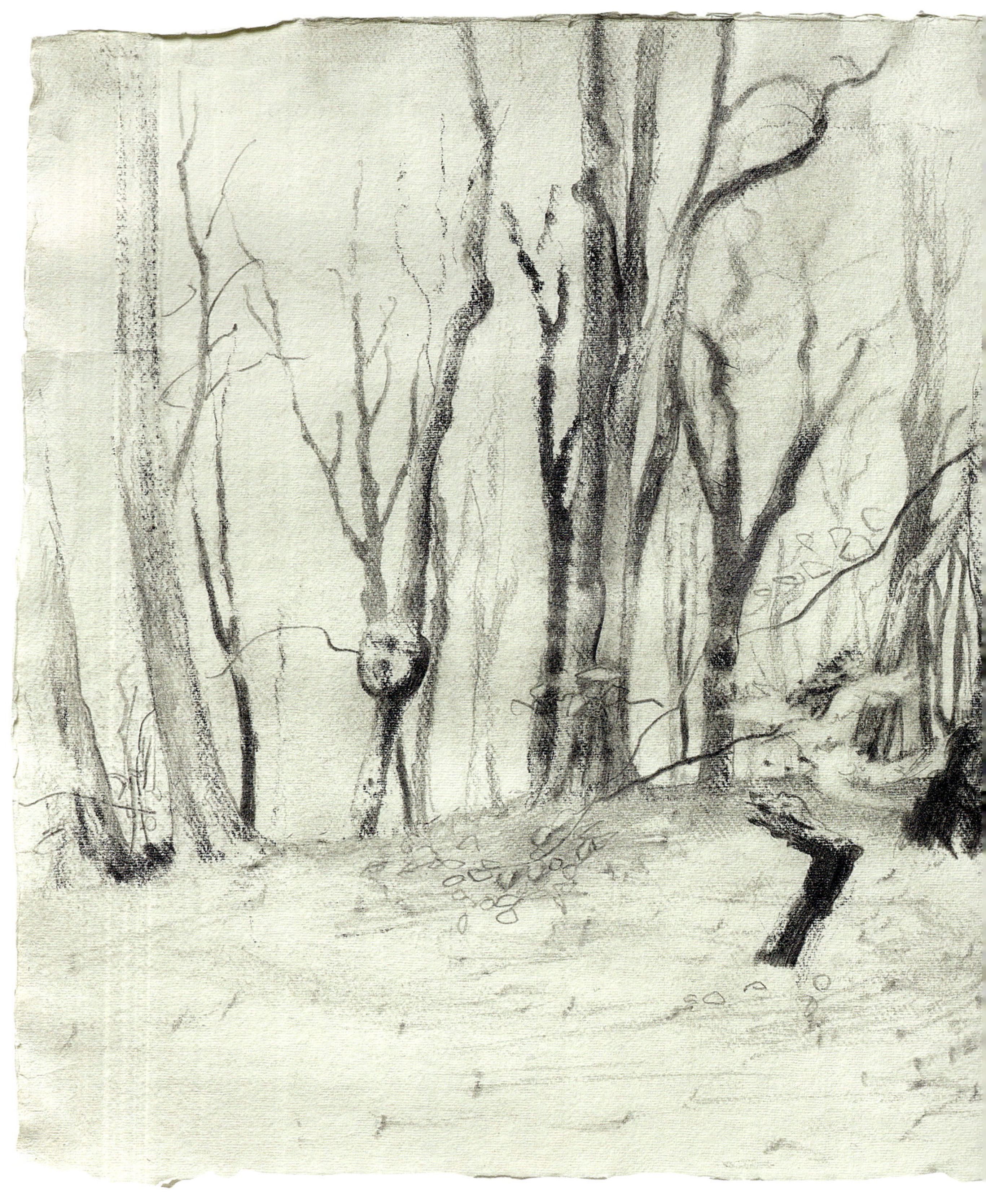

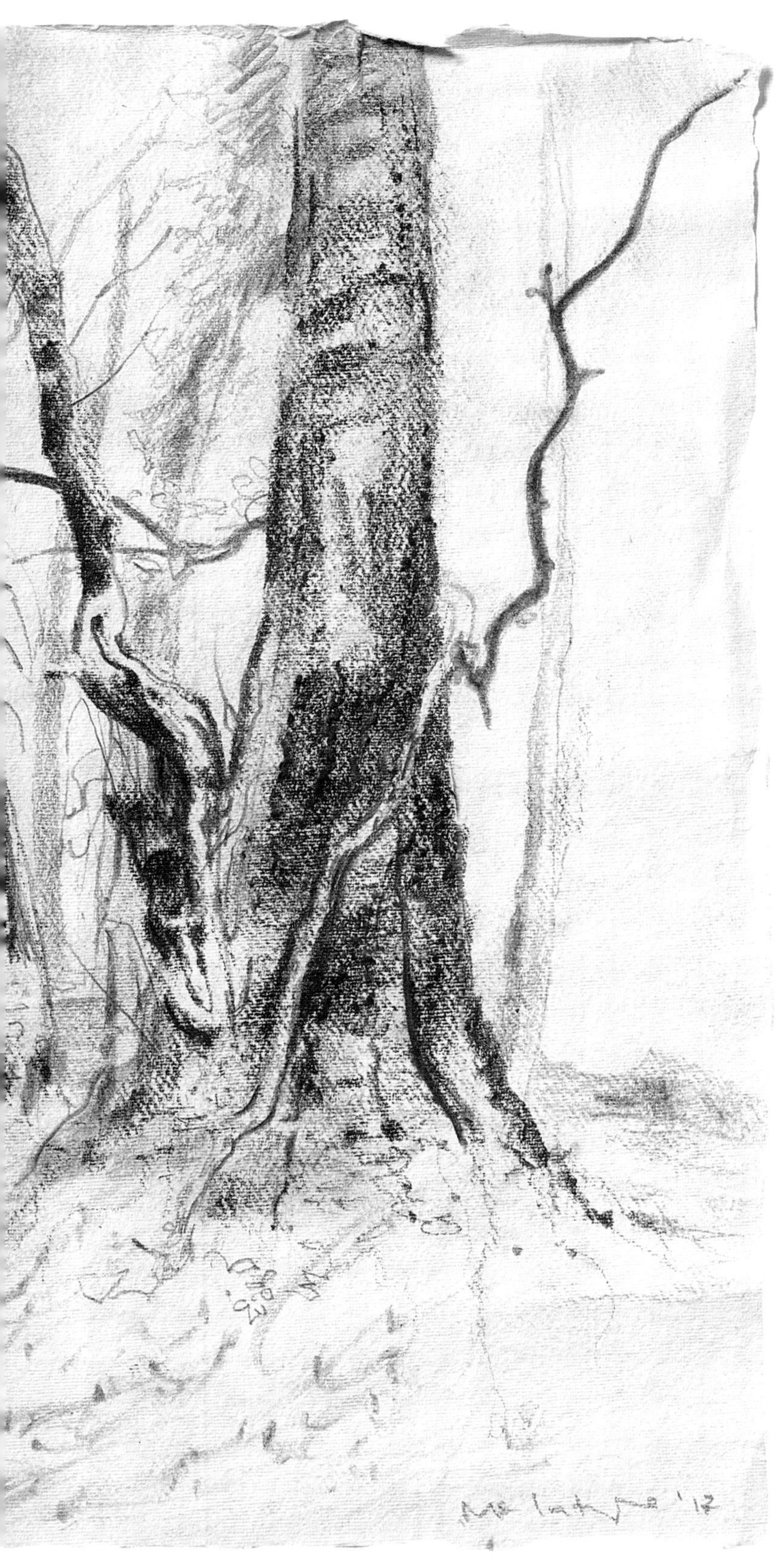

(fig 43)
FIONA McINTYRE
To the Edge 2017
Graphite on Khadi paper
62 x 72 cm
Private collection

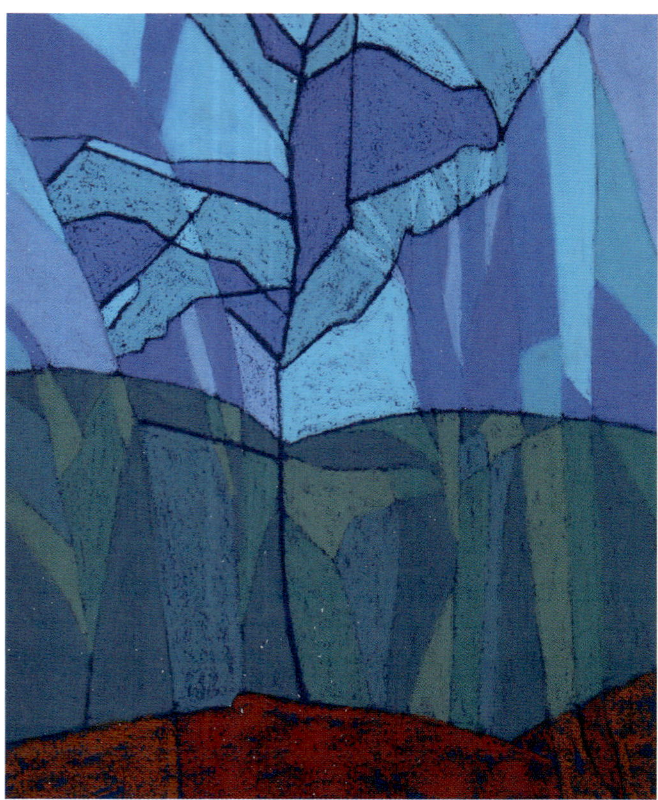

(fig 44)
SUSAN PETERKEN
On the Edge of the Cliff, 2018
Pastel on paper
46 x 34.5 cm
Artist's collection

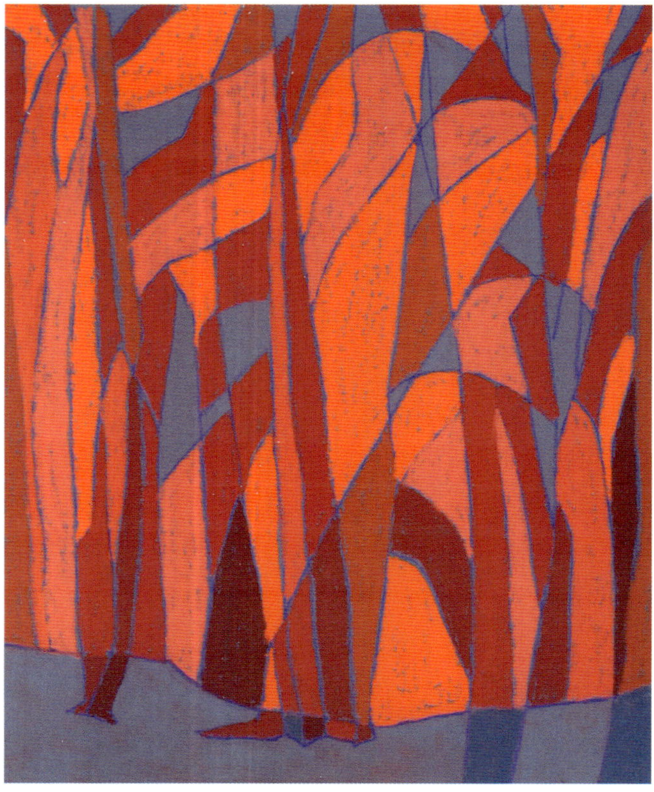

(fig 45)
SUSAN PETERKEN
Red Interspatial, 2018
Pastel on paper
46.5 x 38 cm
Artist's collection

WOODLAND SPACE

SUSAN PETERKEN

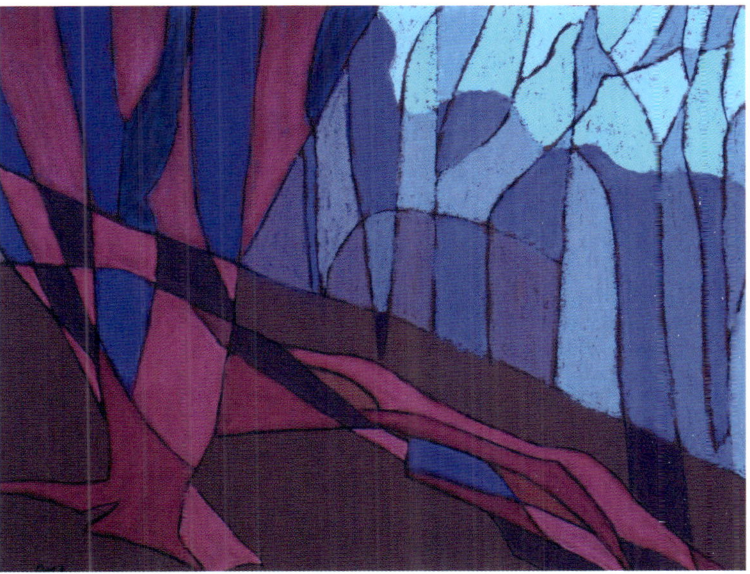

(fig 46)
SUSAN PETERKEN
Interspatial, 2018
Pastel on paper
47 × 37.5 cm
Artist's collection

Woods are defined by their trees. Collectively, they form a dominating presence, reducing the sunlight to sun flecks and deep shade. Their size and structure gives each wood its personality. Individually, the largest inspire awe and wonder by their sheer bulk and complexity of form.

So it is astonishing to find that the trees themselves occupy only a small amount of the volume of the wood. The basal area of natural stands is usually in the range 20–40 m²/ha, which, since 1 ha is 10,000 m², means that the ground actually occupied by tree trunks is just 0.2–0.4% of the total ground area. In fact it is a little more because basal area is calculated by measuring trees at 'breast height', whilst trunks splay out at the base. Even allowing for this, from a plan view, 99.5% of the area of a wood is space between the trees. Further, this must be true in a vertical dimension. However much trees may branch, most of a wood's volume is space.

These stained-glass-window paintings express that logic by depicting trees as thin, monochrome lines, reducing trees to mere boundaries between spaces. Most of these spaces are vertically elongated diamonds through which we see the trees beyond. Trees fill the view, even though they occupy so little of the wood.

Taken together, the three images show the variety of space shapes in different positions and stages of growth. *Red Interspatial* (fig 45) illustrates the small, narrow spaces between branches in a dense hazel coppice, which contrasts with the mature woodland of *Interspatial* (fig 46). In *On the Edge of the Cliff* (fig 44), some of the branches are almost horizontal, creating yet another pattern.

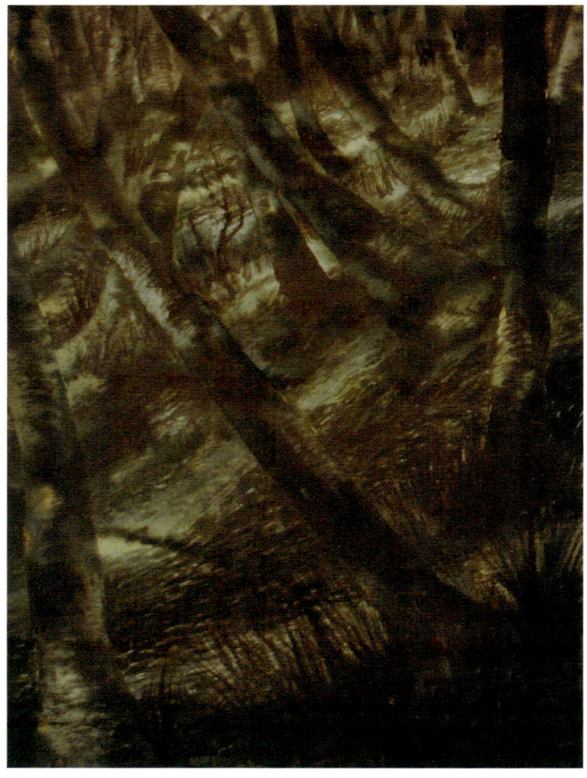

(fig 47)
LESLEY SLIGHT
Slope, 2017
Ink on Arches Aquarelle
300-gsm paper
35 x 25 cm
Private collection

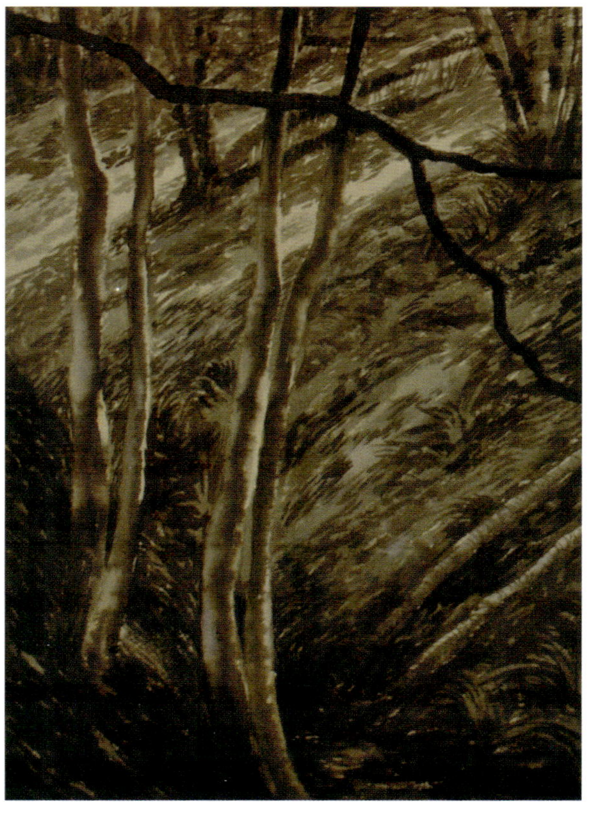

(fig 48)
LESLEY SLIGHT
Bank, 2017
Ink on Arches Aquarelle
300-gsm paper
35 x 25 cm
Private collection

SLOPES

LESLEY SLIGHT

In most woods the ground line is horizontal, but in Susan Peterken's *Interspatial* (fig 46) (see 'Woodland Space' section) it descends from high left to low right. The trees still grow upright, yet the slope leaves its mark because trees on slopes tend to produce stronger branches on the downslope side. You can see this asymmetric distribution of light and shade easily enough. Look upslope and the internal view of a wood is dark, because the backdrop is the ground, whereas downslope, the backdrop is the sky. Looking upslope, trees like beech appear as pale verticals against dark backgrounds, but looking downslope the trees are silhouettes, and the structure of their branching is correspondingly more prominent. The view is across the contour, and so the dark to the left grades through to the light to the right. The growing tree is more shaded by trees further up the slope than by trees further down. Ultimately, this one-sided branching increases the likelihood that a tree will topple.

In *Slope* (fig 47), Lesley Slight presents younger, and therefore denser and darker, woodland on a much steeper slope where the asymmetric environment has impressed itself even more on the form of the trees. They grow towards the light and, as they grow, their lean becomes ever more pronounced as the crowns develop to one side, soil creep tilts their base and perhaps objects falling from above knock them to one side. All the forces of nature work in the same direction and eventually the trees will fall downslope. Very rarely, the forces of nature work the other way. When the beech woods of the Noar Hill Hanger, near Selborne, faced the truly exceptional storm of October 1987, a few great trees were actually blown upslope, their roots coming to rest a metre above where they grew.

In *Bank* (fig 48) Lesley presents much the same kind of scene, but with a significant difference. Here we are looking down a narrow channel deeply etched into the slope, where the trees are neither curved at the base nor leaning because the shade from one side of the valley balances the shade from the other side. Instead, we see a hint of a common feature of natural woodland, that dead trees fall downslope from both sides and will accumulate in the bottom, where they will accumulate, collect twig-and-leaf dams and eventually hold up the flow of water after heavy rains. In managed woodland, headwater channels remain clear because the trees are harvested, so the water runs rapidly into the main rivers. As flooding becomes an ever greater problem, so woodland managers are starting to reinstate log and debris dams in wooded headwaters.

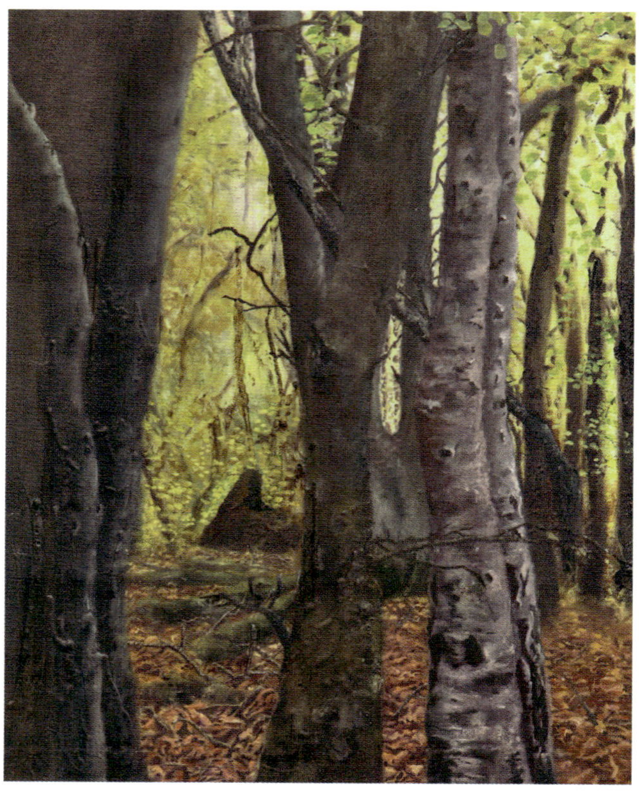

(fig 49)
JACQUELINE WEDLAKE HATTON
Presence, 2018
Oil on canvas
50 x 40 cm
Private collection

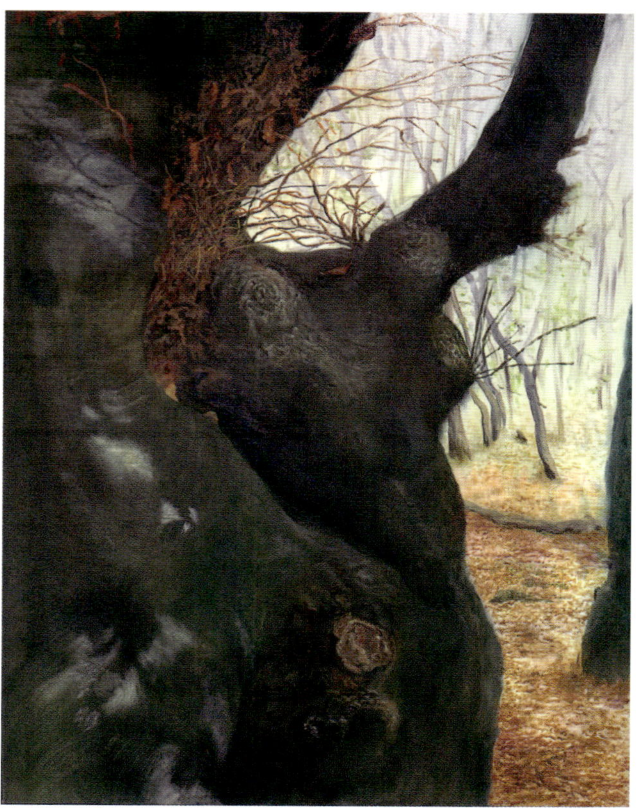

(fig 50)
JACQUELINE WEDLAKE HATTON
Shooting – Lady Park Wood, 2018
Oil on canvas
120 x 100 cm
Private collection

WOODLANDS FOR HUNTERS AND THEIR QUARRY

JACQUELINE WEDLAKE HATTON

Woodlands are places to hide. Outlaws and free spirits, the prime example of which in English mythology was Robin Hood, took to the woods in search of independence from the constraints of civilisation. Even today, criminals on the run attempt to secrete themselves in woodland; and I suspect that many law-abiding woodland visitors are seeking privacy as much as the visual delights of woodland.

This desire to hide is shared by deer and the hunters. Both need to see, but remain unseen. Both of these paintings by Jacqueline Wedlake Hatton, *Presence* (fig 49) and *Shooting – Lady Park Wood* (fig 50), view the wood from a position of concealment into a clearing where deer may come to browse, so these are more a hunter's views than a deer's. Concealment is achieved in one work (*Presence*) within a beech grove, in the other behind an old stub beech surviving from the era of management. Framed in portrait format, both feel even more like a restricted view than the standpoint requires, but this is not how the hunter or a fallow deer will see it, for both are constantly aware of the wood to left, right and behind. For the deer this is an essential survival mechanism; for the hunter it's a key to success; and for any individual woodland walker, the heightened awareness that walking in a wood invariably generates must be a legacy of our evolution as both hunters and hunted. Alone in and around natural woodland we walk softly, glance left and right, jump at any sound behind, and pause where we will not be seen against the dark trunk of a large tree.

Jacqueline's *Presence* (fig 49) shows the apparently random patterns of trees in natural woodland. Unlike plantations, where the orderly lines remain obvious for decades and detectable a couple of centuries after the planters have passed away, trees in natural woodland are distributed where the seed happened to fall; where the deer happened not to browse the saplings; where an old tree fell to admit enough light for the saplings to grow strongly. The result is that trees of a particular species or age tend to grow in clusters, or groups, and we can see this here. The vantage point within a group of beech looks out into a distant canopy gap where saplings are starting to grow strongly, and right to another group of beech, which would be the inheritors of a gap formed decades ago.

The grouping of trees in natural woodland has interesting implications for photographers, including ecologists searching for a 'typical' view to illustrate a publication. Much more so than in plantations, the precise position of the photographer and the exact direction in which he/she aims the shot makes all the difference to the result. Move ten steps, or change the direction slightly, and the resulting image is quite different. One can see this in collections of monitoring photographs, which are taken from fixed points in pre-determined directions: the images are invariably ordinary at best and confusing at worst. It is amazing how carefully one must select the viewpoint when one tries to record a typical image of a wood! The artists, incidentally, tell me that this applies equally to a painter's choice of viewpoint. Many spent a great deal of time wandering and looking before they settled to a particular composition and viewpoint.

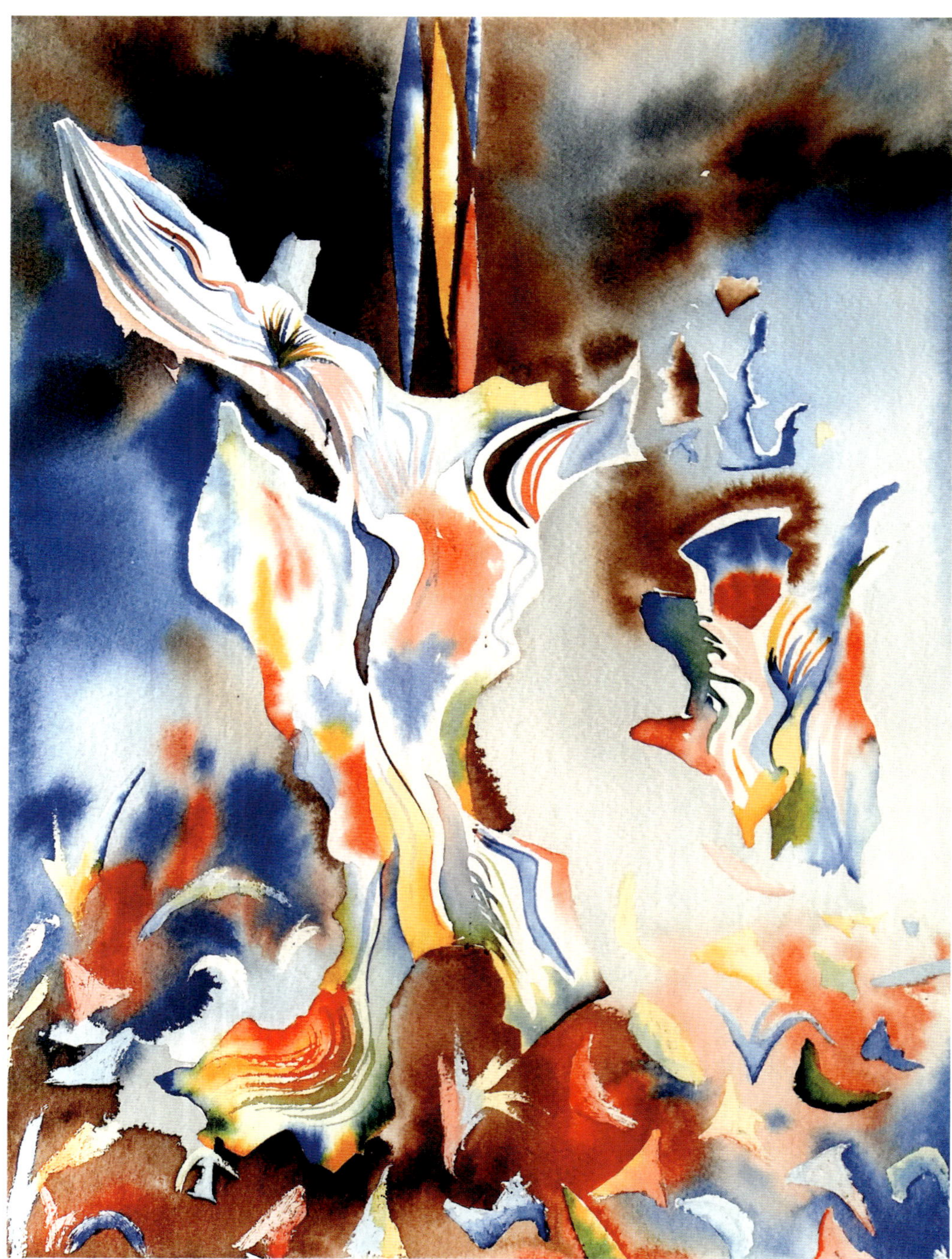

(fig 51)
ABI KREMER
Lady Park Wood 2, 2018
Watercolour on paper
50 x 45 cm
Artist's collection

FANTASY WOODLAND

ABI KREMER

Abi Kremer sees woodland in a way that might surprise a down-to-earth ecologist aspiring to publish a paper in, say, the *Journal of Ecology*. Her fantastical images nevertheless comprise actual components of woodland, but in vivid colours and rearranged from their conventional places. I hesitate to make unecological comments, but they put me in mind of Salvador Dalí or Terry Gilliam's sequences in Monty Python. Or we might see them as scenes from a forest ecologist's dream – all the components real enough, but mixed, moving and coloured in ways that can never be found with one's eyes open. The flying root plate (fig 53) in a blizzard of falling leaves must count as a nightmare.

Abstract though it is, the 'flying root plate' *Lady Park Wood 3* (fig 53) is the only opportunity in this collection to contemplate the wood from below. Normally we see woods from a height of about 1.5 metres, but, if we could see them from a metre below the soil surface instead we would see a scatter of star- or starfish-like objects that are the underside of the large trees. We see this 'worm's-eye' perspective for real when wind or gravity uproots a tree without breaking the trunk and the root plate emerges buried in soil, leaf litter and a mass of fine roots. Over the following years the soil washes off, the rocks drop away and we see the splay of roots, like a many-fingered hand with which the tree grasped the ground when it grew upright. The falling tree creates a pit where the root-plate and its load of soil and rocks used to be, and when the root-plate has completely decayed, it leaves a small mound of soil and rock beside the pit. Over several centuries and the fall of many trees, the result is a hummocky ground surface which ecologists know as 'pit-and-mound microtopography'. When the Swede Peter Kalm travelled through eastern North America in the eighteenth century he used the presence of pits and mounds to identify those woods that the settlers had never cleared for agriculture, and this is still the clue that modern American ecologists use to identify ancient woods today. In Britain, such evidence is not available, for time and millennia of coppicing in ancient woods have not only erased the primaeval pits and mounds, but have also prevented them from forming.

The 'lambent flame' *Lady Park Wood 2* (fig 51) image reminded me of driftwood fires in the grate of the hut on Scolt Head Island, a nature reserve on the Norfolk coast. At first glance it has nothing to do with Lady Park or any other broadleaved woodland, none of which will burn. However, the inspiration was a long-dead, bark-free, but still standing stump of an oak mini-pollard that died with one trunk still attached. In real life it will take the best part of a century to decay, oxidising the wood and returning its mineral nutrients to the soil. Portraying the dead tree as a flame and the leaf litter as a carpet of embers shows this essential process of returning mineral nutrients to the soil in accelerated time.

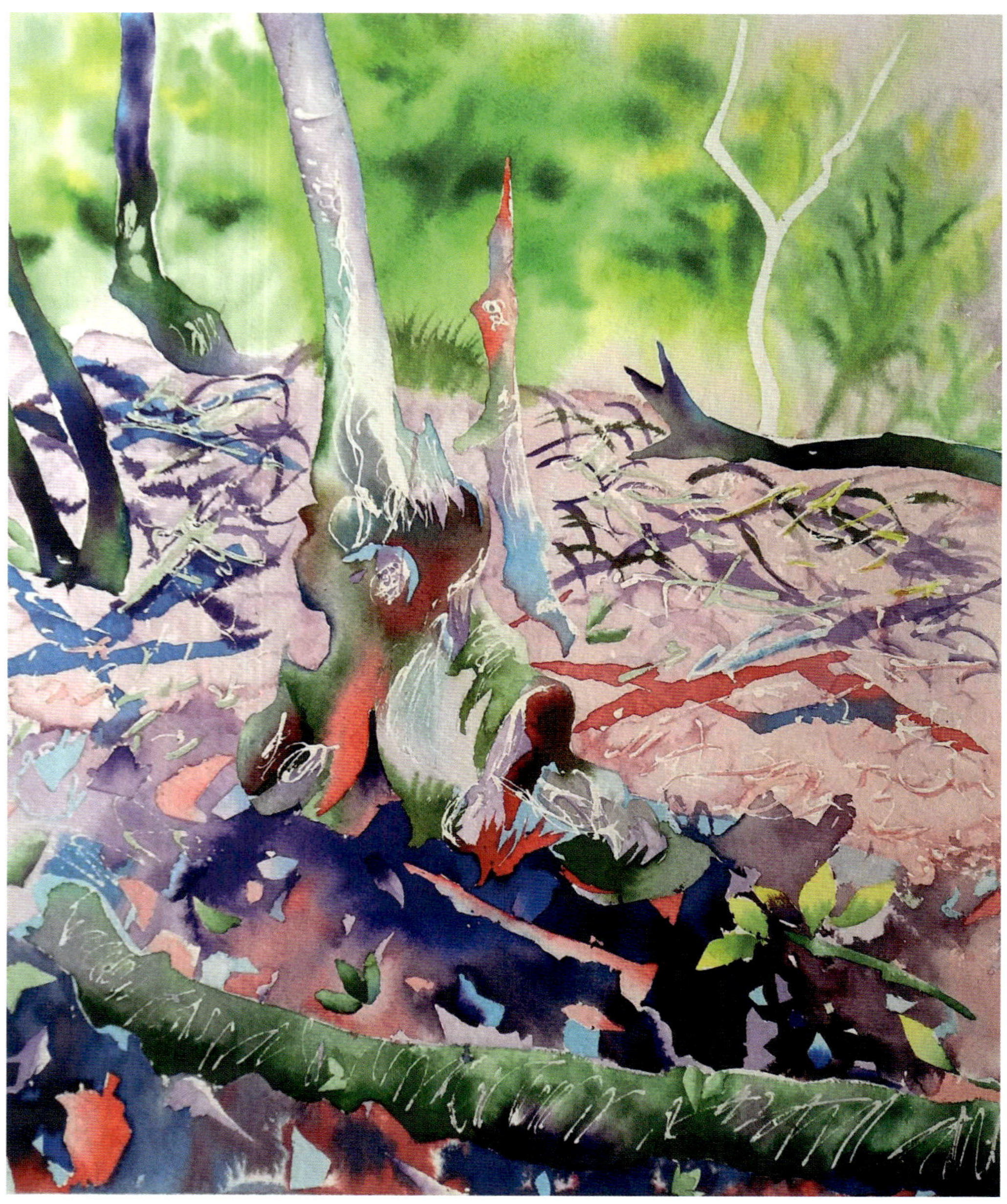

(fig 52)
ABI KREMER
Lady Park Wood 1, 2018
Watercolour on paper
48 x 38 cm
Artist's collection

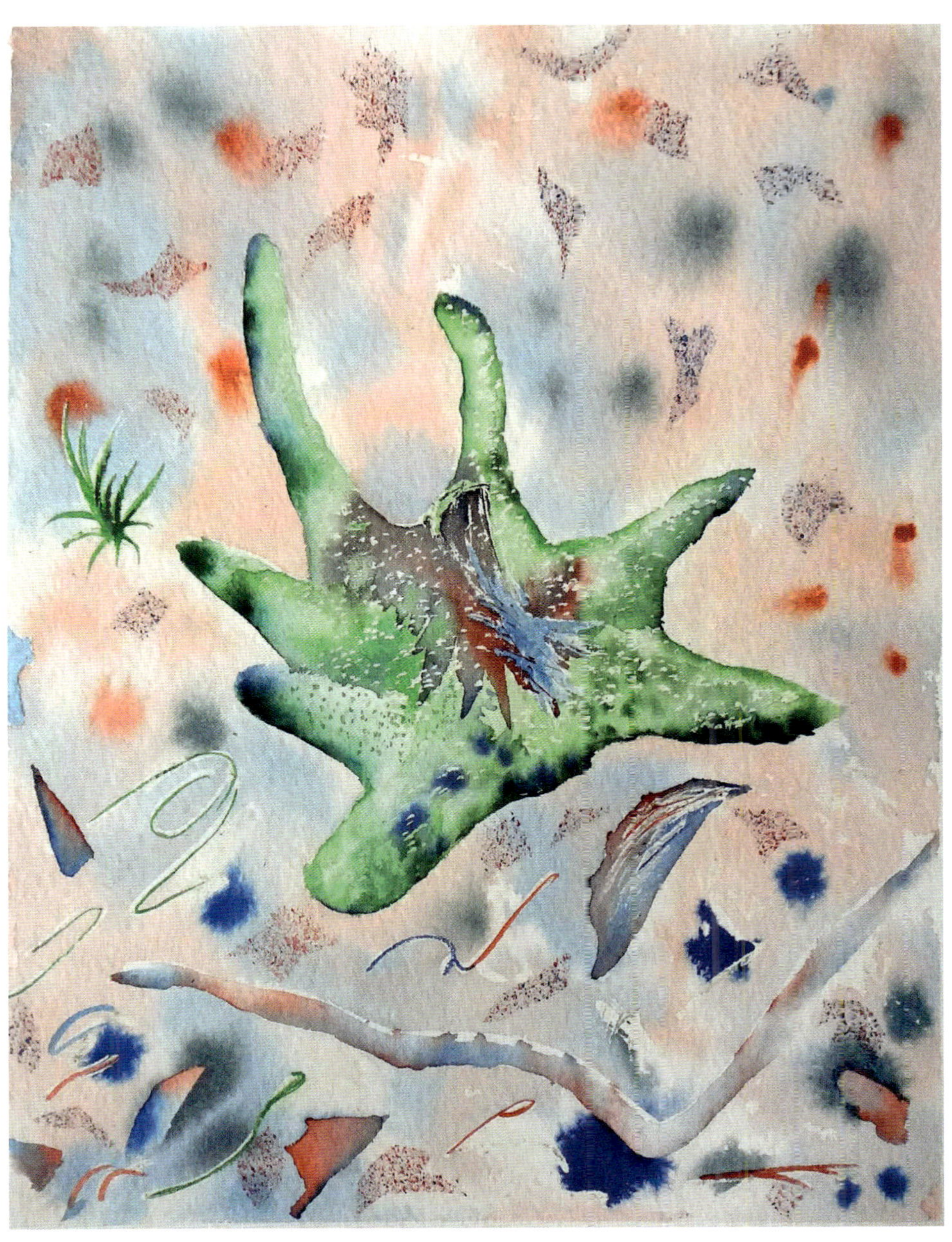

(fig 53)
ABI KREMER
Lady Park Wood 3, 2018
Watercolour on paper
46 x 39 cm
Artist's collection

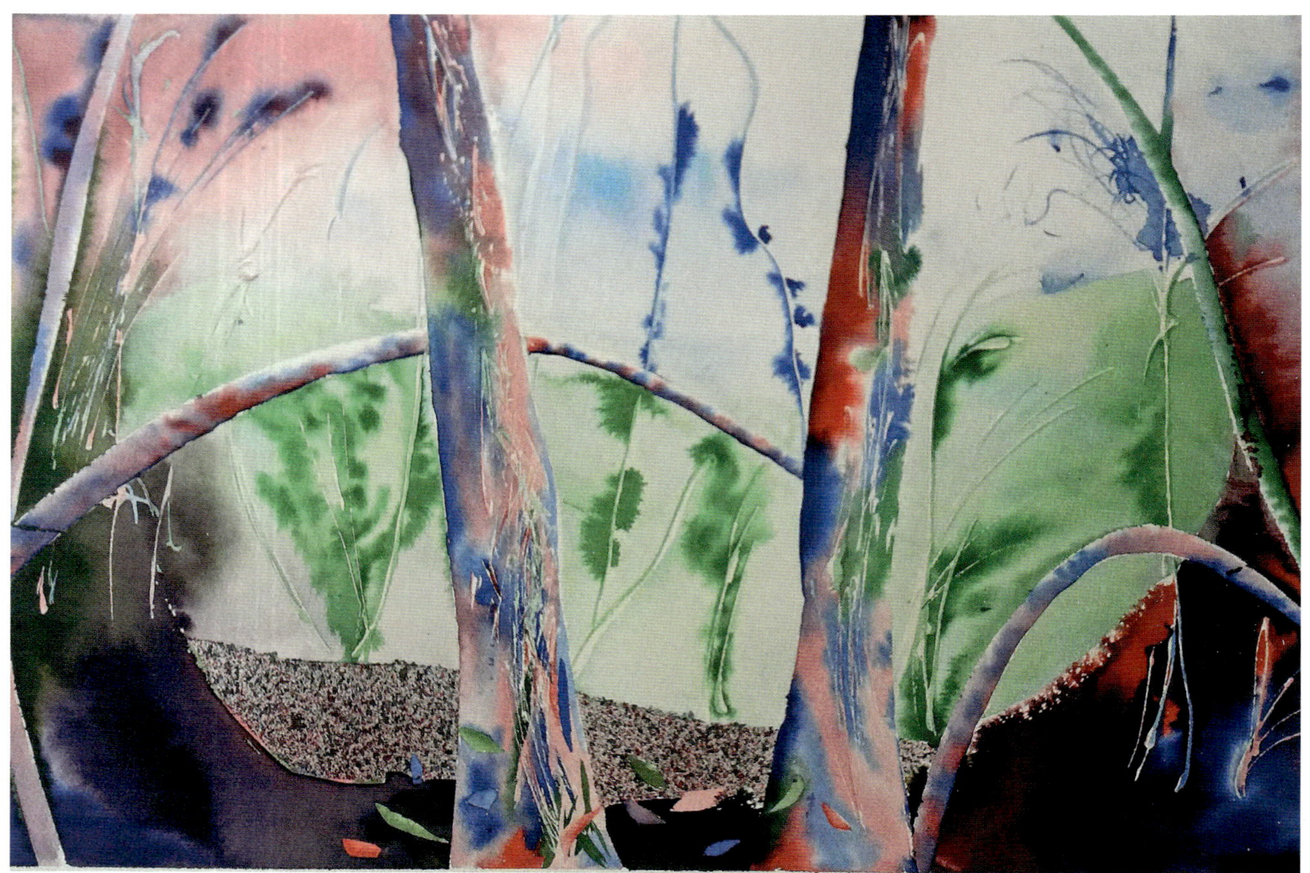

(fig 54)
ABI KREMER
Lady Park Wood 4, 2018
Watercolour on paper
40 x 56 cm
Artist's collection

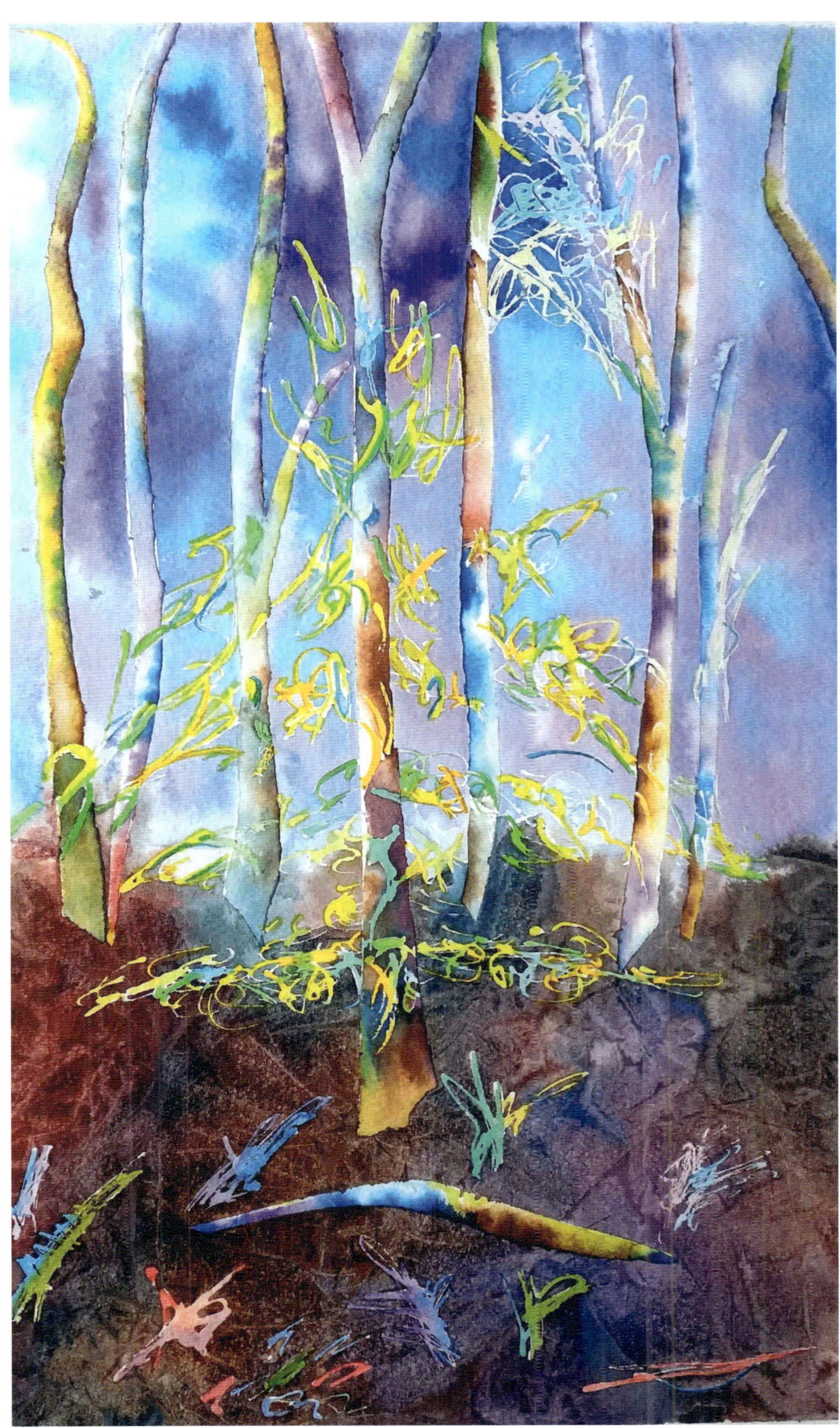

(fig 55)
ABI KREMER
Lady Park Wood 6, 2018
Watercolour on paper
48 x 32 cm
Artist's collection

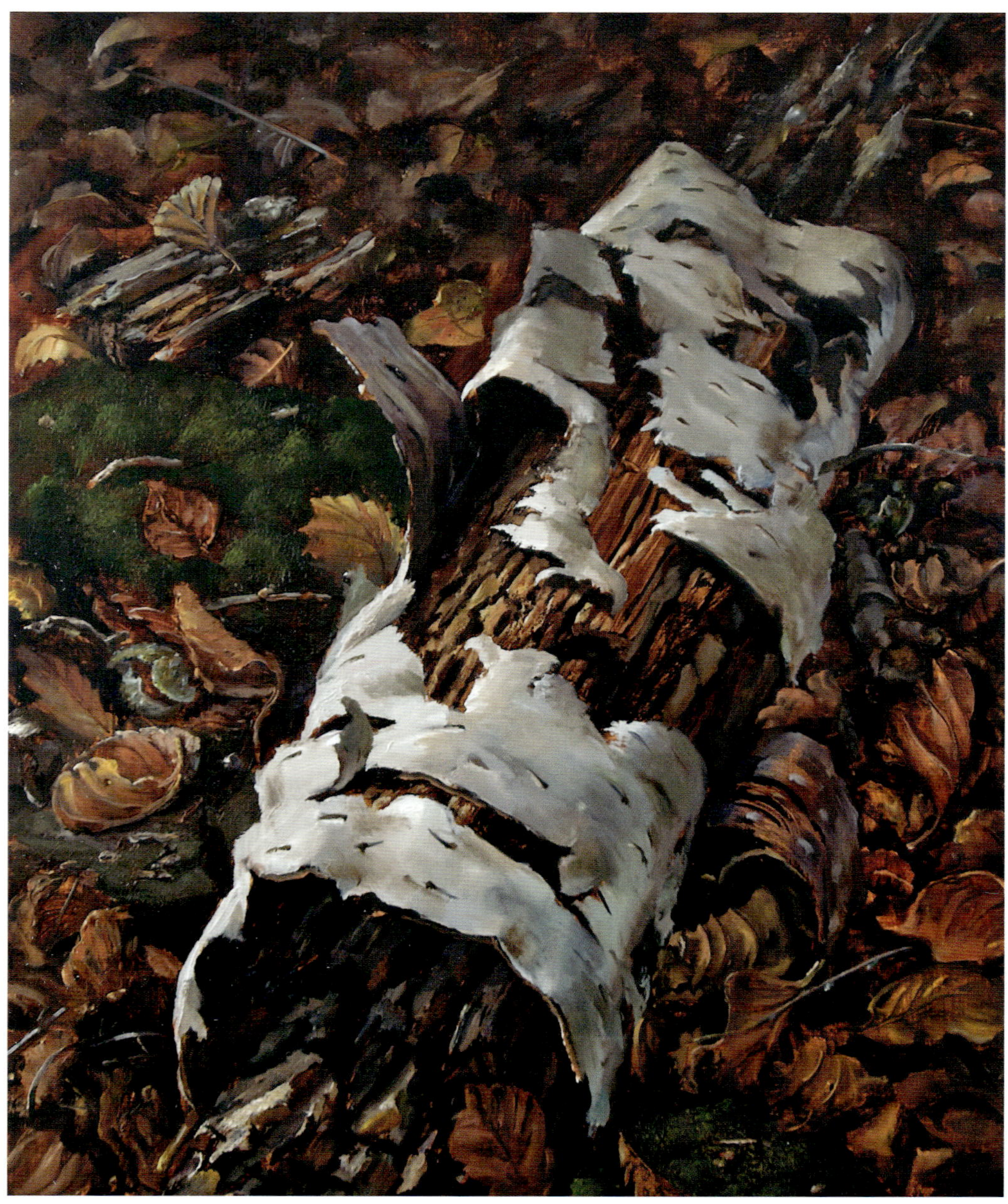

(fig 56)
JULIAN PERRY
Vestigial Birch, 2018
Oil on panel
30 x 25 cm
Private collection

LOOKING DOWN

ANN BLOCKLEY, STELLA CARR, JANE EATON,
FIONA McINTYRE, JULIAN PERRY

Woodland visitors tend to have restricted views. Tree people look up; flower people look down; bird people hear birds; deer people see droppings, browsed leaves and broken twigs. Most people look horizontally; hence the idea that, if you want to hide, you should climb a tree. In the present case, the artists were tree people, but in a few instances they looked down and saw features that are just as interesting as the trees themselves.

Two artists looked at fallen leaves in autumn when, as luck would have it, they were still dry, fresh and colourful. In *Fallen Leaves* (fig 58), Ann Blockley chose the bronzed leaves of beech, which produce a monochrome carpet under large beech trees, partly because beech tends to exclude other species from its vicinity. Jane Eaton chose a place where oak has been accommodating enough to take ash and a few beech for company. Part of her *Calligraphy Trees* (fig 60) work, showing autumn leaves on the ground, presents a shuffled image of what, for the previous seven months, has been the pattern above. Through summer, if we look up beneath an oak tree, we gaze through the mass of leaves of a single species, or possibly two if a beech sapling is struggling on beneath, and on that basis the woodland canopy is a mosaic of single-species patches. In autumn, the leaves twist and turn as they fall and later, if they have not been dampened by rain, will be scattered and shuffled by passing breezes. The result on the ground is a mixture, an integration of all the species in that part of the wood, though the tree overhead will still be better represented than others. In the fresh, dry leaf litter we see woodland trees as an integrated community.

As one walks round the wood, counts the fallen leaf assemblage and observes how it changes, one sees an expression of the variety of ancient woodland tree communities. Also, for a few weeks in autumn, the less-common trees can easily be found by looking at the ground, where wild service leaves glow orange, whitebeams form a carpet of white, crabs are recognised as small trees in a circle of tiny apples and the large-leaved lime can still be distinguished from the surrounding small-leaved limes for much of the winter.

Fallen leaves temporarily cover fallen twigs and small branches, though not in Eaton's image. Leaves fall at a single season, but twigs fall all the time (though more in winter than summer). So, at other seasons, as the leaves decay into humus, the light rain of twigs continues and the ground cover changes. In fact, the appearance of the soil surface of any wood is every bit as seasonal as the canopy itself.

The ground is also scattered with the remains of trees past. Some, such as birch, rot rapidly; others, notably oak, last for years. Long after a living ash has been lost from the recording charts, its dead remains can be found as a blackened stump and a line of

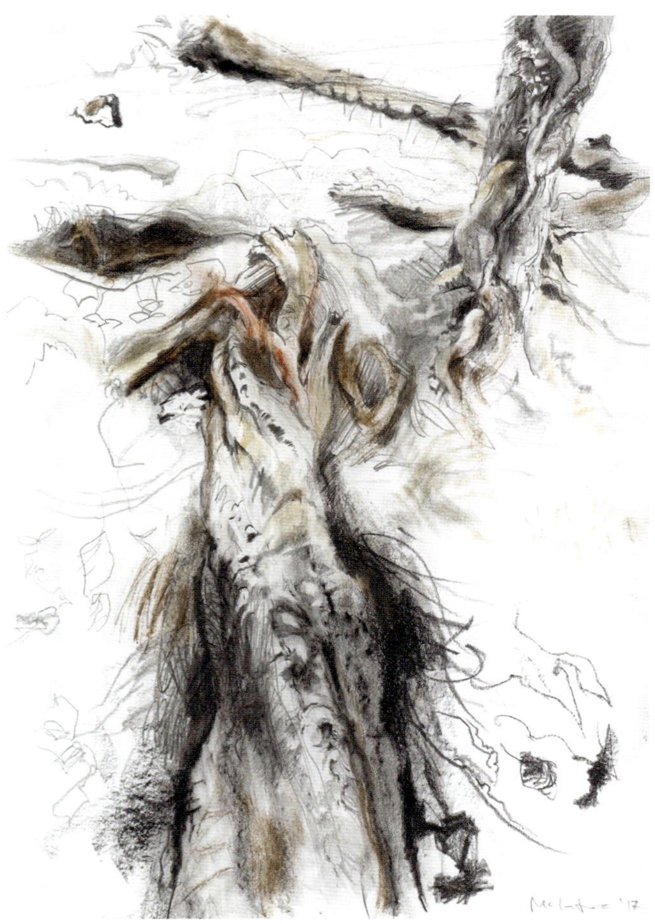

(fig 57)
FIONA McINTYRE
Carcass, 2017
Graphite and earth from the
forest floor on paper
72 x 62 cm
Artist's collection

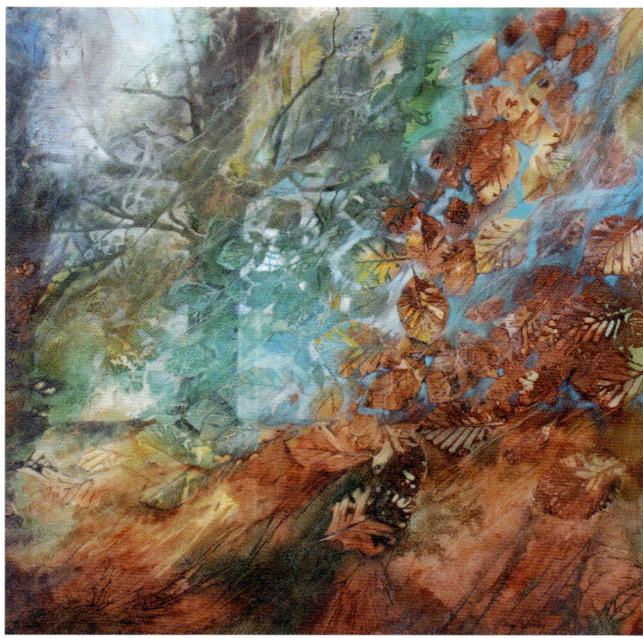

(fig 58)
ANN BLOCKLEY
Fallen Leaves, 2018
Water-based media on paper
73 x 69 cm
Artist's collection

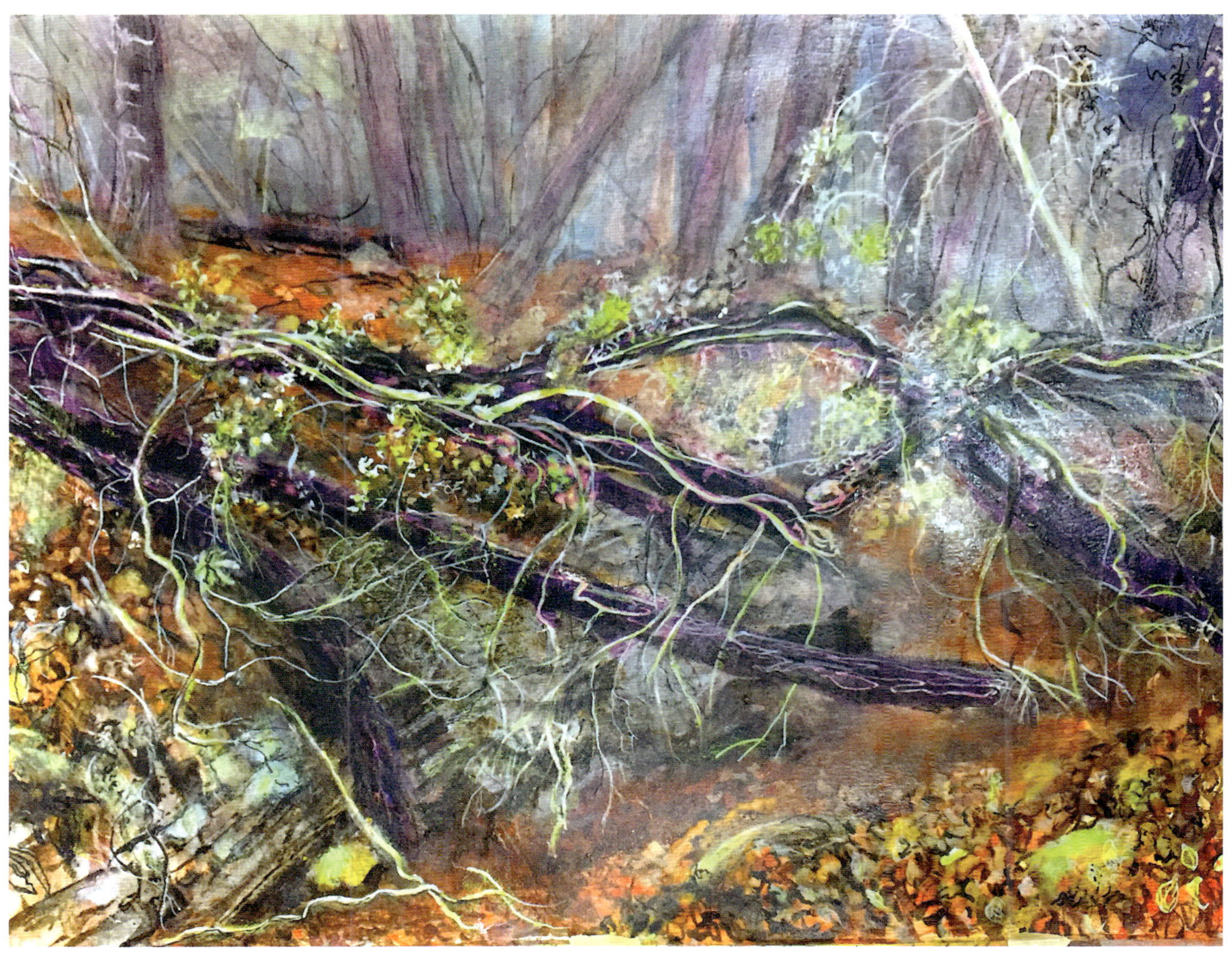

(fig 59)
STELLA CARR
Infinity, 2018
Ink and raw pigment on paper
32 x 45 cm
Private collection

fragmenting, black wood. The most remarkable dead-wood survival is a wartime stack of branch wood that was never carted away: cut and stacked in 1942, two parallel oak logs were still visible in the autumn of 2019. Fiona McIntyre's *Carcass* (fig 57) displays some very average 'coarse woody debris', as some ecologists call it, both seemingly trees that died standing, only to fall when their roots had decayed and almost vanished.

Julian Perry's closely observed study of a well-rotted birch log – *Vestigial Birch* (fig 56) – captures and symbolises a transient phase in the long history of Lady Park. Such logs are a signature feature of the wood as we see it today, but they would have been rare before the 1980s and may just possibly be more abundant now than they have been since woodland returned after the last retreat of the ice sheets.

How can I explain this? When part of Lady Park was felled in 1942, the vacated ground was quickly occupied by a thicket of mainly birch, ash and sallow saplings in a matrix of hip-high brambles. Birch and sallow grew much faster than other species, but birch was so much more abundant that it comes as no surprise to read descriptions from the 1950s saying simply that Lady Park was a birch wood. And so it remained until 1976, when much of Europe endured – or enjoyed – the most severe drought of recent times, and this killed the birch in droves. The 30–35-year-old trees stood as leafless snags for a few years, but the roots quickly rotted, the remaining trunks fell and the ground through the 1980s was littered with rolls of birch bark and fragmenting logs. Thereafter, surviving birch enjoyed a respite, for they had much more room to grow, but by the Millennium, neighbouring trees had grown taller and stronger, and the birch were approaching their allotted span. Birch logs again became a conspicuous feature. Today, the post-1942 birch generation is nearing its end, with only a few clusters of birch saplings in gaps to renew their presence. For the time being, the bark endures as rolls of parchment preserving the memory of a World War II generation that has almost passed – natural woodland operating on a human timescale.

Lady Park was cut down regularly throughout the seventeenth, eighteenth and nineteenth centuries, so surely birch saplings sprang up in droves after each felling, just like they did after 1942? The only direct evidence we have comes from a forester's description recorded in 1897, 27 years after the last coppicing in 1870. Then, Lady Park comprised coppice of beech, ash, lime and hazel with some oak around 10 metres high, and an admixture of field maple, service tree, aspen, birch, sallow and wych elm – in that order. Birch not only had to compete with new coppice growth, but may well have been cut out by the woodmen to make bundles of birch brushwood – faggots – to burn in bread ovens and fill ruts in roads. Birch hardly ever got a chance to grow old and, when it did, the logs were too useful to leave them rotting in the woods.

In *Infinity* (fig 59), Stella Carr has noticed one of the limestone rocks that litter the surface of Lady Park. The main feature, however, is a small tree recently overwhelmed by an ivy. Dishevelled though it is, the ivy retains its sinister, sinuous, seemingly anastomosing form. Raindrops flowing down a window produce a similar pattern, but here the ivy is 'flowing' upwards towards the light. It will not last long in this form: deer will browse the leaves and eventually the ivy will wither.

HAIKU

Calligraphy trees
Dancing light, a tender breeze
Nothing gold can stay

Jane Eaton

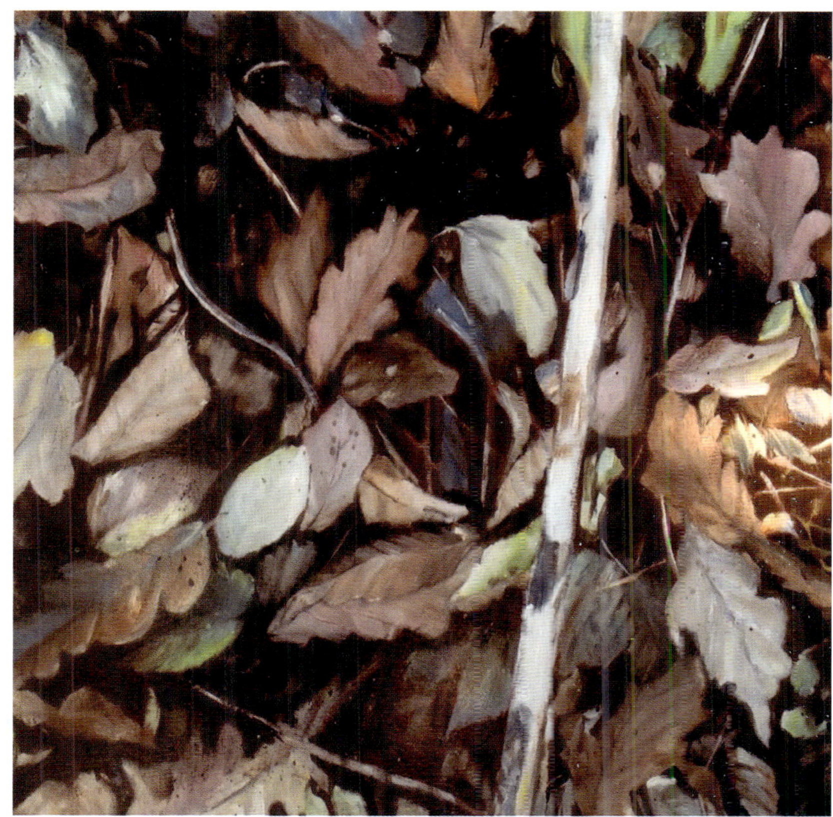

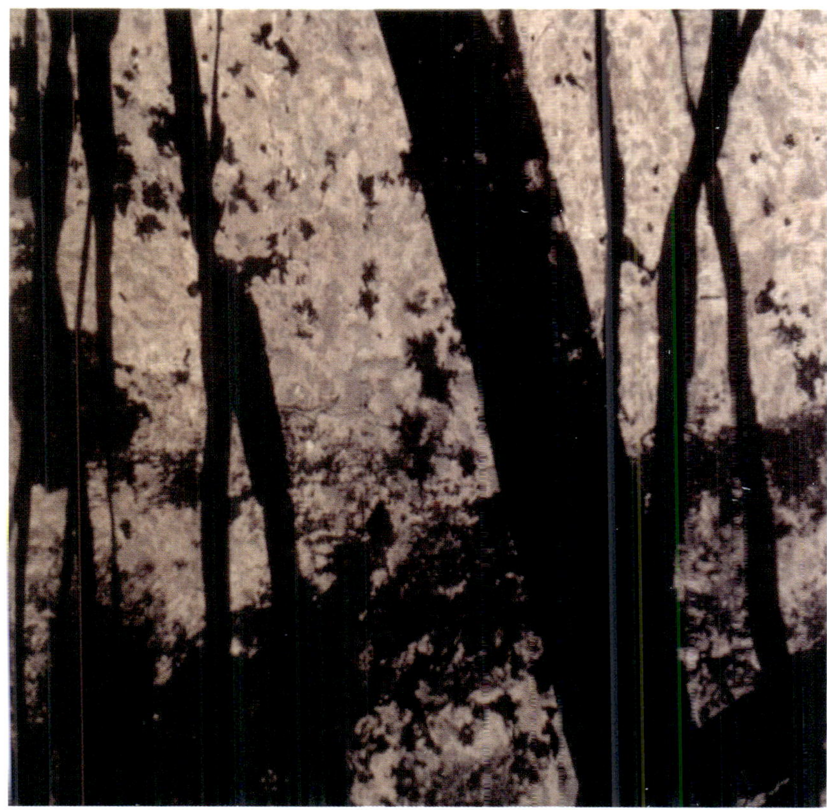

(fig 60)
JANE EATON
Calligraphy Trees Diptych, 2018
Oil on panel
30 x 30 cm
Artist's collection

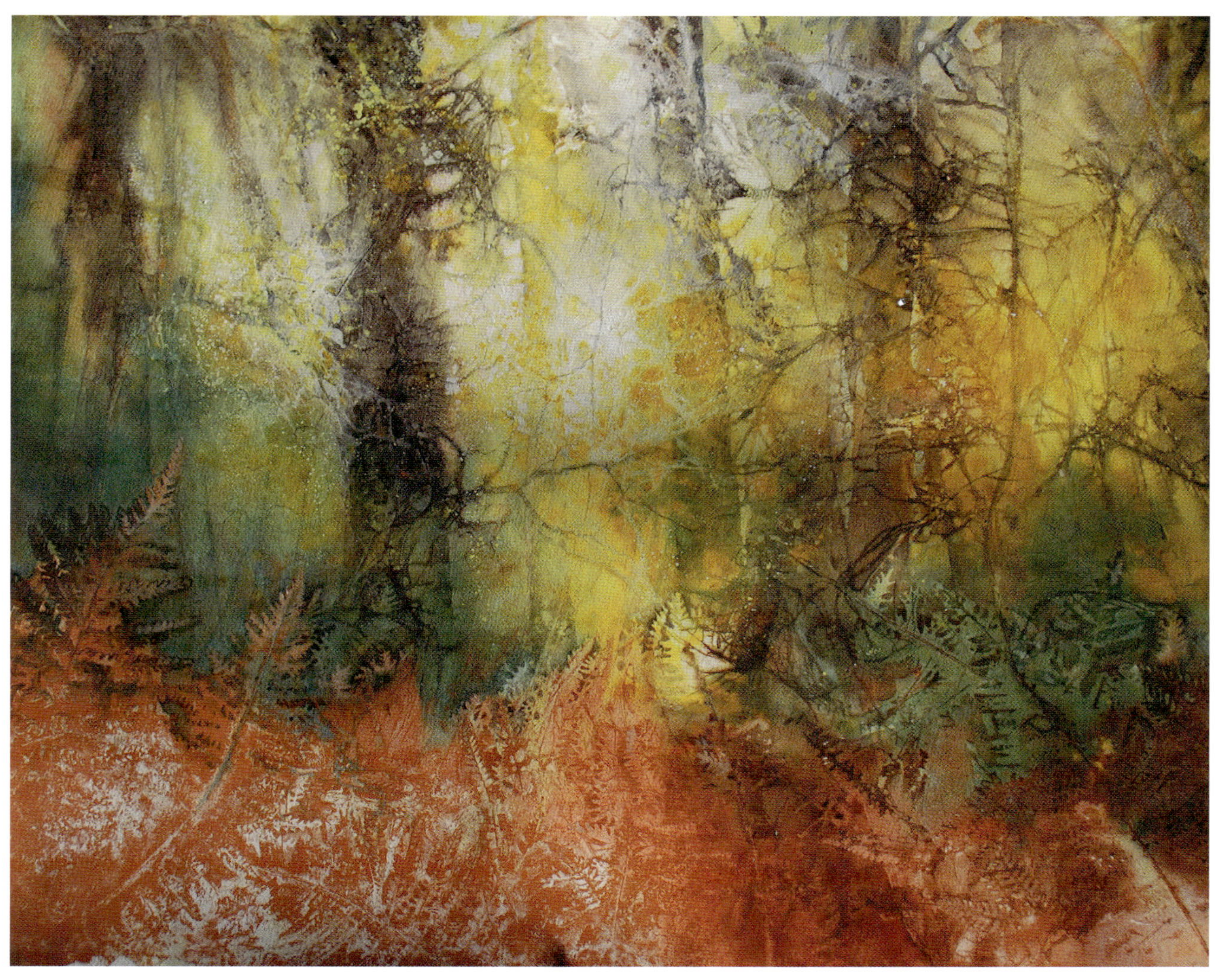

(fig 61)
ANN BLOCKLEY
Woodland Light, 2018
Water-based media on paper
80 x 96 cm
Private collection

LIGHT IN NATURAL WOODLAND

ROBERT AMESBURY BROOKS,
ANN BLOCKLEY, JANE EATON

All the paintings and drawings are about light, an important element in woodland. From the human level of perception, woods differ from other habitats in being dark (though from the perspective of a ground beetle a meadow must also look dark), but the degree of shade varies in time and space. Light intensity on the woodland floor reaches a seasonal peak just before bud-break in April, which explains why bluebells and anemones produce their spectacular displays then. At any season, light intensity decreases from the canopy downwards and in any day it peaks at noon. In closed woodland it varies laterally, being least under beech, holly and yew, and most under birch. In managed woodland, it reaches a maximum in the centre of rides and in recently felled compartments. In natural woodland, it reaches a maximum on the north side of large canopy gaps. However, we should not forget the accumulating effects of several layers: the darkest place may be under a vigorous bramble bush growing below an ash tree.

Jane Eaton's stark and simple image – from *Calligraphy Trees* (fig 60) – means dusk in a natural woodland to me. There is a moment as the light fades when the trunks are black, but the sky, though dull, seems bright by contrast. It is the time when the last of the human visitors go home and the first of the night foragers stir.

We also see a strong hint that this is not just any wood but actually Lady Park, specifically the trees on the edge of the cliff leaning out over the Wye gorge, with the woodland on the opposite face still illuminated by the last of the light. In *Woodland Light* (fig 61), Ann Blockley shows dense, fundamentally dark woodland which is lit up at intervals by the setting sun. A little higher in the sky and with the wood wreathed in mist, this sun would produce the cone of searchlight rays that would stop anyone in their tracks. The old beech of Robert Amesbury Brooks' *Trees and Rocks* (fig 62) shows the brightest location of this collection – reasonably enough, for it grows on a slope that steepens to the right until it appears to reach the cliff. The steepening slopes above the cliff are unsafe places for a human visitor, though they were the favoured route for deer passing through the wood in the 1940s. Here, poor growth, irregular ground and frequent tree falls conspire to create a zone of well-lit ground where bilberry, cow-wheat and even heather can grow. This is just one example of a general point: that the wood is full of niches, any one of which may be exactly what a particular species may need to survive in a natural wood.

The ancient beech coppice stool in Robert's second image, *The Claw on the Rock* (fig 63) clings to a similar, well-lit position, but it tells a different story. It was cut many times by woodmen who thought nothing of working at the top of a vertiginous slope. Today, in the fast-moving world of machines and health and safety, trees on such ground cannot be harvested.

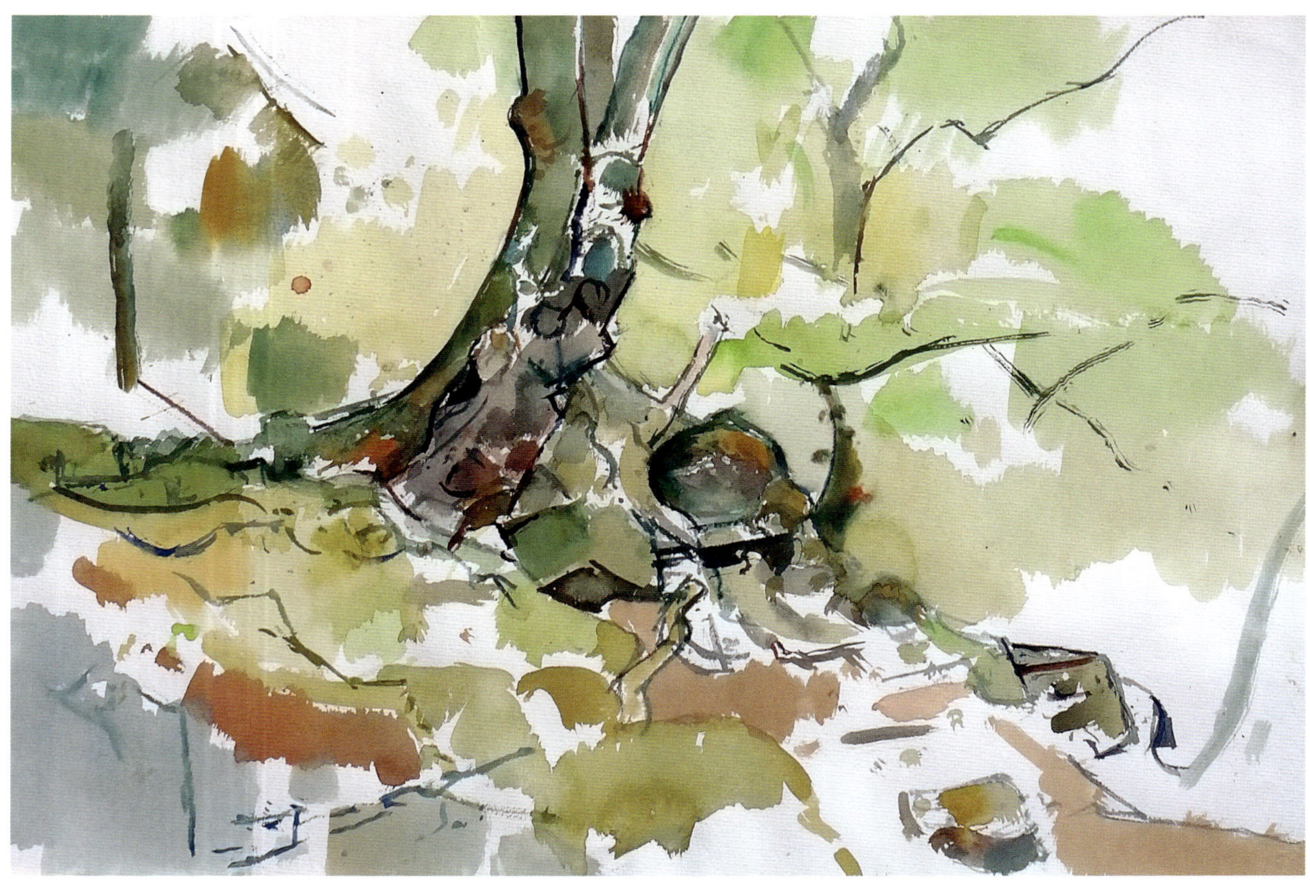

(fig 62)
ROBERT AMESBURY BROOKS
Trees and Rocks, 2018
Watercolour on paper
38 x 56 cm
Private collection

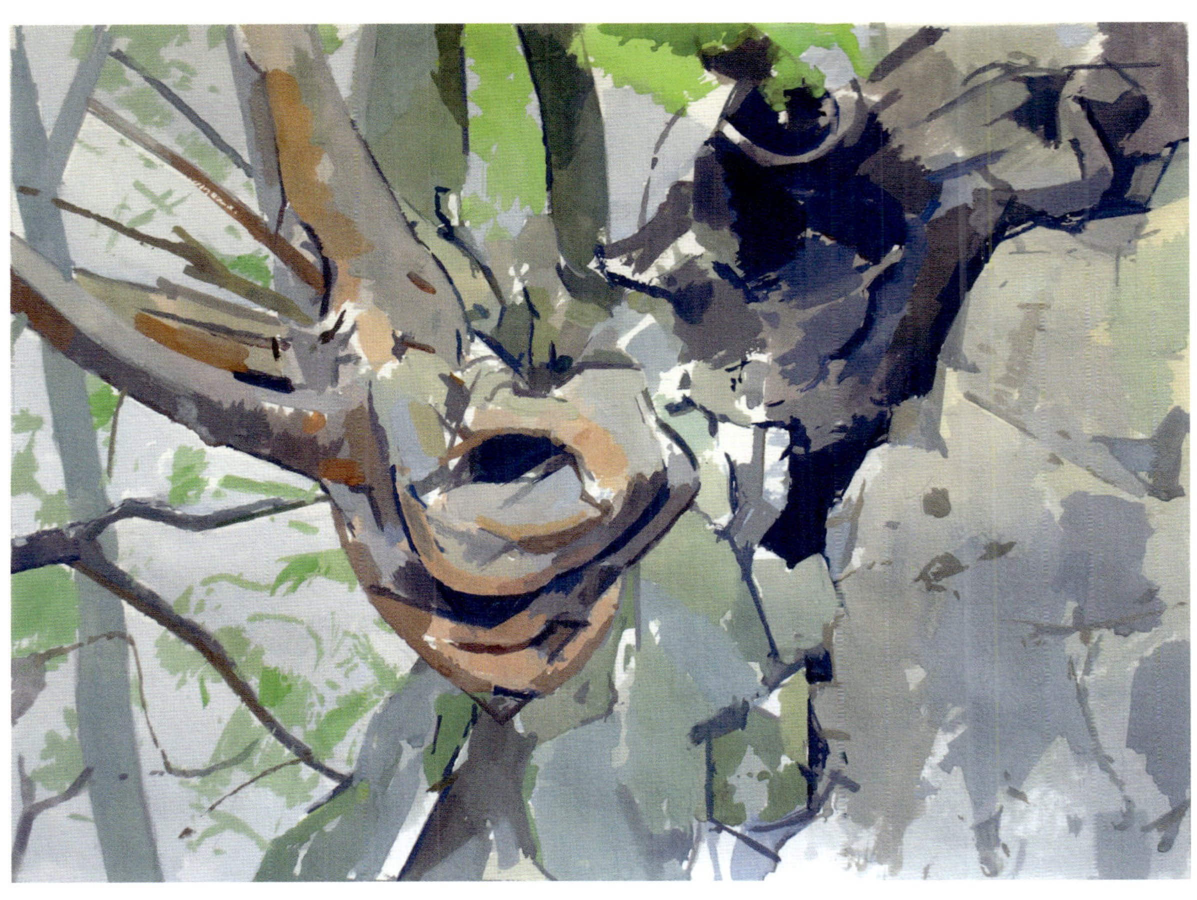

(fig 63)
ROBERT AMESBURY BROOKS
The Claw on the Rock, 2020
Watercolour on paper
54 x 41 cm
Private collection

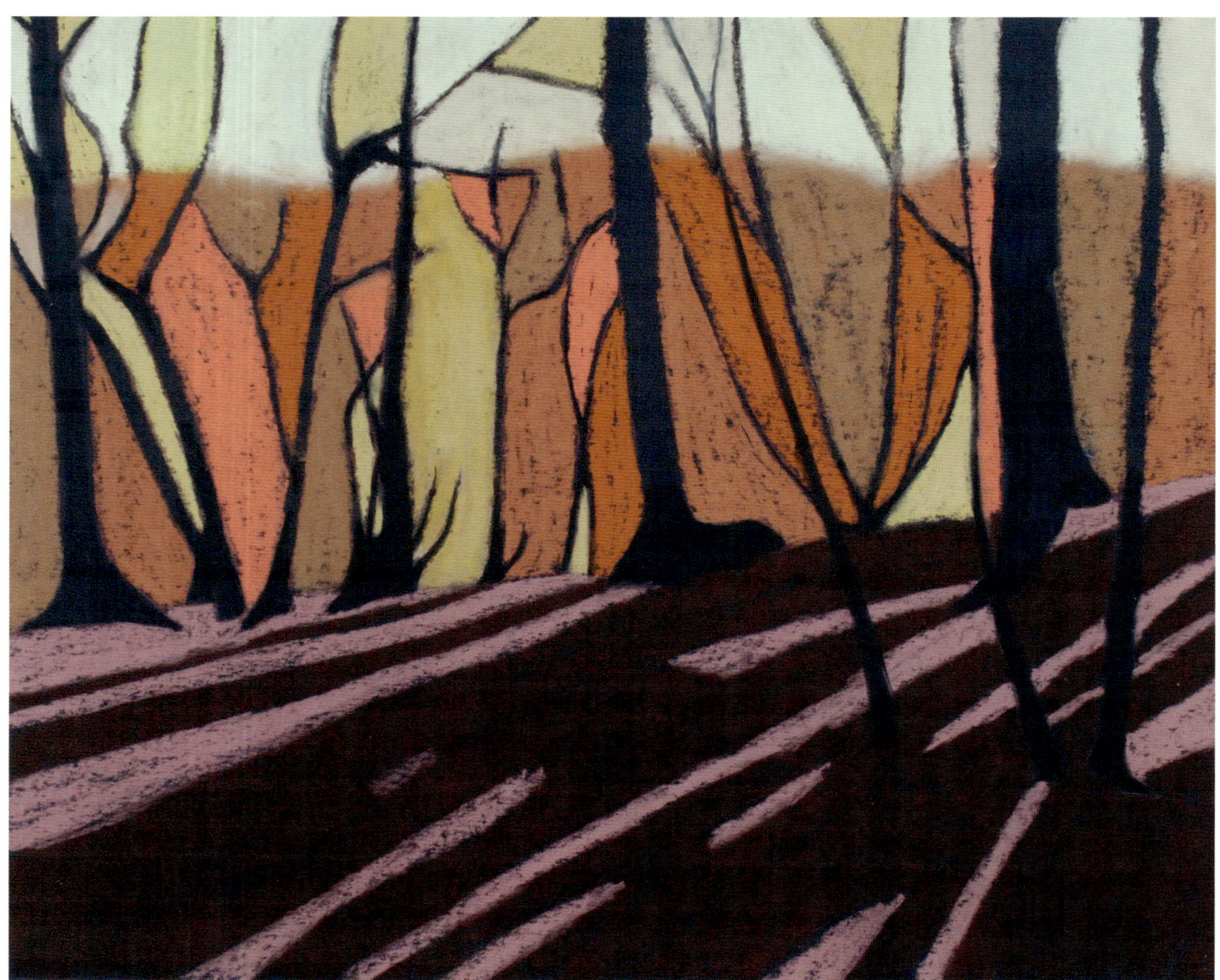

(fig 64)
SUSAN PETERKEN
The Light Beyond, 2018
Pastel on paper
37.5 x 47 cm
Artist's collection

EDGES

FIONA McINTYRE, SUSAN PETERKEN

Edges are important woodland habitats. Not least because many species cling to these borderlands and would be lost if they did not have this half-lit world to survive in and retreat to. Lady Park has both natural edges in the form of cliffs that exceed the height of trees growing below and artificial borders onto a cycle track by the river and a forest road along the top. Outside Lady Park, there is managed woodland on three sides. Indeed, the plantations forming the top edge were mostly felled a few years ago.

These artificial edges are one reason why, despite our best efforts, the reserve can never be totally free of human influence, for what happens outside inevitably influences what happens within. The original natural woodland only had natural edges, of course, but ecologists are not sure how many and what form these took. If primaeval forest was wall-to-wall trees, only rivers, large cliffs and swamps would have been open. If it was full of temporary glades, kept open by deer and primitive cattle, edges would have been common and all-pervasive. This is what forest ecologists debate – hotly – when they get together. Images by Fiona McIntyre and Susan Peterken give us some sense of Lady Park's edges. Susan's *The Light Beyond* (fig 64) is the only painting in this collection to show shadows clearly, an important woodland feature. Here they are elongated from late afternoon sunshine, shining in from beyond the cliff, and sharply defined because the shadows are formed by tree trunks. Sun flecks that pass through small holes in the canopy foliage are much more diffuse. They constantly move and change shape, ruining many photographs by camouflaging tree shapes. Tree seedlings live in a world of feast and famine – in shade they remain cool and receive perhaps 5 per cent daylight, but, brightly illuminated and hot in a sun fleck, they may be scorched. They must be physiologically prepared to leap into photosynthetic action when the sun fleck passes.

Fiona McIntyre's *Ash Carcass and Yew* (fig 65) shows a tight group of trees close to the upper, artificial edge. It is an overcast day, but light intensity in the wood is still higher than it is in the woodland interior. This is the edge effect which in isolated woods on farmland extends perhaps 50 metres into the wood, thereby generating a marginal zone of high tree and shrub density, and a special niche for shrubs that cannot stand deep shade. If a small wood is no more than 100 metres across, wild species experience all of it as edge.

Fiona's *Yew on an Ironstone Heap and Fallen Ash* (fig 66) was located near the cliff: we can see the other side of the Wye gorge in the background. The wood and hereabouts is almost park-like in its lack of low growth, but that is because the beech – the great shade-caster – dominates the canopy. The most prominent feature, though, is the mound, which brings to mind the mounts created as vantage points in landscaped parks. Here, however, the heap is spoil left behind by nineteenth-century miners prospecting for ironstone, an ineradicable reminder that not everything that happened in woods was to do with trees.

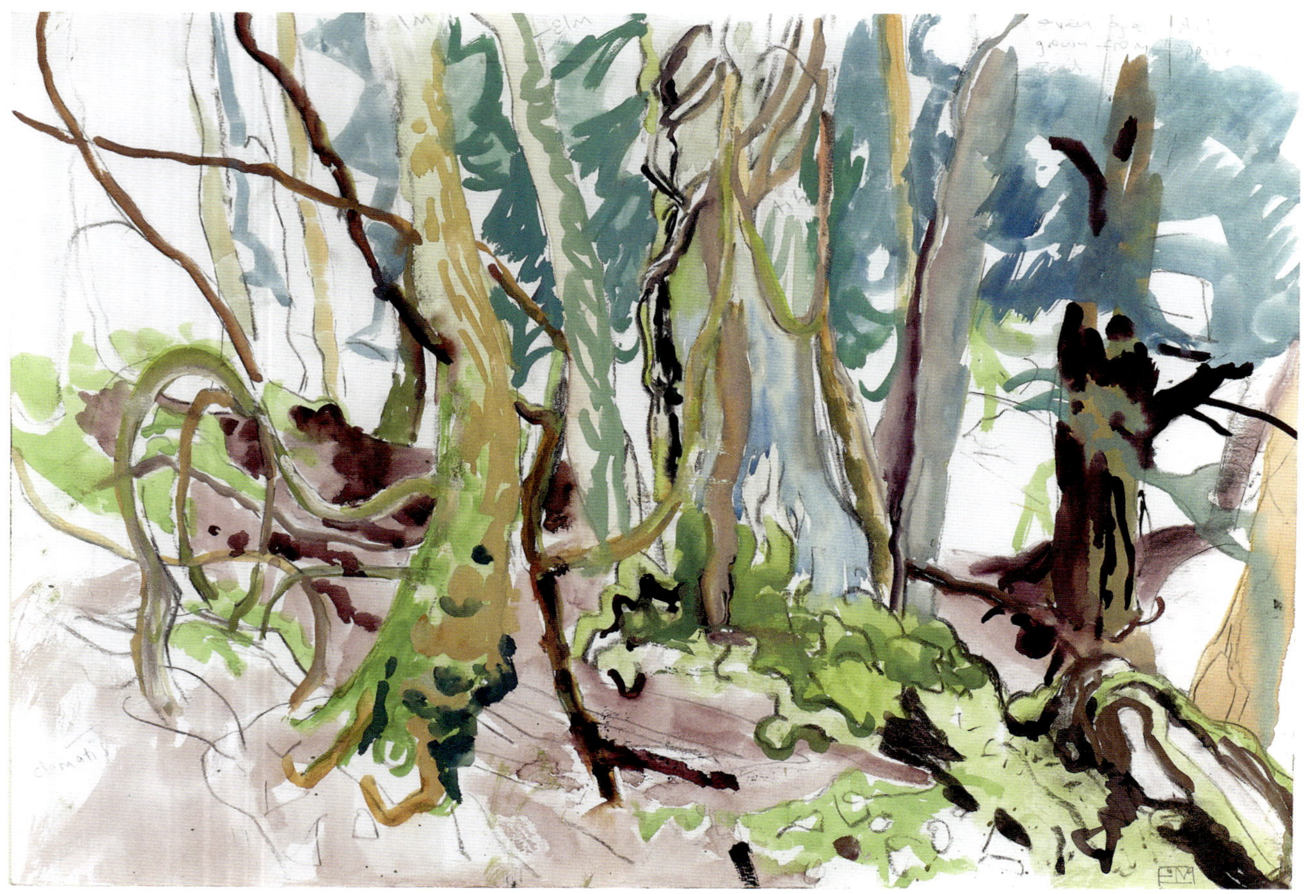

(fig 65)
FIONA McINTYRE
Ash Carcass and Yew, 2018
Gouache on paper
29.7 x 42 cm
Artist's collection

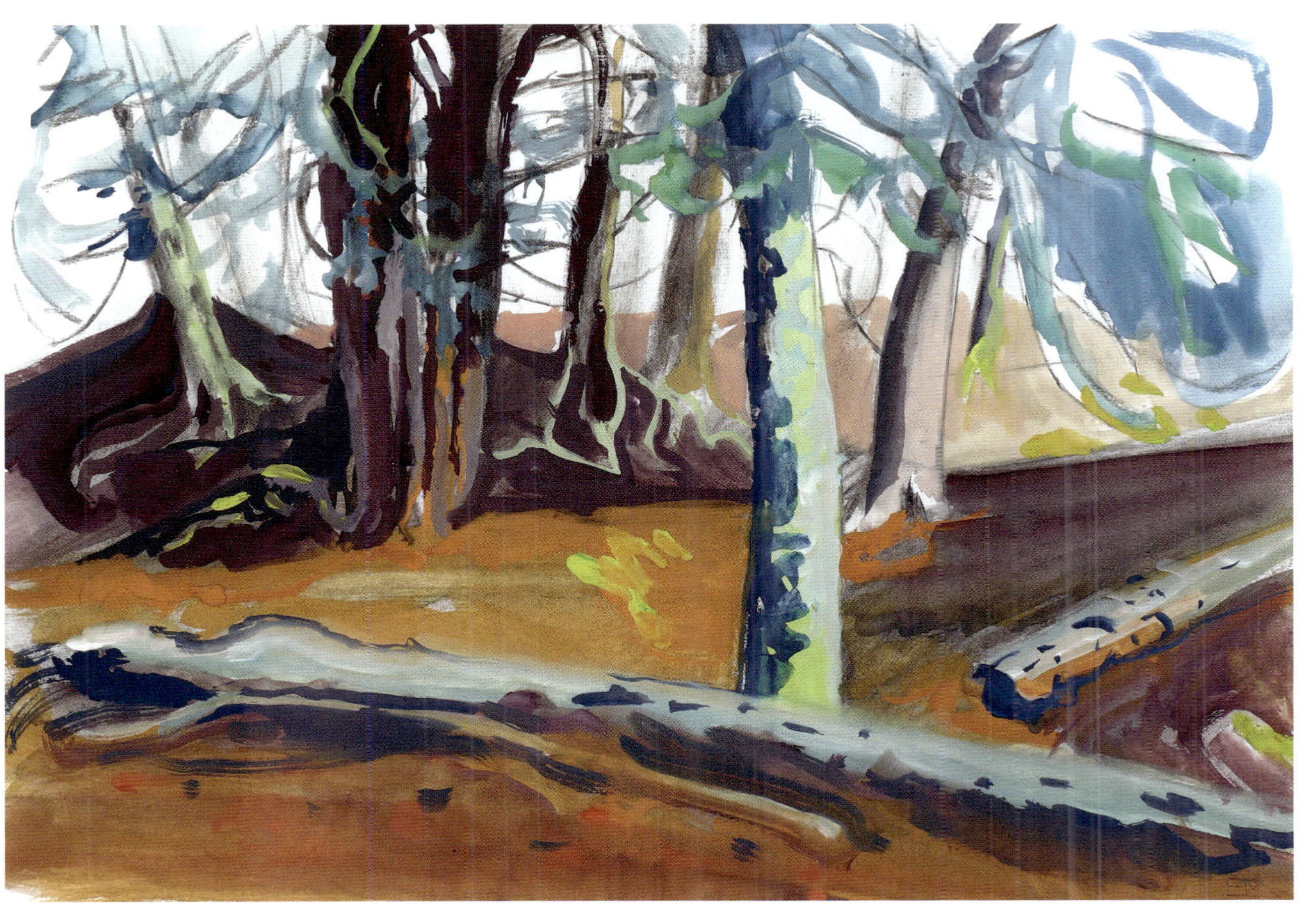

(fig 66)
FIONA McINTYRE
Yew on an Ironstone Heap and Fallen Ash, 2018
Gouache on paper
29.7 x 42 cm
Artist's collection

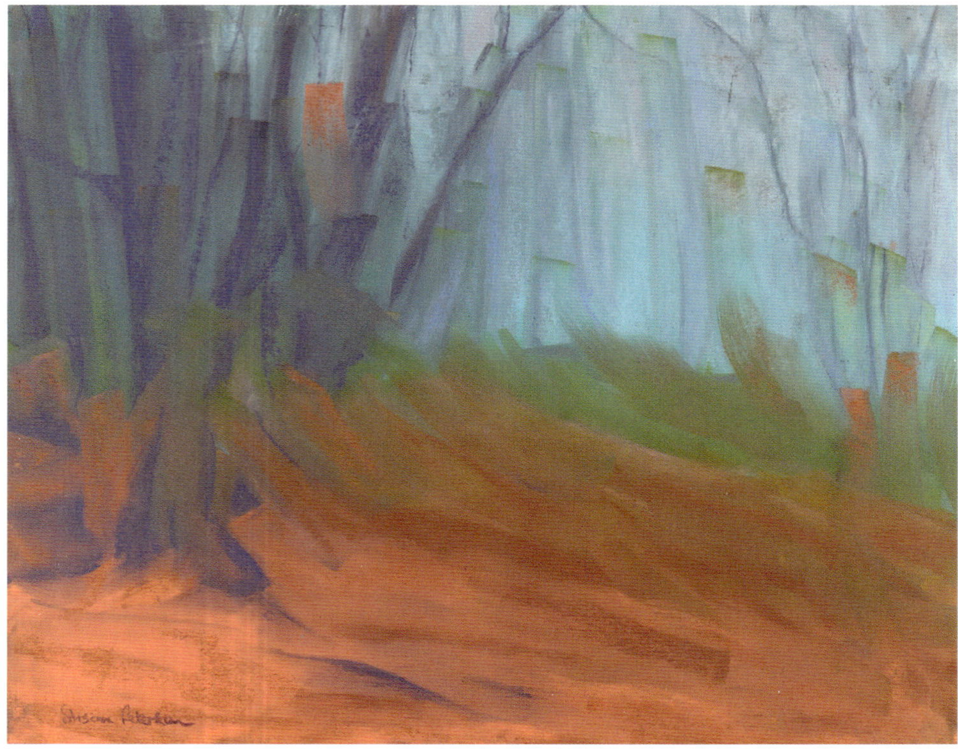

(fig 67)
SUSAN PETERKEN
The Mist Within, 2018
Pastel on paper
37.5 x 47 cm
Artist's collection

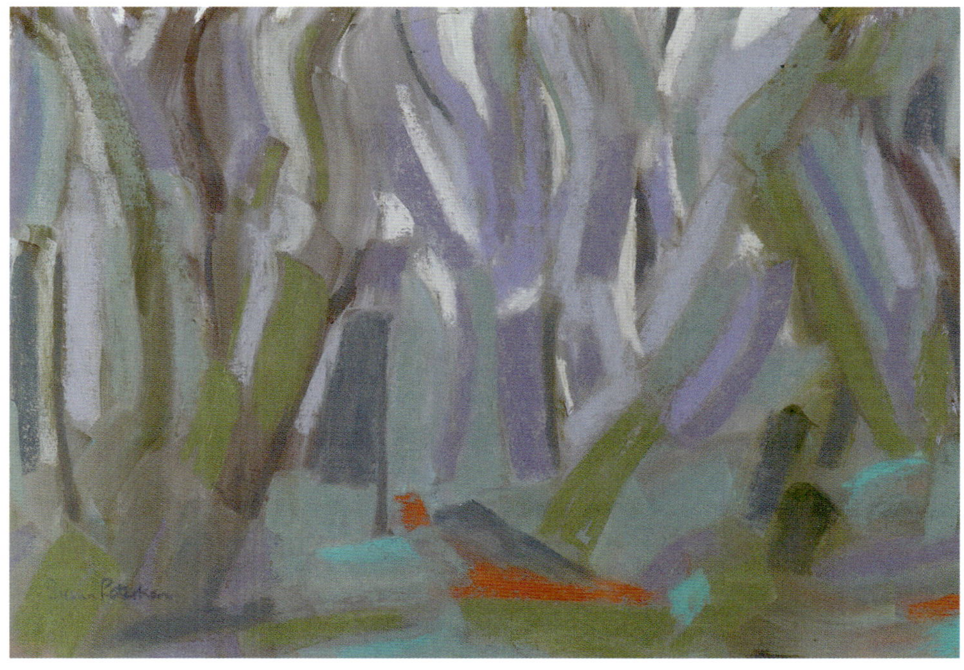

(fig 68)
SUSAN PETERKEN
Blue Uprising, 2018
Pastel on paper
28.5 x 41 cm
Artist's collection

NATURAL WOODLAND AT DUSK

SUSAN PETERKEN

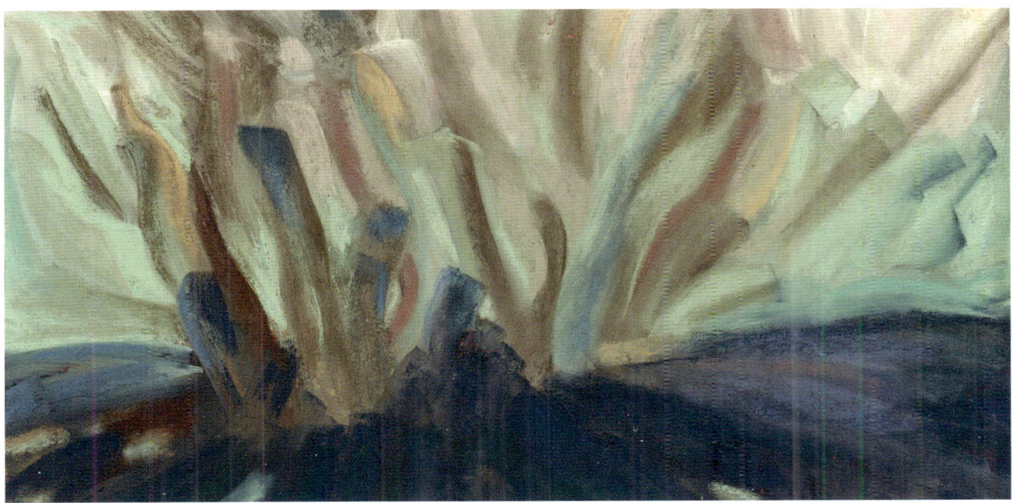

(fig 69)
SUSAN PETERKEN
Green Uprising, 2018
Pastel on paper
23 x 45 cm
Artist's collection

Illustrations in books about trees and woodland are restricted to what a photographer would call 'good' lighting conditions. They would be rejected by publishers if they were not clear, well lit and in focus. This misrepresents the year-round experience of being in woodland, which also includes rainy days, deep winter overcasts, dusk, dawn and night. On these occasions, individual trees lose their definition and almost merge with each other. The wood nearly goes out-of-focus. Most ecological researchers inevitably take this textbook, photographic route. They try to stay in focus, sharply observe particular features, photograph them with 'autofocus' turned on and generally remain oblivious of the atmospherics.

Susan Peterken's *The Mist Within* (fig 67), *Blue Uprising* (fig 68) and *Green Uprising* (fig 69) could be said to demonstrate the alternative experiences of being in woodland. Unlike most other paintings and drawings in this book, these are out of focus, much as one experiences a wood as the light fades at dusk. One can still see the growth forms and for a moment their exploding upward growth may be emphasised, but as night advances the interplay of shapes and shadows can become so confusing that one may blunder into small trees and stumble over woody litter. The artist can bring such experiences to our attention, but the ecologist must keep them private as a tired, end-of-the day feeling.

Even so, although as an ecologist I am always tempted to wait until the light is bright before taking photographs, I find that the shots that best convey the feel of Lady Park are those taken on dull November mornings, when mist and low cloud drift amongst the trees.

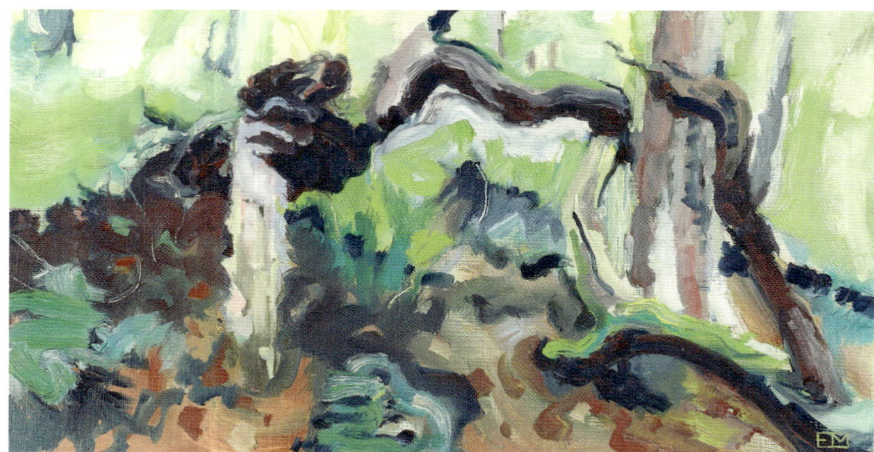

(fig 70)
FIONA McINTYRE
Gateway, 2018
Oil on board
62 x 72 cm
Artist's collection

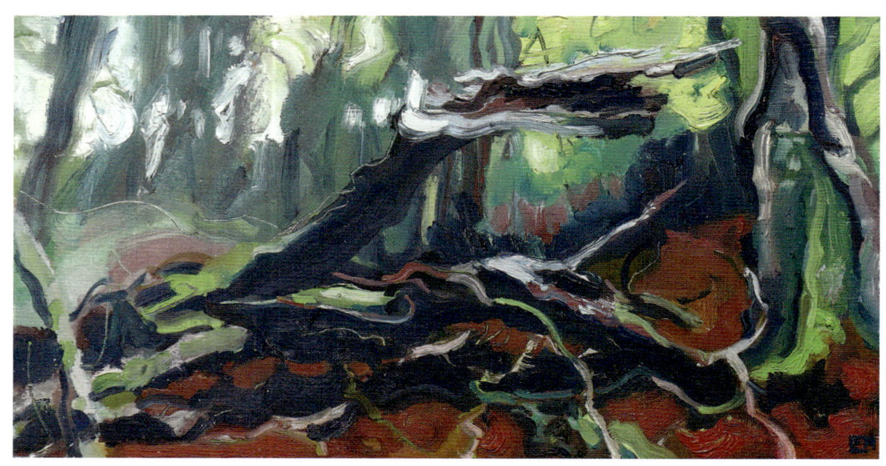

(fig 71)
FIONA McINTYRE
Fallen Split Tree, 2018
Oil on board
62 x 72 cm
Artist's collection

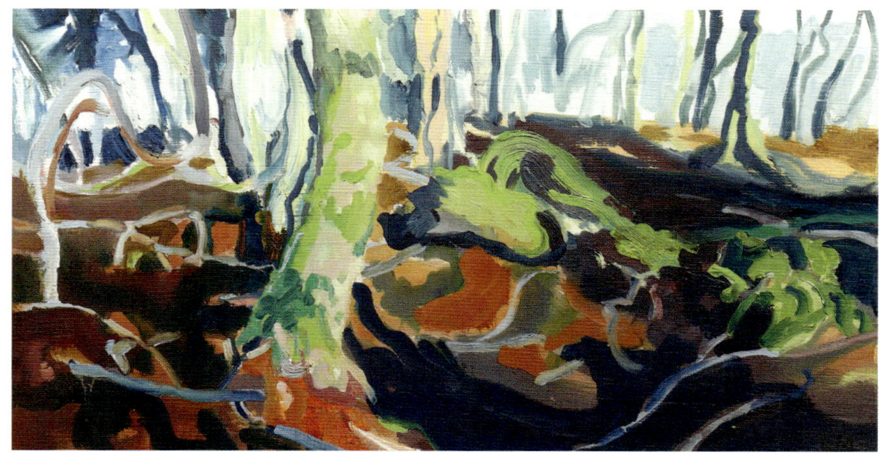

(fig 72)
FIONA McINTYRE
Ash Carcass, 2018
Oil on board
62 x 72 cm
Artist's collection

DISORIENTATION AND CHAOS IN NATURAL WOODLAND

FIONA McINTYRE

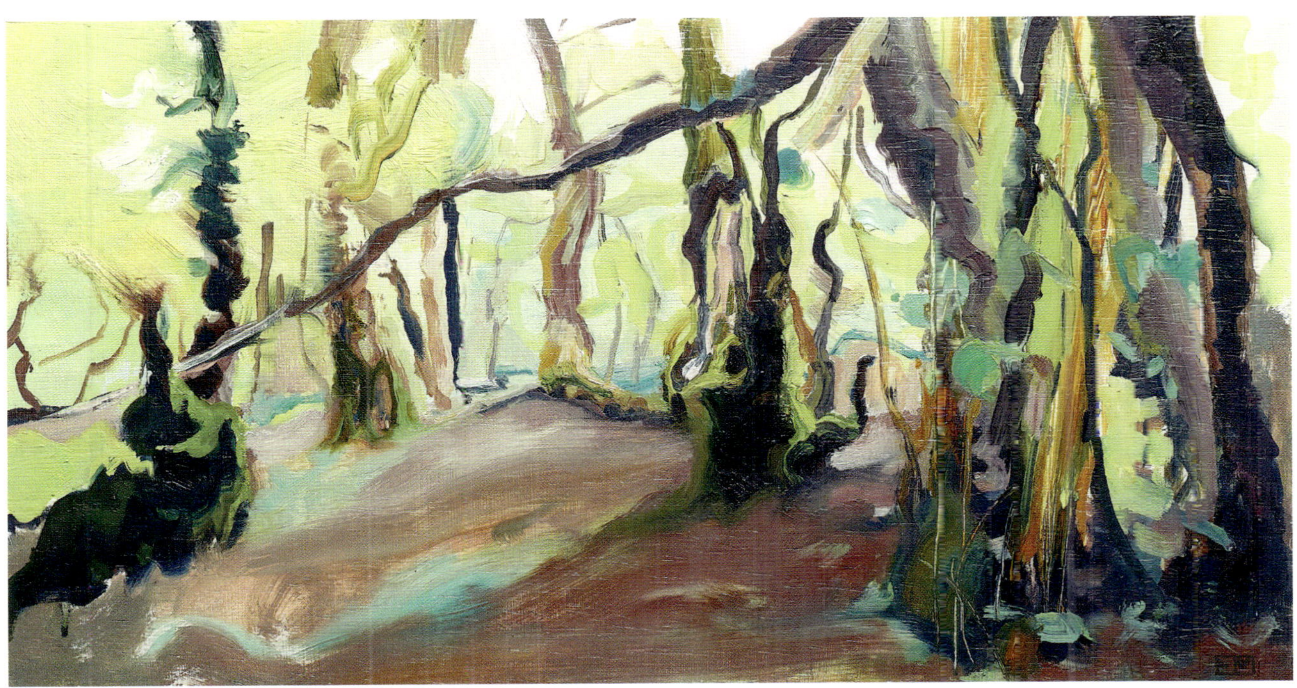

(fig 73)
FIONA McINTYRE
Wild Woodland, 2018
Oil on board
62 x 72 cm
Artist's collection

Fiona McIntyre's stylistically similar paintings *Gateway* (fig 70), *Fallen Split Tree* (fig 71), *Ash Carcass* (fig 72) and *Wild Woodland* (fig 73) have been named to indicate that they portray distinct subjects. The common thread is the impression they convey of extremely irregular ground, which in Lady Park indicates the places where the ironstone prospectors left hollows and spoil heaps.

Elsewhere in the district, where these excavations are deeper and more extensive, they are known as scowles. One such scowle has been developed as a visitor attraction known as 'Puzzle Wood', which is about right, for that and Fiona McIntyre's images induce a feeling of confusion and disorder. Being impossible to use for anything else, these scowles have remained covered in woodland which in the past has been coppiced. Now that the woodmen have passed into history, the woodland is left to grow naturally, dead logs and leaning timber are commonplace, the deep workings are dark ravines, and the ambience is chaos and disorientation.

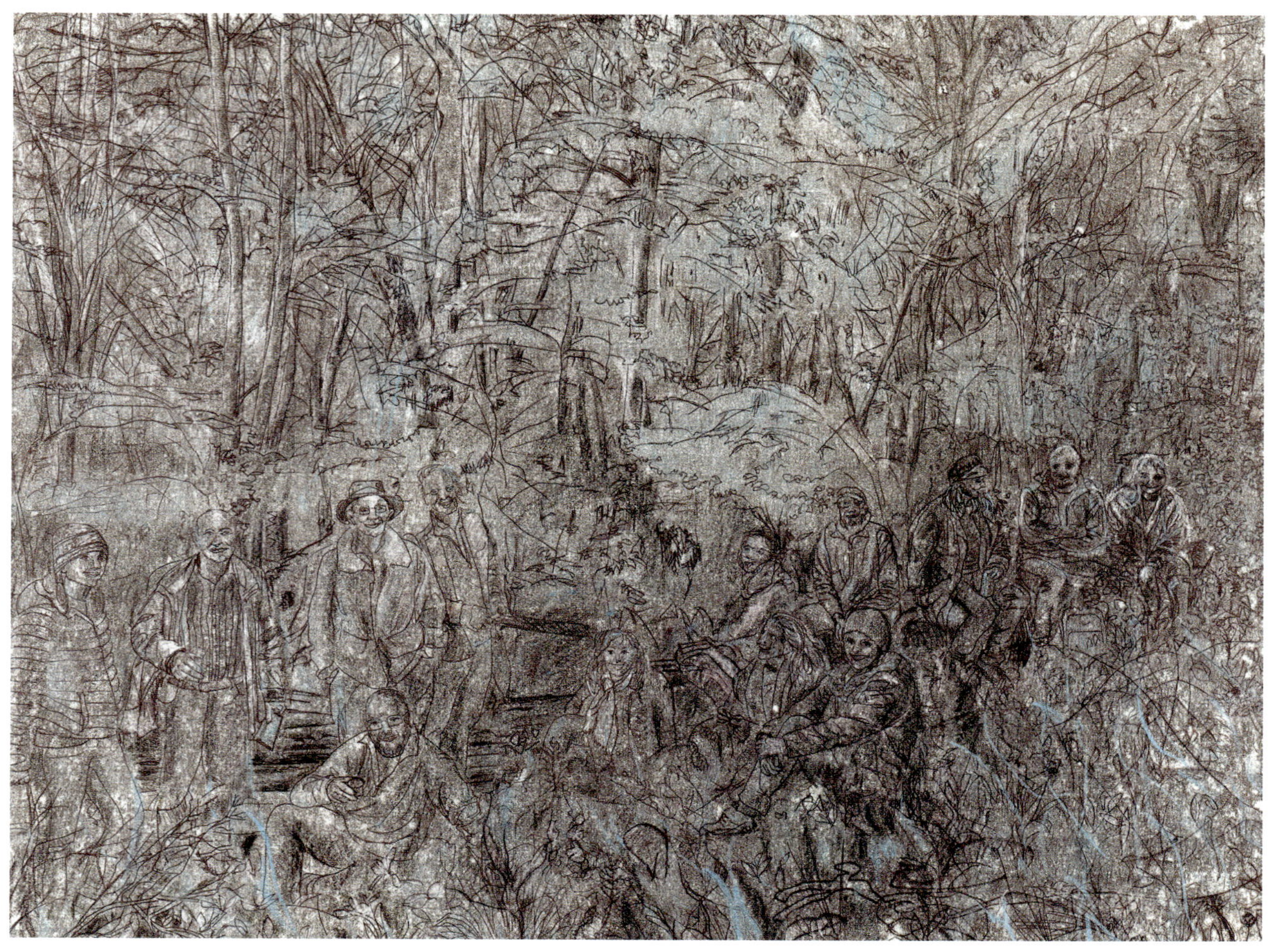

(fig 74)
STELLA CARR
Arborealists in Lady Park Wood, 2019
Monoprint on Washi paper
61 x 76 cm
Private collection

LOST IN THE WOODS

STELLA CARR

In *Arborealists in Lady Park Wood* (fig 74), Stella Carr records a moment at the end of an afternoon in the present project when the artists gathered on a fallen tree l ke migrating swallows on a te ephone line, ate cake, drank tea and chatted. The gathering was just inside the gate at the top of the wood, and in the background is a part of Lady Park that has remained largely untouched since 1870. The accommodating branch fell from a wide-spreading beech that must have originated in the eighteenth century and which, I suspect, had been left standing by the woodmen before 1870 because it grew on the skyline as seen from the river – a nice, if tenuous, link between the Arborealists and the Picturesque tourists who drifted down the Wye in boatloads during the eighteenth and nineteenth centuries.

The branch fe l partly because the tree had been greatly damaged by the prolonged drought of 1976. Until then a healthy, vigorous tree, it was almost killed, but recovered to form a new crown; but it was also left with great scars, fungi entered its core, and ever since it has been slowly falling apart. Just over a year after the Arboreal sts were sitting on the log, another skyline beech (which can be seen faintly in the right background as the large, healthy tree it then was) fell apart completely, leaving only a tall stump and a great pile of shattered branches. Had they been sitting on the log when that happened, the artists would have survived, but they would have departed with a very real appreciation of how natural woodlands work.

At another level, this print symbolises the whole 75 years of the Lady Park scientific project. When I first glanced at this drawing, I saw the trees but not the people, and it was only later that the 'undergrowth' resolved itself into a crowd. This reprises in a flash many decades of ecological and historical studies of natural woodland. When the Lady Park project started in 1944, ecologists could reasonably think in terms of primaeval woodland, completely natural in the sense that people were thought never to have influenced its condition and composition. In fact, the ecological study was started in order to understand how such woodland worked. Now, however, the people have come into view. We realise that our species influenced woodland and the rest of our environment back to the end of the ice ages and before; that pre-Neolithic woodland was not as pristine as we thought. The Lady Park long-term ecological project still seeks to make people self-effacing so that we can learn how woods work when we are not in control, but the 75 years of recording has demonstrated that the wood that we thought of as completely natural has been permanently and irrevocably touched by the past and continuing presence of people in the rest of the landscape. Like my view of the painting, people have come steadily into focus.

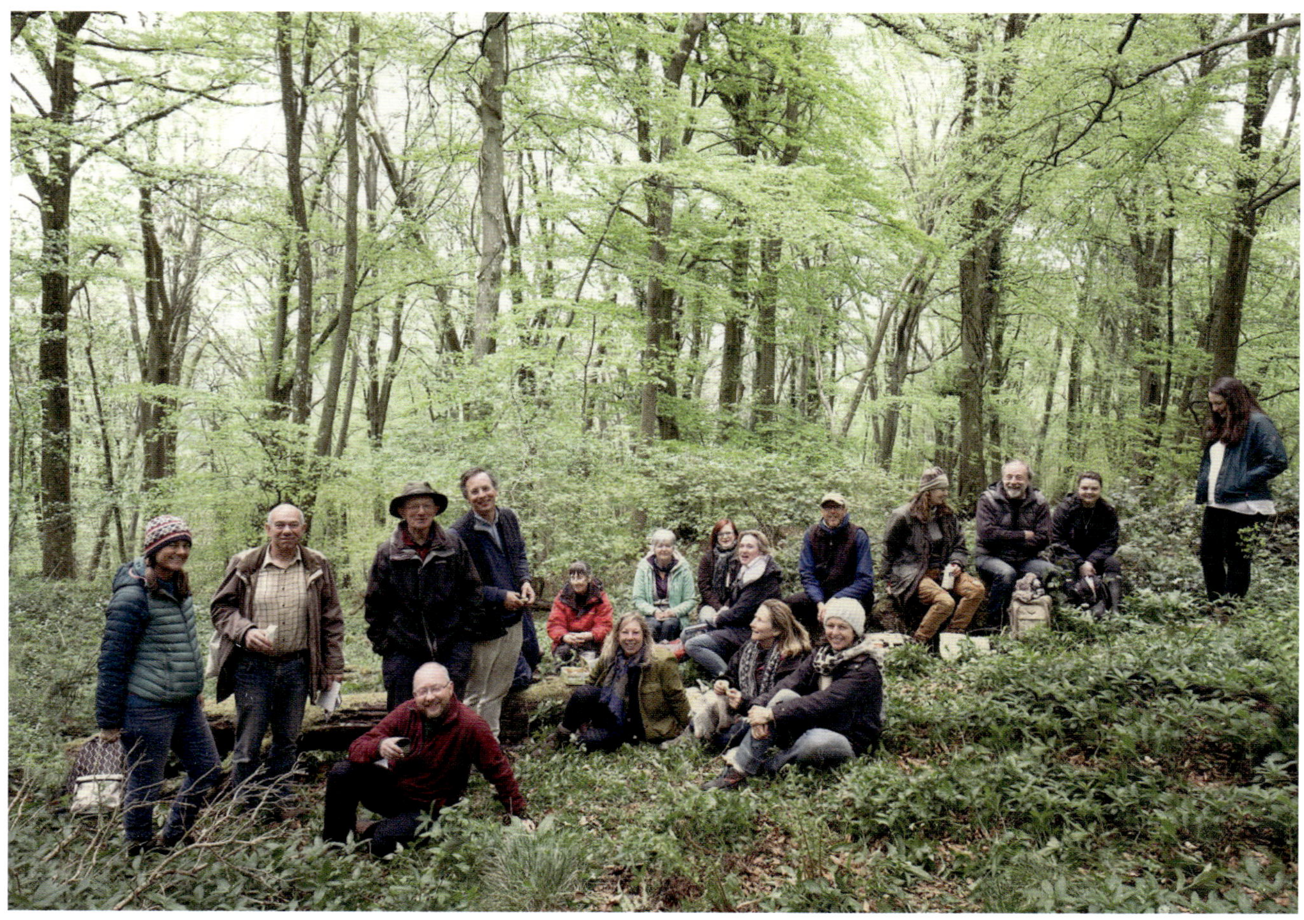

From back, left to right: Sarah Sawyer, Tim Craven, Richard Bavin, George Peterken, Richard Hoare, Susan Peterken, Stella Carr, Jane Bailey, Becca Bratt (ecologist at Worcestershire Wildlife Consultancy), Mary Ann Eyton-Ellis, Alex Egan, Jacqueline Wedlake Hatton, Tom Deakins, Fiona McIntyre, Julian Perry, Blaze Cyan, Jess Vuckovic (Assistant ecologist at Worcestershire Wildlife Consultancy). Photographed by ©Tony Golding.

SOME GENERAL REFLECTIONS

Rather to my surprise, the majority of images were more realistic than abstract. This creates easy points of departure for short essays on ecological features and ideas, but it would have been interesting if more images had been more abstract, especially as the works that hovered between abstract and realistic seemed to generate more lateral associations with ecological matters. Thus, the incomplete trees around Tim Craven's crashed oak – *Crash! (Lady Park Wood)* – help to make a link to images of woodland shattered by the 1914–1918 World War; Abi Kremer's oak stump rendered as a flame – *Lady Park Wood 2* – dramatises the return of mineral nutrients to the soil as trees decay; and Susan Peterken's stained-glass-window paintings – *Red Interspatial, Interspatial* and *On the Edge of the Cliff* – help point to the importance of space in woods. One can think of other possible abstract renderings: it would have been interesting to see, say, a Rothko-style simplification of the woodland scene, blue below and bright green above, to summarise a bluebell-beech wood in late spring.

So, what did attract the artists? Judging by the results, distinctive individual trees and the two characteristic elements of natural woodland – tree-fall gaps and conspicuous piles of dead wood – commanded attention. So, too, the mature structure of stands that have so far remained immune to wind-throw and the collapse of large trees. The violence inherent in natural woodland and the forces unleashed were represented mainly by recently fallen trees, but also by Annabel Cullen's close study of a broken branch (*Forces of Nature*). The confusion and barriers to movement created around major tree falls were made clear by various artworks and the thickets that the wood regenerates in gaps can also be seen. Another feature of natural woodland, the tendency of tree species to grow in clusters and groups, is difficult to capture in a single image, but it can be seen in one painting and is implied in others. The clearest representation of Lady Park as a mixture of tree species was Ann Blockley's detailed painting of *Fallen Leaves*.

The interest in distinctive individual trees seemed to express itself in a predilection for large beech trees and the few large yews, but oaks, which are actually the biggest trees in the wood, were under-represented. Strangely, the clear preference for painting beech, not oak, mirrors their respective influence on the ecology of the wood. Beech makes the ecological weather: it is the species whose behaviour influences the performance of every other species, whereas oaks just stand there quietly, suffering 'in silence' as other species around them grow tall and kill their lower branches. Further, Lady Park is a mixture of tree species, but one gets little sense of this. Lime, the up-coming species, was almost omitted, and there is little sign of ash. Both can be seen in stand profiles, but they remained anonymous.

On the whole the artists viewed the wood through middle-distance eyes. There was no attempt to view the wood from the outside, though in fairness this would have been difficult to arrange. But there was also little attention given to close-up detail, though the few microcosms (the wrenched branch; the fallen leaves; the birch bark) were particularly telling.

Much else escaped artistic attention, or at least proved to be less compelling. The ground vegetation remained largely unrepresented, which is consistent with the Arborealists' interest in trees. Saplings and regeneration, too, were largely ignored, and in one instance the regeneration that was shown clearly in the field sketch was removed in the painting derived from it – perhaps it is age that generates interest, rather like a 'lived-in' face being more interesting than a baby's. Niche features were also unrepresented, though Julian Perry's painting of a well-rotted birch log (*Vestigial Birch*) stood out as a seemingly trivial feature that nevertheless enabled a significant story to be told about Lady Park's history. I found no hint of the one constant process, the relentless, unforgiving, Darwinian competitive exclusion of weaker trees, akin to unregulated free-market economics – the strong get stronger and live, but the weak get weaker and perish – though admittedly this is a particularly difficult process to represent. On the other hand, if any of the artists have been impressed with recent ideas of trees looking after their young, then they left this out, too.

One justification for maintaining a natural woodland reserve is that it provides a sample of the truly wild. As such, it is a baseline which allows us to appreciate the managed and built environment in which we live. This is related to the recent enthusiasm for (re-) wilding, which would allow us into environments where nature is permitted to run free (which is assumed to be good for biodiversity and refreshing for us). On site, the artists expressed enthusiasm for the reserve, which indicates to me that they shared the enthusiasm for a wild place. But did anyone see the wood as threatening or dangerous? In mythology, the wildwood is meant to be a fearsome place, but I see no sign of this in the paintings. Perhaps, like me, no one felt at risk.

Completely pristine original woodland has rarely been painted. The most convincing – to an ecologist – depictions of natural woodland were painted by the Hudson River school of artists in the nineteenth-century USA. The painting I selected as a cover illustration for a book, *Natural Woodland*[1] was *In the Woods* by Asher B. Durand, even though I knew it was not an objective representation of a real place but a confection of elements put together to represent the idea of pristine woodland as the unadulterated work of God. Since then, I have seen identical elements used in other, similar, paintings by the same artist, some of which represent woodland that is even more convincingly natural. Other artists of the period tended to paint woodland that ecologists would now describe as 'semi-natural', notably the wood-pastures of Fontainebleau painted by the *Barbizon* school and the Russian woodlands painted by Ivan Shishkin (though some of Shishkin's paintings of boreal conifer forests look pristine). From the sixteenth century onwards several Flemish and German artists painted what most people would happily accept as natural woodland, but in most cases ecologists can see features that are obviously the work of unseen people, or they actually show people doing improbable things in apparently natural woodland.

Artists of the Hudson River school and their like sometimes included people as observers of an otherwise completely natural scene, which gave one a sense of how people reacted to the wild. The film *The Arborealists in Lady Park Woods*[2] of the artists working in Lady Park – an integral part of the associated exhibitions – dwells on the artists' responses to the wood, but the paintings almost exclude people from the scene. One, Alex Egan's *The Forester*, may well show me, and I hope my presence in the wood has been as small as the painting suggests. Stella Carr's *Arborealists in Lady Park Wood* shows a crowd, but it helps to make several ecological points.

Finally, an admission of relief that the artists did not find Lady Park boring. I say this because, many years ago, when I was searching for paintings of virgin forest, I visited the Kunsthistorisches Museum in Vienna, where I hoped to find a painting of an Urwald by Gillis van Coninxloo. I found it in a corner, looking dark, featureless and anonymous, surrounded by contemporary paintings of rural scenes showing people and farmland. I watched for thirty minutes, but it attracted not a single glance from other visitors. Literally, it lacked personality. This reinforced earlier experiences in real virgin forests. Thus, my first contact with tropical rainforest in Lamington National Park, Queensland, was exciting at first, but tedious by the end of the day. My first experience of a European *Urwald – Boubínský Prales* in Bohemia – left me prostrated with over-stimulation, but by the time I had seen thirty of them, I was yawning. Even the famous *Białowieża* Forest, Poland, was interesting as much for the relics of human usage as for the demonstration of natural processes. It is the human element that gives woodland much of its interest, and my perspective on the Arborealists in Lady Park is that many would agree.

None of this is criticism, just observation. For both artists and myself as the ecologist, the project was a revelation. After a lifetime in woods with ecologists, foresters, natural historians and historians, it was heartening indeed to hear woodlanders from an entirely different background express interest in my subject and voice the same concerns for the future. We were all learning that there is more to woodland than had so far met our eyes, and realising that there is still more to learn.

Notes

[1] George F. Peterken, *Natural Woodland, Ecology and Conservation in Northern Temperate Regions* (Cambridge University Press, 1996).

[2] The *Arborealists in Lady Park Woods*, filmed by Kashfi Halford and produced by Fiona McIntyre (15 minute documentary, 2018) ©McIntyre/Halford.

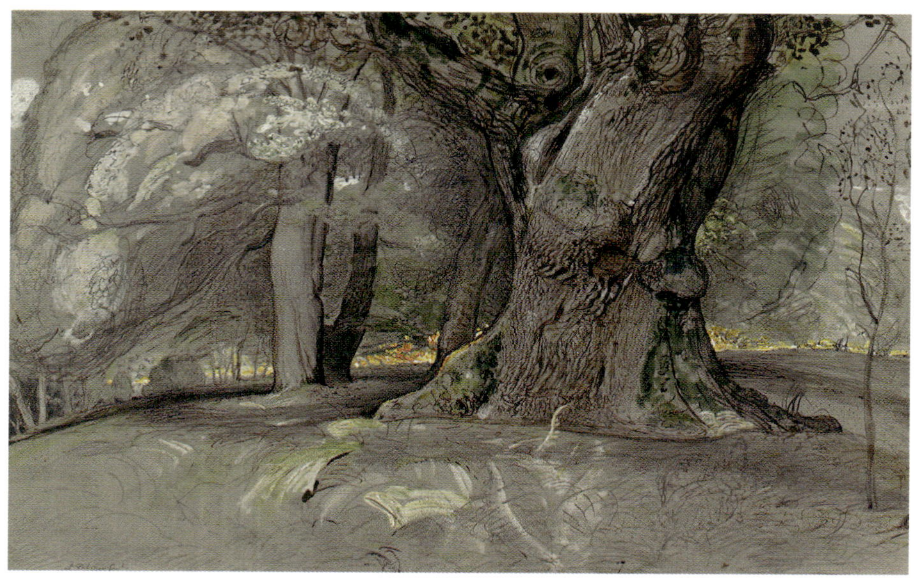

SAMUEL PALMER
Oak Trees, Lullingstone Park, 1828
Pencil, pen and brown ink and
watercolour, heightened with
bodycolour, on grey paper
29.5 x 46.8 cm
©Bridgeman Images 6322894

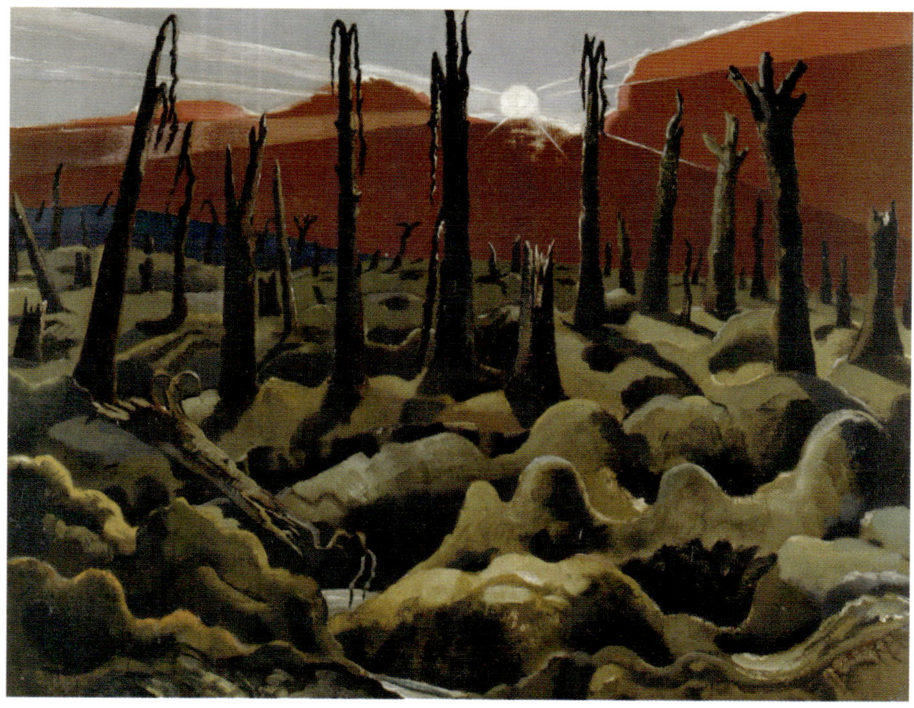

PAUL NASH
We Are Making A New World, 1918
Oil on canvas
56.4 x 38.9 cm
©Imperial War Museum
(Art.IWM ART 1146)

ROOTS IN THE PAST

CHRISTIANA PAYNE

It was a wonderful idea to get together a group of artists and an ecologist in a wood with a unique history: full of evidence of human land use in the past, yet unmanaged for 75 years. As George Peterken observes in his commentary on the artworks, the artists rose to the challenge by picking out many of the features that an unmanaged wood presents: fallen and leaning trees, new trees growing out of fallen trunks, characterful older specimens, a profusion of tangles and thickets, a rich understory. He rightly points out that the artists who have painted natural woodland in the past were not British: he mentions sixteenth- and seventeenth-century Flemish artists including *Gillis van Coninxloo* and nineteenth-century artists such as the French group in *Barbizon*, *Ivan Shishkin* in Russia and, above all, the American *Asher B. Durand*, who was able to paint forests in the eastern United States before they had been irrevocably changed by European settlement. Yet he also shows that the distinction between 'virgin' and managed woodland is not clear-cut. We now know that so-called 'primitive' peoples have exercised sophisticated management techniques, such as controlled burning, and Lady Park Wood, like other areas of ancient woodland, shows evidence of coppicing, pollarding and the soil disturbances caused by mining.

Earlier British artists have mostly drawn and painted managed woods and parkland, yet there are echoes of their works in many of the paintings in this book. This is most obvious in the paintings of trees that seem to have individual personalities. Stella Carr's *Fagus Metanoia* reminds me of *Samuel Palmer*'s drawings of the ancient oaks and beeches of Lullingstone Park, executed in the late 1820s. The paintings of yew trees by Alex Egan, Blaze Cyan and Robert Amesbury Brooks can be related to the British tradition of making 'tree portraits', exemplified in the paintings of Paul Sandby and James Ward, the etchings of Jacob George Strutt and the drawings of John Constable. George Peterken comments that the tendency to see trees as individuals, with a distinct character that grows as they age, is tempting even to the 'dispassionate' ecologist: anthropomorphism and subjectivity 'intrude'. Yet modern science, summarised in the writings of Peter Wohlleben, appears to provide some justification for this approach. Trees really do behave like humans in many ways, caring for their community and their descendants, as well as competing with their peers for light and air.

Artists in nineteenth-century Britain, from John Sell Cotman to Myles Birket Foster, showed a particular fondness for the 'chequered shade' of enclosed woodland, especially beech woods, with well-marked paths and pleasant glades that were suitable for picnics. The fall of sunlight through the canopy, and the varied shapes and textures of dead leaves on the ground, inspired them, as they have also inspired Ann Blockley,

Jane Eaton and Stella Carr. Perhaps it is Cotman who comes closest to suggesting the profusion of natural woodland, in his watercolours of the Greta Woods in Yorkshire (1803–5), which immerse the viewer in a sea of different shades of green. But Cotman's watercolours have a strong sense of pattern and order, giving them a very different character from Fiona McIntyre's *Rewilding*, suggestions of the disorientation that can be experienced in truly wild woodland.

Annabel Cullen's drawing, *Forces of Nature*, leads George Peterken to reflect on the dangers of unmanaged woodland and the great forces that could be unleashed at any moment. Its twisting forms and close-up focus may refer to drawings and photographs of dead trees and tree roots by Paul Nash and Graham Sutherland, produced under the shadow of the Second World War: the sight of mangled trees can be all too reminiscent of human suffering. Similarly, Richard Bavin's painting and sketch, simply entitled *Fallen*, can be compared to Paul Nash's depictions of trees shattered by the trench warfare of the First World War, most notably in his painting, *We Are Making A New World* (1918, Imperial War Museums). These wartime artistic echoes seem particularly appropriate for Lady Park Wood, which lost two-thirds of its trees in order to supply the war effort in 1942.

Many British artists in the past combined a quasi-scientific study of the different species, and the behaviour of individual trees, with a more emotional and aesthetic response to these remarkable beings. The combination of artistic and ecological perspectives in this book, therefore, has its roots in the past, but it offers hope for a future in which we will treat trees with the care and respect they deserve.

References:
Christiana Payne, *Silent Witnesses: Trees in British Art*, 1760–1870 (Bristol: Sansom & Co, 2017).
Peter Wohlleben, *The Hidden Life of Trees: What They Feel, How They Communicate* (Vancouver: Greystone Books Ltd, 2016).

ARTISTS IN
THE WOODS

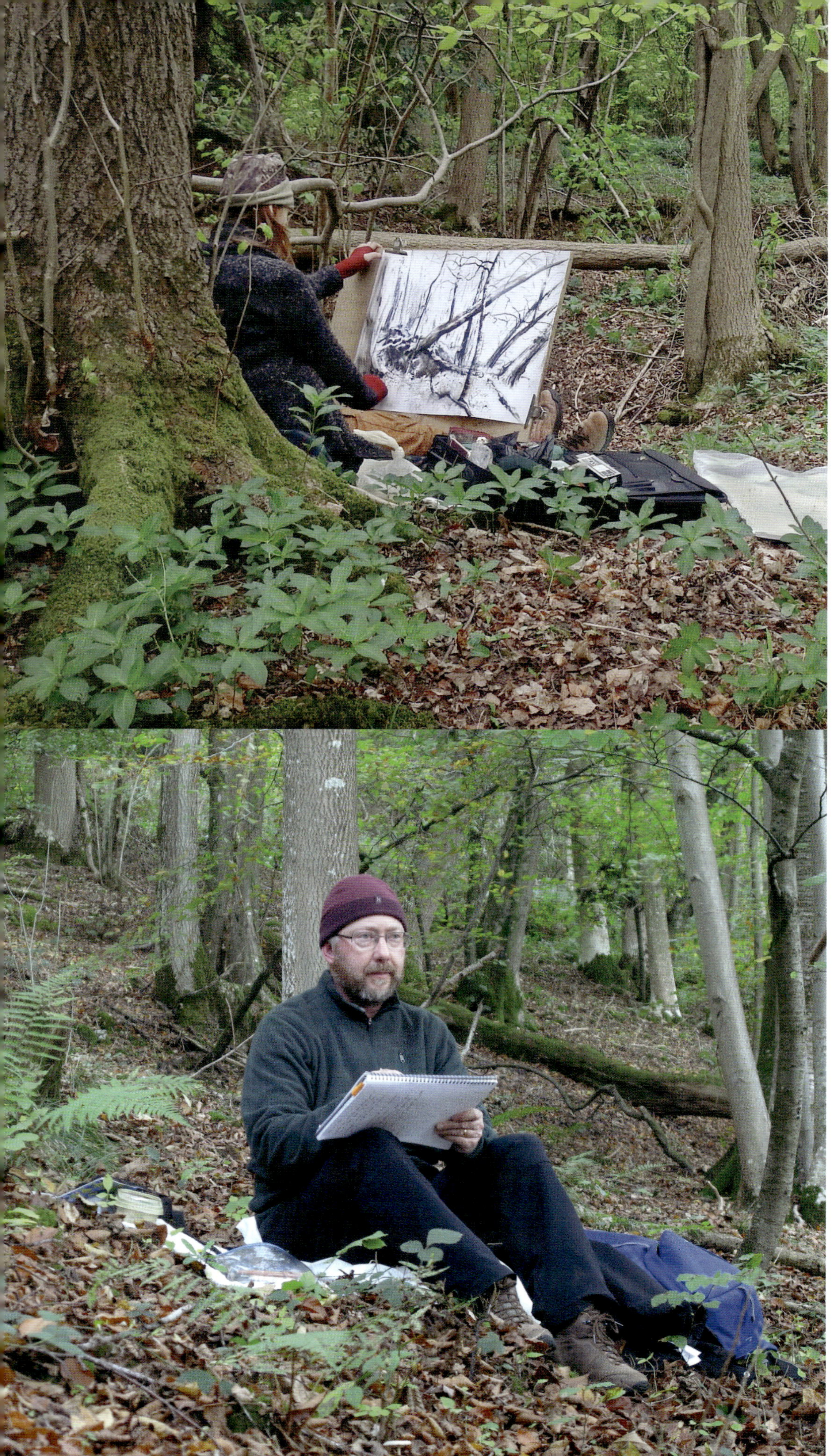

Fiona McIntyre
April 2017

Richard Bavin
April 2017

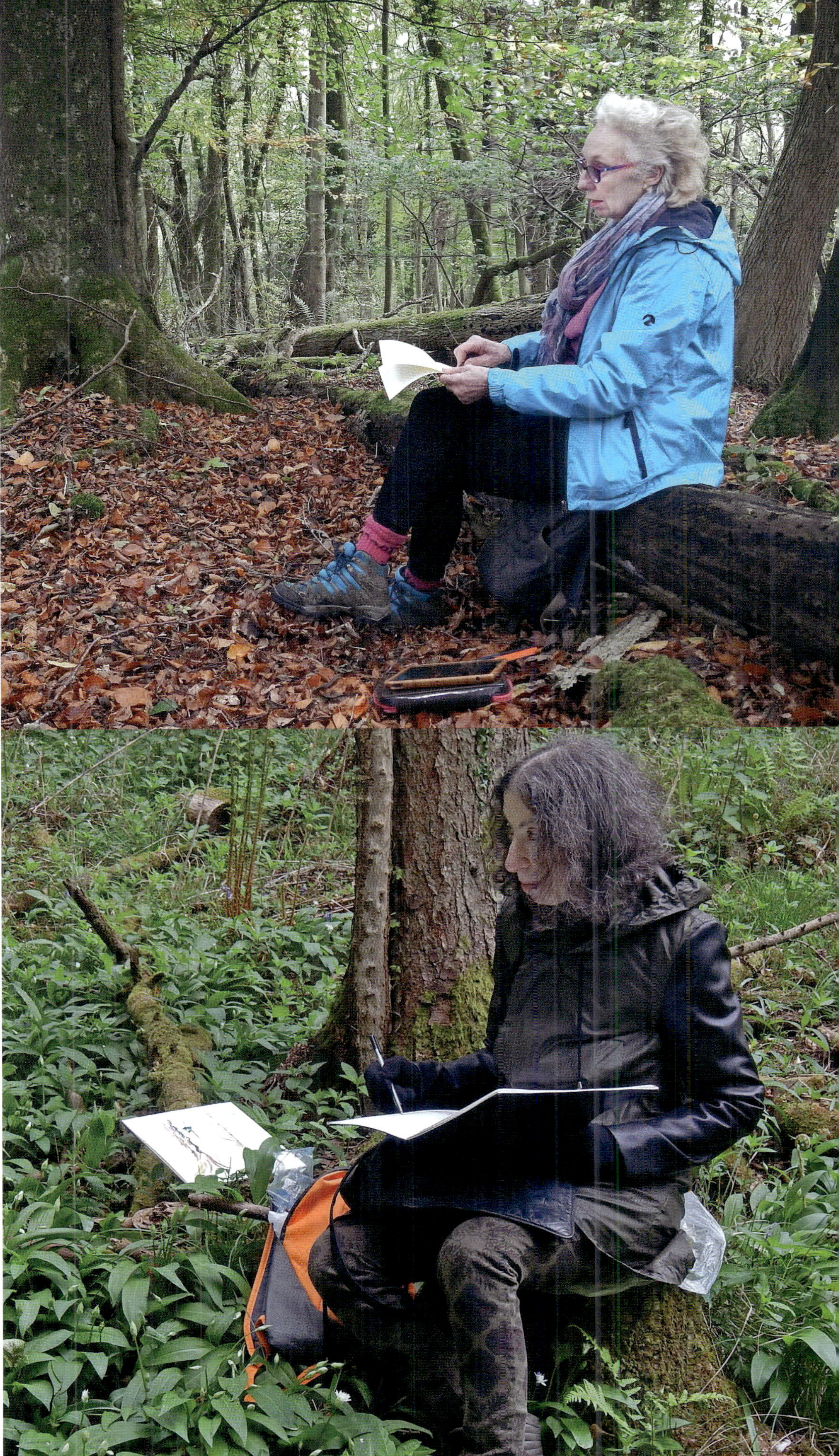

Jane Eaton
September 2017

Abi Kremer
April 2017

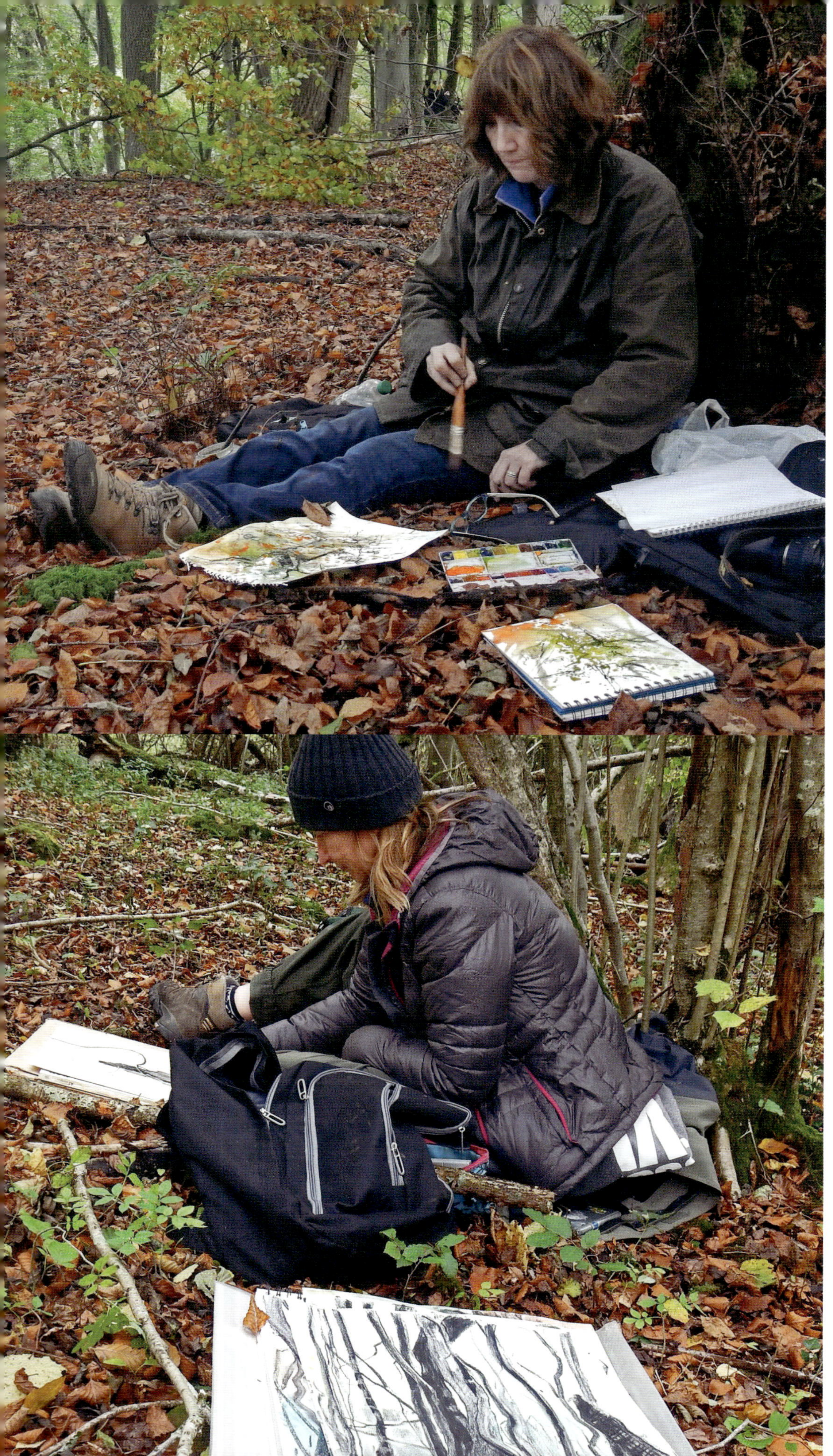

Ann Blockley
September 2018

Alex Egan
September 2018

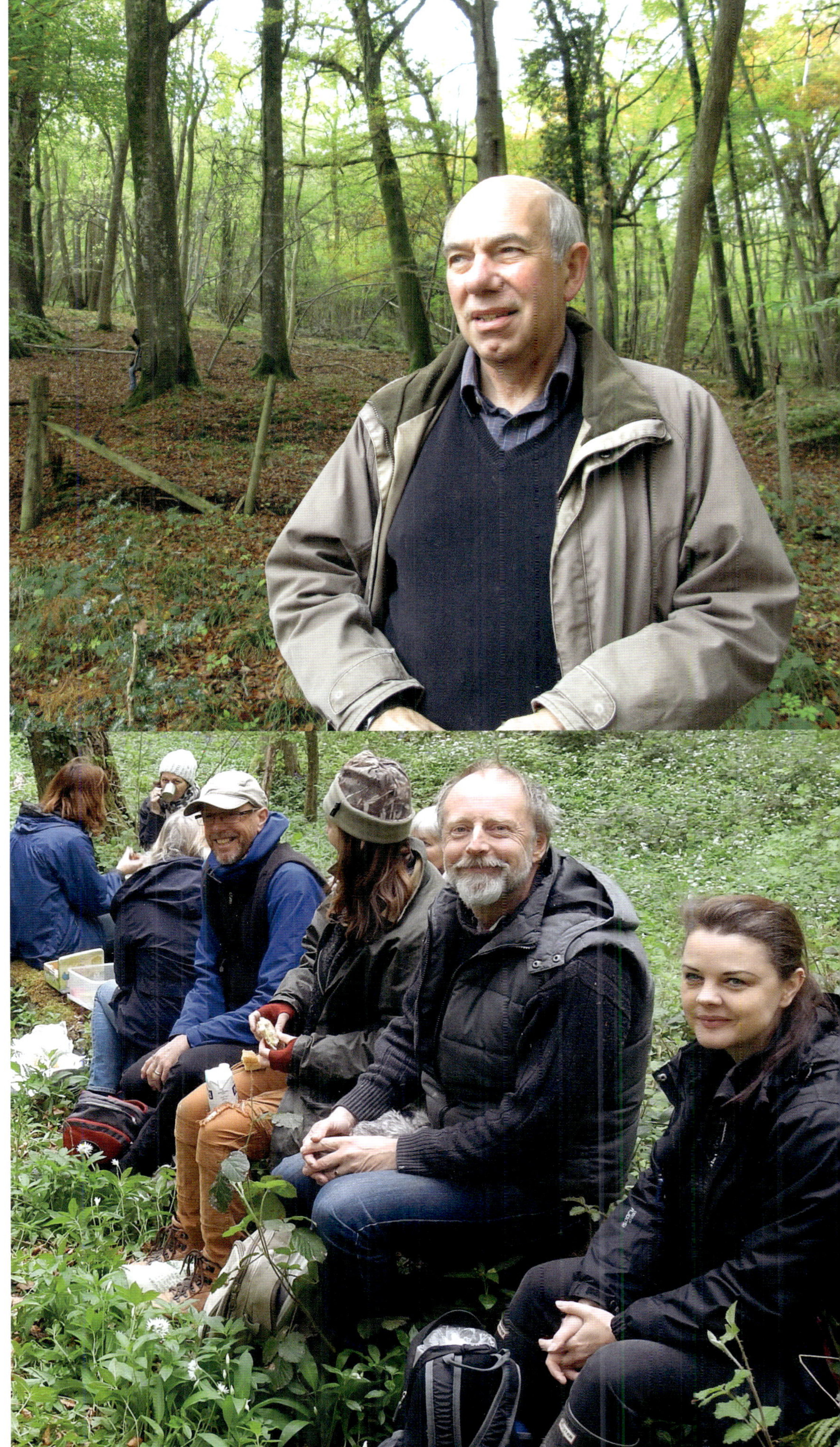

Tim Craven
September 2017

From left, Ann Blockley,
Jaqueline Wedlake Hatton,
Mary Ann Aytoun-Ellis,
Tom Deakin,
Fiora McIntyre,
Julian Perry, Blaze Cyan,
September 2018

Artists' Biographies

Richard Bavin

Born 1957, based in Herefordshire, where he is resident artist with Herefordshire Wildlife Trust. EDUCATION | 2002 Hereford College of Arts | 2008 Cheltenham School of Art (Gloucestershire University) | Works in watercolours, oils and drawing media on long-term projects about specific habitats and nature reserves. His practice combines year-round outdoor sketching and information-gathering with studio series which pare down and distill these outdoor experiences. See www.richardbavin.com

Ann Blockley

Born 1959, UK. Lives in Gloucestershire. EDUCATION | Gloucestershire College of Art and Design, Brighton University, BA (Hons) Illustration | Member of Royal Institute of Painters in Water Colours | 'I use water-based mediums to interpret the sense of the subject; alluding to the facts rather than precisely representing them; aiming to subtly alter reality into something poetic and elusive. I sometimes use plant materials carefully foraged from the site to imprint textures within the paint and create an alliance between myself, the painting and nature.'

Robert Amesbury Brooks

Born 1964, UK. EDUCATION | 1983 Foundation in Art and Design, Shelley Park College Bournemouth | 1987 BA Fine Art, Slade School of Fine Art, London | 'When it comes to looking I am forever searching, hoping to bring out the best in what I see. Colour is so powerful, but it becomes even more so when, like an orchestra, warm and cool relationships sing off one another. Being so overwhelmed I guess is one reason why I continue to paint, never fully grasping but always hungering for more knowledge and enlightenment.'

Stella Carr

Born 1962, Liverpool, UK. EDUCATION | Kingston School of Art, Kingston upon Thames | Brought up among artists and scientists, Carr explores regenerative relationships between species as infinite interconnections; fundamentally the works are about coming home to the fact that we are all nature. This seeing is layered like a network throughout Carr's printwork, drawing and painting, emphasised by scratching, scraping and glazing, with colour applied in complementary opposites. 'Being an artist in this time, with global readjustment, we need no evidence that we are all one organism on this earth.'

Tim Craven

Born 1953, Birmingham, UK. EDUCATION | Fine Art at Stourbridge College of Art and the Conservation of Easel Paintings at Gateshead Technical College | Tim joined the staff at Southampton City Art Gallery in 1980, working in conservation, collection management and as Curator. He left the Gallery in 2017 to concentrate on his own art practice and to curate exhibitions. He founded the The Arborealists in 2013 and was elected a member of the London Group in 2015.

Annabel Cullen

Born 1953, Surrey, UK. Lives and works in London. EDUCATION | 1978 Camberwell School of Art and Crafts, London | 1983 Royal College of Art, London | 'As a painter of the human figure, my interest in trees arises in part from their anthropomorphic and emotive qualities. I enjoy the correlation between their sinuous, jointed limbs and human anatomy, and look for the suggestion of movement in their seemingly static forms. I generally make the work on site, using charcoal, graphite, ink, lithographic crayon and conté.'

Blaze Cyan

Born 1969, in rural Wiltshire, UK, and now lives and works at her studio in London. EDUCATION | BA in Fashion Design, MA in Fine Art (specializing in printmaking) | Fellow and Honorary Secretary of the Royal Society of Painter-Printmakers | Blaze's practice includes the mediums of etching, drawing, woodcut and wood engraving. Her work is about the beauty and complexity of trees in nature and their importance in supporting and enriching lives. See www.blazecyan.com.

Tom Deakins

Born 1957, Barnet, Herts, UK. Has lived in and near Great Dunmow, Essex, since 1965. EDUCATION | Newport [Essex] Grammar School | 1980 BA (Hons) Fine Art, University of Newcastle upon Tyne | 1982 Art Teacher's Certificate, Leeds University | 1982–91 Taught Art, History of Art and Architecture and Silversmithing at Felsted School and local adult education centres. Currently gardening part-time and occasionally leading cycle-tours. Works mainly in oils on canvas panels, with a balance of fine detail and broader atmosphere: small in scale – emphasis on light and a sense of place in the landscape.

Jane Eaton

Born 1947, Epping, Essex, UK. EDUCATION | 2002 BTEC Professional Development Award (Design and Crafts), Outstanding Student | 2010 FDA (First Class) | 2015 BA (Hons) Creative Arts (First Class) | 'My work is both exploratory and expressive, using a variety of processes and media reflecting aspects of a cross-cultural aesthetic (Western and Eastern). Line and the chance mark are key aspects within my imagery. I also employ repetition and simultaneous mark making, studying the relationship of repetition and difference. Since 2014 my work has predominantly been made in response to ecological issues affecting the world; however, my creative practice remains open, inquisitive and curious to visual expression within many areas.'

Alex Egan

Born 1964. Grew up and educated in Hong Kong until age 12 then educated in England. EDUCATION | 1981 Full-time dance course, the Arts Educational School London | 1983 Arts Foundation course, Salisbury College of Art | 1986 BA (Hons) Fine Art Bristol | 'For the detailed drawings and commissioned portraits of trees I work from my car in front of the trees (subjects) during the winter months. When weather permits I draw/sketch and paint outdoors. I use these to either create new paintings or finish off in the studio.'

Jelly Green

Born 1992, Ipswich, UK. EDUCATION | The Royal Drawing School, London | Mentored by artist Maggi Hambling since she was 16 years old | Her paintings, which are imbued with a deep passion for nature and landscape – whether it's the Brazilian rainforest where she lived in a treehouse for several months, or the bucolic English garden of her childhood – explore the passion and wonder of the natural world. Her most recent work is focused on raising awareness of the deforestation that is occurring throughout the earth, primarily in tropical rainforests.

Richard Hoare

Born 1967, Ipswich, UK. Lives and works in south-west Britain and France. EDUCATION | 1989–91 Kent Institute of Art and Design | 1992 Postgraduate Diploma, Cyprus College of Art | Richard Hoare is a painter of light in the landscape, working directly in front of nature. By Dennis Creffield he was taught the 'spirit in the mass' approach, which was developed by Creffield's master, David Bomberg. Recently returned from Japan as Artist in Residence at Koumi-Machi Kougen Museum of Art, Richard is currently working in specific locations in Ireland, Scotland and Wiltshire, UK. See www.richardhoare.com and www.thesongofkoumi.com.

Abi Kremer

Born 1955, London. Lives and works in Bournemouth, Dorset. EDUCATION | 1974
Harrow College of Art | 1977 Bournemouth College of Art | Abi Kremer has had a
varied artistic career spanning public and private practice, including collaborations with
contemporary dance companies. Currently the energy of woodland spaces and structures
inspire work which reflects an interest in prismatic colour and arabesque movement.
Translation into paint of organic phenomena addresses the subconscious, resulting in
fantastical landscapes. Influences include the Surrealist Eileen Agar and colourists such as
Winifred Nicholson and Bridget Riley. See www.abikremer.com.

Fiona McIntyre

Born 1963, Nairobi, Kenya. Grew up in Dublin, then Sweden as an adult. Based in
Gloucestershire. EDUCATION | 1985 BA (Hons) Drawing and Painting, Edinburgh
College of Art | 1992 Printmaking, Grafikskolan Forum, Malmö, Sweden (mentored
by Imaginist Prof. Bertil Lundberg) | 1993 MA European Fine Art, Winchester School
of Art | 'McIntyre has proved a versatile artist eager to reinvent her visual iciom and to
engage with motifs, material and forms in subtle and sophisticated ways ... an artist whose
roots reach deep down into the layered strata of English art and its sense of a collective
organicity.' Prof. Catherine Bernard, Université Paris Diderot (Permission Cerles).

Julian Perry

Born 1969, Worcester, UK. Lives and works in London and Suffolk. EDUCATION |
Studied at Maidenhead School of Art and Bristol Polytechnic | 'Julian Perry ... paints
images of genuine topicality in an immaculate high-definition realist style. His ... show in
2007 dealt with the allotment sheds bulldozed [to make way for the Olympic site]. Since
then he has been painting pictures of coastal erosion, visiting locations around England
and composing hallucinatory images of deracination and loss.' Andrew Lambirth, *The
Spectator*.

Susan Peterken

Born 1943, Watford, UK. EDUCATION | BSc Botany University College, London |
'Colour is my main inspiration, and an intense love of landscape impels me to draw out
colours, forms and patterns from my surroundings, often leading towards abstraction. A
similar approach underlies my painting of still-life subjects. Starting nearly fifty years ago
in oils, I now work mainly in soft pastels. I exhibit around the Wye Valley, and have won
prizes in two open art exhibitions.'

Lesley Slight

Born 1939, Wells, Somerset, UK. Lives and works in rural Dorset. EDUCATION | 1960 Fine Art Painting and Printmaking, Nottingham College of Art | 1961 Textiles, Leicester College of Art | Established a design career in London, then moved to Dorset to work as a painter. 'Her paintings invoke a magical, mystical, mythical world in which absolutely anything is possible. These are views that are slightly out of reach, just over the hill or around the corner – at once some place and no place, everywhere and nowhere.' Interview with Nick Churchill, *Dorset Life – The Dorset Magazine*, 2018. See lesley@ lesleyslightpaintings.com.

Jacqueline Wedlake Hatton

Born 1964, St Austell, Cornwall, UK. Lives in London and Cornwall. EDUCATION | 1997 Art Foundation, Shrewsbury | 2001 BA Falmouth College of Arts | 2012 MA University College London | 'I am most inspired by trees that have a distinctive form. Such trees are beautiful to me in their resilience and natural "intelligence". My paintings are created in the studio, where I reimagine my encounter with the trees; my recollection of them; their environment; their place in the world – all are equivalent to meeting interesting people. These impressions are the most important aspect of the paintings.

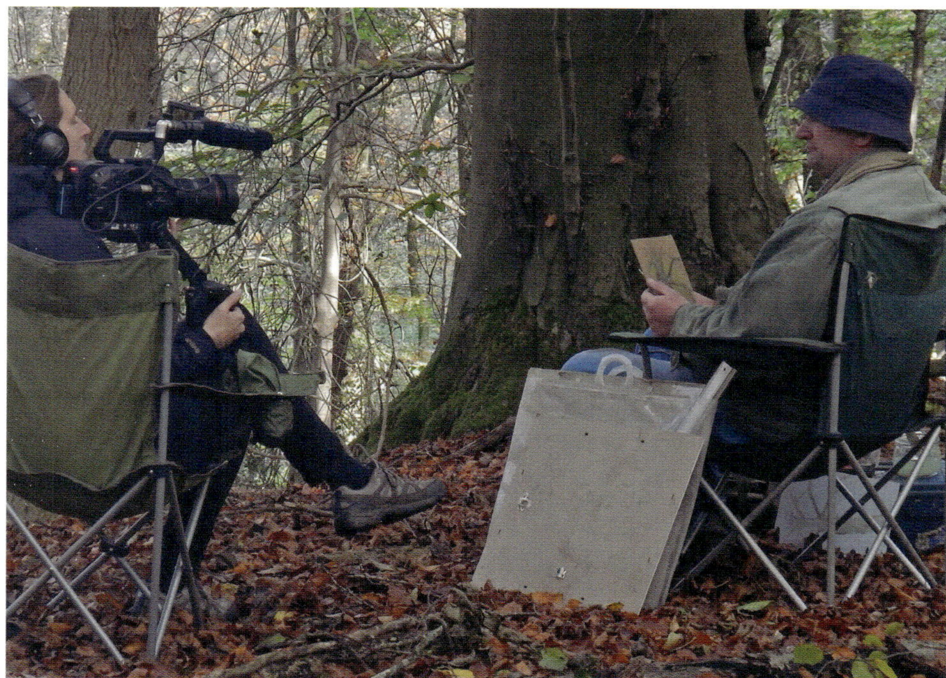

Robert Amesbury Brooks being filmed by Kashfi Halford for *The Arborealists in Lady Park Woods*, September 2018